M000040219

The Sex
You Want

The Sex You Want

A LOVERS' GUIDE TO WOMEN'S SEXUAL PLEASURE

MARCIA DOUGLASS, Ph.D.
and LISA DOUGLASS, Ph.D.

Marlowe & Company
New York

$m \uparrow (97)$

JUN 2003

THE SEX YOU WANT: *A Lovers' Guide to Women's Sexual Pleasure*
Copyright © 1997, 2002 by Lisa Douglass and Marcia Douglass
Illustrations by Marcia Douglass

Published by
Marlowe & Company
An Imprint of Avalon Publishing Group Incorporated
161 William Street, 16th Floor
New York, NY 10038

An earlier edition of this book was originally published in hardcover in 1997 by
Hyperion under the title *Are We Having Fun Yet?*.

All rights reserved. No part of this book may be reproduced in whole or in part
without written permission from the publisher, except by reviewers who may quote
brief excerpts in connection with a review in a newspaper, magazine, or electronic
publication; nor may any part of this book be reproduced, stored in a retrieval
system, or transmitted in any form or by any means electronic, mechanical,
photocopying, recording, or other, without written permission from the publisher.

Library of Congress information is available.

ISBN 1–56924–495–2

9 8 7 6 5 4 3 2 1

Designed by Nicola Ferguson
Printed in Canada

For our mother,
Marilyn Wise Douglass

and for all the women who came
before us

CONTENTS

ACKNOWLEDGMENTS

This book grew out of the ongoing conversations we have had over several years with a number of women and men about sex. Marcia wants to especially thank Robin Bernard for her brilliant insights and great times laughing about sex. Kevin Fitzsimmons and Khoi Dang also spent hours talking with me about sex and reading the manuscript. Their comments greatly improved this book.

Many of Marcia's friends and students, including Skye, Debra Isaacson, Erma Jean Sims, Rubbie McKeever, Marcia Spires, Silvia Dominguez, Nancy Feezel, Yelba Gonzales, Susan Montrose, Naomi Eilat, Lorna Spencer, Dolores Padilla, Merryl Sinclair, and Shoshana Kornfeld, generously commented on drafts of the book.

Marcia would also like to thank all the women who shared their experiences in focus groups. Their input was invaluable: Many of these women found talking with other women about sex—for many, their first time—very empowering. Several also spent many hours talking with me about sex one-on-one. Their experiences greatly enrich this book.

Marcia is also grateful to Rae Blumberg, Lee Meihls, Rosemary Griffith, Jane Simpson, Carole Hann, Margot Dashiell, Becky Platero, Graciela Platero, Guadalupe Friaz, Alessandra Chacham, Linda Walker, Suzanne Decker, Diane Beeson, and our cousin, Susan Hass, for their comments and encouragement. Thanks especially to my intimate partner Louis, who gave me the emotional and sexual support and love I needed to write about sex.

The biggest thanks goes to my sister, Lisa, who made this book happen.

Lisa first thanks Marcia for getting me to think more seriously about the pleasures of sex and for encouraging me to keep on learning. Gratitude is only one of many warm feelings I have for my sex companion, intellectual partner, lover, friend, and husband, Bob. He and our son, Ian Douglass, are daily sources of joy to me.

This book could never have been written without the help of the large community of teachers and friends who have helped Ian grow. They include brothers Ben Nelson and William Nelson, sister Hannah Nelson, his highly skilled and affectionate teachers Stephanie Athey, Vélika Simonovski, and Ondine Weber, Julie McGonagle, as well as Cheryl Andrist, Joshua Pelton-Stroud, Alisa Coccetti, Shawnette Hanna, Jennifer Nissen, and Sharon Hickey. Suzanne Pelton went beyond the call of duty as a friend and fellow parent. Naomi Eilat and Patrick Douglass contributed their extraordinary humor and energy to making Ian's and my stays in California fun for him and productive for me.

I am deeply indebted to Lori Andrews, whose faith in me and in this project was crucial to the launching of this book. I hope it meets her own high standards. Other friends both near and far provided input that has enriched this book. Mary Kate Driscoll, Mindie Lazarus-Black, and Leah Feldman each read with an eye that was critical but kind. Audrey Wilson, Ritu Frankel, Leslie Lim, Lori Spear, Gayle Hall, Althea Bailey, Susan Masters, Toni de la Motta, and Susie Brown offered frank and insightful comments when they met with me to talk about several chapters. Laura Rogerson, Angela Alston, Elke Weinstein,

Chris Grabarek, and J. W. Bennett contributed various forms of expertise by e-mail, snail mail, and telephone. I am also grateful for ongoing conversations about sex and everything else with friends Morny Joy, Karen O'Kain, and Jennifer Hopwood.

Both of us would like to thank Betty Dodson, Carol Queen, Joani Blank, Beverly Whipple, Louisa Daniels, and Norma Wilcox for lively interviews. Each of them generously shared her hard-earned knowledge with us out of a desire to get the word out on women's sexual pleasure.

We are also greatly indebted to Josephine Lowndes Sevely, whose book, *Eve's Secrets: A New Theory of Female Sexuality,* with its new vision of women's genital anatomy, helped inspire this one. Sevely's groundbreaking work has never received the recognition it deserves. Her book is now out of print, and our efforts to locate Ms. Sevely were unsuccessful. We hope this book serves to credit her work.

A New View of a Woman's Body, by the Federation of Feminist Women's Health Centers, has also been an important influence, especially its revolutionary depictions of the female clitoris by illustrator Suzann Gage.

Several chapters benefited from the skillful editing of Sandra Little and Kathy Glimn. Patricia Wortner's secretarial skills helped us through endless drafts. Lorrie Wessel provided skilled transcriptions in short order, and Tamara Kay and Michelle Van Natta gave excellent editorial help. Michelle also contributed a fine critical reading of several chapters and brought important points to our attention.

All of the above people helped strengthen this book, but none of them is responsible for any weaknesses or errors. Those reside with us.

At Hyperion, our editor, Leslie Wells, gave us enthusiastic support and cheerful direction. Her assistant, Jennifer Lang, patiently helped move the editorial process along. Our agent,

Gail Ross, and her colleague, Howard Yoon, not only made the book possible but made it better by providing detailed suggestions and useful advice along the way.

No book about sex by women would be complete without acknowledging the supportive role of the cats (Beryl, Easy, Leonita, and Oyo), the coffee (Peet's), and the chocolate (special thanks to Fernando at Godiva Chocolates on Fifth Avenue).

We dedicate this book to our mother, Marilyn Wise Douglass, who has provided many types of support and unlimited love over the years, who was the first person to read the completed manuscript, and who wonders aloud to us, "How did I end up having two girls who write about sex?" after every time she is asked to explain more about the book by the other ladies at the Y.

PREFACE

The Sex You Want is a book about female sexual pleasure. It asks why sex is typically more fun for men than it is for women. Most sex books suggest ways women should change to have better sex. Our book turns this question around and asks how sex should change to be made better for women.

Women deserve to enjoy the erotic power of their bodies as much as men enjoy their own. Yet it is rare for a woman to assert her right to sexual pleasure, to stop and ask herself, "Am I enjoying this?" and "What do *I* want?" These are questions that we, like many other women, only started asking ourselves after many years of sexual experience. As sisters, the two of us began to talk and to look back over past relationships with men. We realized that, although sex had sometimes been great, it had more often been so-so or even frustratingly bad. From talking to friends and reading books on sex, we knew that our experiences were fairly typical. Either some or all of the time, women have sex that is far less pleasurable for them than it is for their partners. We wondered why it was that, even amidst rising feminist self-awareness, the fun of sex still eludes many women. We came to the conclusion that it was because the sexual culture to which we all subscribe orients itself toward satisfying men, while women's pleasures are neglected.

Knowing that things could be different, we began to write this book and to imagine what sex designed *by* and *for* women might

be like. We spoke at greater length and depth with friends, with
our partners, and with many of the students Marcia knew from
the college sociology courses she teaches. In conversations and
in focus groups, we talked with women who range in age from
their early twenties to late fifties and in socioeconomic status
from working to upper middle class. They are from many cultural backgrounds, including Latina, Asian American, white
American, and African American, and many are immigrants
from other countries, including Mexico, Vietnam, Nicaragua,
Jamaica, India, South Africa, and Israel. These women are heterosexual, lesbian, and bisexual. Virtually every woman who
had had a male partner said that sex was far more likely to be
orgasmic for him than for her. When so many women experience the same pleasure imbalance, it cannot be explained as an
isolated, *personal* problem. Instead, it is clearly a *social* problem,
but one that, once recognized, is within women's power to do
something about. This book initiates that project.

The Sex You Want: A Lovers' Guide to Women's Sexual Pleasure
is much more than a sex guide: It is also a social critique and a
call to action. Rather than guide women to sex done in the usual
way, this book shows women how to guide sex their own way. It
combines our experiences with those of other women and with
the results of sex surveys and other published research to examine the current state of sex. We tell the story of Nikki, a character who is a composite of many women we know, and how she
grows sexually by challenging the unspoken assumptions in the
sexual culture. We then present a wholly new framework for sex
from the point of view of women's pleasure.

We focus especially on heterosexual sex because women are
least likely to have orgasms in sex with men. This is not because
men, either as individuals or as a group, intentionally keep
pleasure from women, but because sex is often reduced to intercourse and other sexual activities that make men come but not
women. When sex is changed so that women come too, both

partners will expand their sexual horizons and have more fun.

Women today may be both more pessimistic *and* more opti-mistic about sex than ever before. The fear of AIDS and of sex-ualized violence forces some to gravitate either to dangerous and self-destructive, unsafe sex, or to adopt antisexual feelings and behavior. Meanwhile, many other women ignore the pleasure imbalance and believe that they now enjoy a sexual freedom of expression equal to men's.

We believe that the extremity of these views indicates an ur-gent need to rethink sex. We also believe that women can lead the way to a new view of sex, pulling the sexual culture out of its slump of fear and complacency. By re-creating sex from their own perspective, women can fight sexual violence and make safer sex practices standard, while ensuring their orgasm and en-hancing sex overall. *The Sex You Want* shows women how they can even the balance of pleasure in sex by stirring up the sexual culture and turning up the sexual heat.

INTRODUCTION TO THE PAPERBACK EDITION

The book you hold in your hands is unlike any other sex book. Other books help you deal with the sexual status quo. *The Sex You Want* shows you and your partner how to change it.

The Sex You Want: A Lovers' Guide to Women's Sexual Pleasure includes everything you need to know to make sex better than ever before. Whether you are the proud owner or the appreciative lover of a female body, you are sure to find surprises here. This book brings you insights from sex research that rarely gets public attention but that we think are too useful to remain secret. This is information you can put to immediate use and enjoy the results. For when it comes to sex, knowledge is bliss.

Lovers want sex that gives both partners orgasms, yet many heterosexual couples face an orgasm gap. The orgasm gap is our name for the huge pleasure rift between women and men. For men, sex would not *be* sex without orgasm, yet according to surveys, more than 70 percent of all women typically go without!

Men are not to blame for this orgasm gap—most want nothing more than to bring a woman to orgasm—nor is it women's fault—with the right stimulation, they have orgasms as easily as men. The reason orgasm eludes so many women is that sex is designed for male sexual anatomy, while female anatomy is overlooked.

The current focus of sex between a woman and a man is

intercourse, an activity that is sure to stimulate a man's most sensitive organs. But the kinds of contact that give women orgasms—namely, oral and manual clitoral stimulation—are relegated to foreplay, as if they were only a warm-up for *real* sex, a.k.a. intercourse.

In *The Sex You Want,* we propose a new way of having sex that incorporates women's anatomy and pleasure. We say, "Forget foreplay!" Instead, we give oral and manual sex top billing. This new emphasis does not displace intercourse. Rather, it puts "ladies first." When a woman's first orgasm precedes intercourse, and when intercourse is combined with manual clitoral stimulation, penetrative sex becomes a dance of truly mutual pleasure. Her arousal combines with his, propelling both partners into sexual terrain they never even knew existed.

Our new view emerges from the recent boom in medical research on female sexuality, which includes findings that will forever change the way you think about—and have—sex. For example, *The Sex You Want* gives you new information about the clitoris, including its full size (5+ inches, from the external tip to its long legs inside), its shape (a large wishbone or Y), and its ability to become erect.

You will discover that the clitoris is just the tip of the iceberg in knowing the female body. You will learn that the urethra is a sexual organ and that it becomes erect along with the clitoris and other areas during sex. Once you try it, you will agree that a woman's erection, like a man's, is a prerequisite for the most satisfying intercourse. You will find out how the G spot and female ejaculation deepen sexual pleasure. And this book is the only place you will read that the core of pleasure for men is also the clitoris, which makes up one part of the penis!

Most sex guides encourage you to talk with your partner, but only *The Sex You Want* offers a language for sex that will make true communication possible. The terms we provide give women and their lovers the specific words they need to say exactly what gives them pleasure and where they want to be touched. We propose words like *clittage* for clitoral massage, the activity that is most likely to bring a woman to orgasm and the secret of success among men who know how to use their hands. We suggest that "down there," "vagina," and other common terms for women's sexual anatomy are either too vague or off the mark. So we coined *cligeva,* shorthand for the trio of the clitoris, G spot, and vagina, the three keys to maximum pleasure.

We think women and their lovers are ready for a new sexual reality. Their readiness is obvious in the ever more open talk about women's sexual pleasure in movies, TV, music and popular culture. For perhaps the first time in history, the woman's view is center stage in productions like the *Vagina Monologues* and *Sex and the City,* in magazines like *Bitch* and *Bust* and *On Our Backs,* in books of women's erotica and at Web sites like CakeNYC.com and gynomite.com. Despite seemingly permanent mountains of T & A elsewhere in the popular culture—in music videos, beer commercials, and men's magazines, especially—there are also many men who want to know: What really makes a woman come?

You will find the answers here so that both you and your lover can have the sex you want. As we move toward a new definition of sex that includes women's pleasure, there's probably never been a more exciting time to be a sexual person. Sex itself seems like a woman on the verge of orgasm—highly aroused, but not yet satisfied. Our book will give you what you need to take sex—and you—over the top. *Enjoy!*

CHAPTER ONE

The Orgasm Gap

Nikki and Joe lie naked in their bed, kissing in passionate embrace. As they caress one another, Nikki slowly glides her hand down Joe's chest and abdomen to his penis. She delights in the way it responds to her touch and savors its warm, firm feel in her hand. Joe reaches between Nikki's legs and slides his finger into her vagina. Nikki tilts her hips so that his fingertip meets her clitoris. She closes her eyes to focus on the rush of excitement his touch sends through her genitals. As Joe rubs her clitoris and kisses her neck, shoulders, and nipples, Nikki's pleasure borders on orgasm.

After a few minutes on this erotic edge, Nikki begins to worry that Joe wants to move on. She gets up, straddles him, and together they roll on a condom. Nikki massages on some lubrication then slips Joe's penis into her vagina. She caresses his penis inside her, alternately tightening and releasing her vaginal muscles. As Joe's excitement builds, Nikki senses that her own arousal is not keeping pace. The intensity of her pleasure dissipates, and she feels her orgasm slipping away. Nikki does not want to deny Joe his pleasure, so they flip over. Joe thrusts rhythmically and deeply inside her, then quickly comes. Nikki is disappointed that she has not had an orgasm, but as they rest in each other's arms, she takes pleasure in their intimacy.

For Nikki, as for most women, orgasm in sex is like a mirage: It appears on the horizon one minute, like a delicious glass of water to a thirsty traveler. But the next minute—poof!—it is gone. Sometimes, especially when she is on top during intercourse, Nikki comes, too. But at other times, she fakes orgasm. (Actually, she just lets Joe believe she has come.) Occasionally, when Joe asks, Nikki tells him, "It felt great! Really, it's OK. I love just being close to you." These are words that Joe has never uttered. He never has to: Like most men, Joe always has an orgasm when he has sex. As Joe begins to snore in satisfied slumber, Nikki lies awake trying to convince herself that it really was good for her, too.

Most men would not see the point of sex if their orgasms were so elusive. Yet Nikki and millions of other heterosexual women put up with unsatisfying sex on a regular basis, and the sexual culture—the way people in our society define sex—seems undisturbed by this fact. Both women and men expect sex to be a physically satisfying experience, but for many women it is not. Although sex virtually always includes *his* orgasm, hers is optional—nice, but not necessary.

The orgasm gap disrupts the pleasure of sex for both Nikki and Joe. When Joe comes but Nikki does not, they both feel frustrated or somehow deficient. Nikki thinks it is her mood. *I just could not let go tonight.* Sometimes she blames how she looks. *If I could just lose ten pounds.* Joe feels he has not "performed" adequately. *Maybe if I had lasted longer. Maybe if my penis were bigger.* Nikki and Joe tell themselves that orgasm is always harder for women to achieve. *Women just do not come as easily as men.*

What Nikki and Joe never blame is the *way* they have sex. For them, sex is synonymous with intercourse. They never have sex that does not include it. Intercourse gives Joe direct genital stimulation and virtually ensures his orgasm. Nikki loves the way intercourse feels, too, but most of the time it does not lead to her orgasm.

Nikki knows that she comes every time she masturbates by massaging her clitoris. But in partner sex, she never touches herself there. Joe pays her clitoris some attention during foreplay, but the stimulation he gives her usually stops short of orgasm. When they move to intercourse, the clitoris is all but forgotten. Nikki enjoys the feeling of Joe's penis inside her, but because penetration bypasses the clitoris, it does not make her come. Sometimes Nikki is tempted to ask Joe to keep his fingers on her clitoris a little longer or to give her cunnilingus. But having an orgasm from manual or oral sex is seen as inferior somehow. Both Nikki and Joe have learned that orgasm should come from intercourse. So they cut foreplay short and begin penetration, even though it is likely to mean that sex will soon culminate in his, but not her, orgasm.

The orgasm gap between women and men is not just an individual problem. Nikki's experience of hit-or-miss orgasm is typical of sex for heterosexual women in the United States today. Seventy-five percent of men have orgasm in partner sex on a regular basis, but only 29 percent of women do. Two-thirds of women have orgasms only sometimes or not at all. It is difficult to imagine men accepting sex that excluded their orgasm. Yet because women have learned to accept this double standard, the orgasm gap has hardly budged over decades of social change—the sexual revolution of the 1960s, the women's movement of the 1970s, the antisex backlash in the era of AIDS in the 1980s, and into the sexual quandary of the 1990s. The 29/75 gap continues today in a social environment that appears to be more open than ever about sex. Intimate details of sexual activity are now discussed in safer sex instruction, on television and radio talk shows, and explicit sex acts are regularly portrayed in the popular media. But the orgasm gap is rarely discussed. It is simply accepted as the way sex is.

The orgasm gap between women and men is not restricted to any particular group of people. It crosses all lines of income,

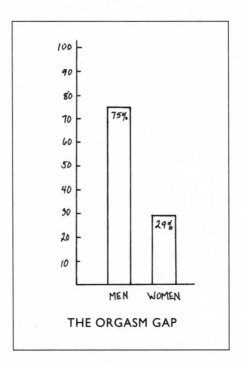

THE ORGASM GAP

race, and ethnicity. It exists not only in every region of the United States but in every society around the world. Its near universality is not, however, proof that the orgasm gap is inevitable. Women are not inherently less orgasmic than men. In fact, women are physically capable of multiple orgasms, and most women who masturbate reach orgasm without fail. Women who have sex with a female partner come 83 percent of the time. Clearly, the problem lies not with women themselves, but in the way *heterosexuals* have sex.

Most people attribute the orgasm gap to biology and ignore the fact that people learn to have sex and to have orgasms according to the beliefs of their particular culture. In the United States, people believe that there is a difference in hormones that

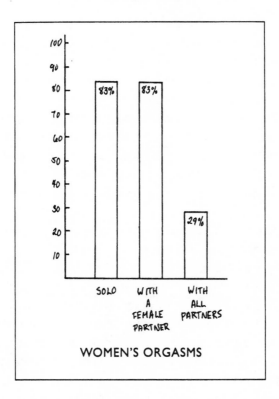

WOMEN'S ORGASMS

makes men want and need sex more than women. They believe that it is a natural fact that men reach their sexual peak at age eighteen, while most women's sexuality surges at thirty-five. They believe that women have a harder time having orgasms than men as a result of some evolutionary master plan of nature, when the real culprit is the way women and men are taught to have sex. It usually takes a woman decades before she figures out that the model of sex she was taught was wrong: It leaves out her orgasm.

Other people, including many sex experts, attribute the orgasm gap to women's psychology. In this view, women do not have orgasms because they have psychological hang-ups about sex. If women can just learn to relax in sex, they will have orgasms. But even the most carefree and uninhibited woman will not have an orgasm unless she gets the appropriate stimulation. Yet the sexual culture defines sex in such a way that women and men either never learn to use or are discouraged from using the kind of stimulation that works.

At the start of a new millennium, most young women face the same confusing path toward orgasm their mothers and grandmothers encountered. They must make their way through a morass of inconsistent messages about sex. The most damaging of these is that sex is essentially intercourse and every other kind of sexual activity is not the real thing, even when they are more likely to give women orgasms. The sex = intercourse message leaves a woman to flounder through a long series of unsatisfactory sexual encounters before she finally figures out that clitoral stimulation, not intercourse alone, will bring her to orgasm. Although the role of the clitoris in women's orgasm is mentioned in sex manuals and sex education texts, a woman can easily miss this important fact. Most women eventually discover the clitoris-orgasm connection. But then they face the higher hurdle of making this knowledge mesh with the way their partner (and the sexual culture) expects them to have sex.

The information a woman receives about orgasm is often so garbled and contradictory that she gives up trying to have one. Orgasm should come from intercourse, she is told, yet for most women it never does. Orgasm comes from clitoral stimulation, she reads, but a woman should nevertheless try to come from intercourse. Don't worry if you have never had an orgasm or only have them sometimes, she hears. Sex is so much more than orgasm: It is romance, sensuality, emotional intimacy, and above all, an expression of love.

But love is not enough to make sex good. And bad sex can interfere with love. An intimate relationship cannot thrive and grow where the physical pleasures of sex are as unequal as they are between Nikki and Joe. Some women settle for orgasms that happen now and then, and they focus their energies on romance and intimacy. But for women who find sex more frustrating than pleasurable, more embarrassing than ecstatic, and more of a duty than an opportunity, not having orgasm takes them further away from a loved partner, not closer. When the man has an orgasm but the woman does not, sex is not only less fun, but a gap can develop between two lovers in which doubt, anger, and blame begin to fester. Some women just stop having sex. One woman told us, "I faked it for over twelve years. And then it got to a point where I felt turned off to sex altogether. I didn't even want to deal with it because I wasn't getting anything out of it."

Men suffer from the orgasm gap, too. They have learned that it is up to them to "give" their partner an orgasm with their penis. If she does not come, they feel that it is a failure of either their own sexual prowess or a result of their partner's "frigidity." A man may tell a woman that she just needs to let go. The woman, too, believes that the problem is all in her head. They both accept the sexual culture's explanation that women's psychological hang-ups are the main cause of the orgasm gap. Yet the fault actually lies with a sexual culture that defines sex as intercourse.

Some women manage to defy the sexual culture and learn to have satisfying orgasmic sex. Some stumble upon orgasm by chance or luck. Others make a conscious effort to cultivate their sexuality. Of the women who regularly experience orgasm, some have one orgasm, some have multiple orgasms (more than one orgasm in a sexual session), and some ejaculate, a sexual pleasure most women never even learn about. Because sex is more often alluded to than honestly and openly discussed, women in our society have little chance of growing sexually unless they question the sexual culture and determine to cultivate their sexuality on their own.

There is little social support for women who challenge the sexual status quo. Even though women talk to each other about their periods, their relationships, and other intimate subjects, what they do in sex is a topic even the closest friends fear to broach. Women never take the opportunity to learn from other women about orgasm. Nor do most women talk frankly with their male partners about safer sex, much less better sex.

Nikki and Joe have never talked about what they actually do in bed. Neither of them has ever stopped to think about how they might do things differently because, in spite of their orgasm gap, they consider their sex life to be pretty good. They are equally interested in having sex, they enjoy foreplay, and when they have intercourse, it lasts longer than the national average of two and a half minutes. Yet, at some level, both of them know that sex between them could be so much better if Nikki had an orgasm, too.

Although primarily a problem for straight women, the orgasm gap also affects lesbians, bisexual women, and all men who care about gender equality and who like good sex. When the sexual culture focuses on what gives men pleasure in sex with a woman, all other sexual activities and everyone who is not a heterosexual male gets short sexual shrift. All women are pushed to the margins of sex defined as intercourse—lesbians do not have "real" sex, bisexual women "play around" with women until a man comes along, and straight women are expected to get pleasure from the same things that please men. If the sexual culture considers women's pleasure at all, it is only insofar as it fits into a model for sex designed to satisfy men.

Is Orgasm Important?

> I don't think orgasms are the be-all, end-all, but I sure as hell wouldn't want to live without them.
>
> —BETTY DODSON

Most men never question the importance of orgasm—it is simply their sexual right. Many women cannot say whether or not orgasm is important, however, because they have never had one. A woman who does insist on having an orgasm may be accused of being too unromantic, too male, or too demanding. Yet no man ever has to justify his desire for orgasm. The goal of sex for women, in contrast, is supposed to be intimacy, not orgasm. Yet orgasmic sex improves intimacy. When only one partner's orgasm is important, even necessary, while the other partner's is ignored or denied, true intimacy is impossible.

The Sexual Culture

The orgasm gap can be bridged only by changing the way women and men have sex. Changing the way people have sex means changing the sexual culture and confronting the assumptions upon which it is based. The first assumption is that sex is natural and that people are driven by hormones and genital urges. A person is thought to have a "sex drive" that motivates sexual behavior. Yet, as Leonore Tiefer's 1995 book proclaims in its title, *Sex Is Not a Natural Act.* Everyone who has ever had sex knows that it involves not only the body, but the mind and spirit. They know that it occurs in the context of complex relations with other people. Furthermore, sex is learned.

And it is carried out according to the standards of a particular culture. Although sex takes place in and through the body, it is not governed by people's hormones or gonads. Sex is a social act to its very core, including in the way we define the body and sex itself.

Recognizing that sex is learned, people can act to change it. Until now, women have learned to have sex in ways that favor male pleasure, but they can unlearn those ways and invent new ones that foster more equal and satisfying sex.

To make sex as good for her as it is for him, Nikki and Joe need to examine each layer of their sexual activity to look at what they do and why. This means talking about sex. Already, sex is a popular topic of public discussion, but in the age of AIDS, the talk sometimes gets reduced to a debate about whether to "just say no" or to "do it, do it, do it," without ever asking what are we doing when we "do it"? Why are we doing it? For pleasure? Out of obligation? To demonstrate love? For all of these reasons? And why is one way of having sex considered right, and another considered wrong? The sexual culture promotes intercourse between a woman and a man as something that should "come naturally." But if intercourse "comes naturally," why is only one partner coming?

Recognizing that sex is not natural, but rather a product of culture, opens up exciting possibilities for change. Reinventing sex is a radical project that involves more than just trying new positions or buying a sex toy (although these can definitely add to the fun). Changing the way we have sex requires thinking in profoundly different ways about the body, about power relations between women and men, and about sex itself. It means developing a new language to talk about sex in more equal terms. By imagining a new sexuality, women and men will do much more than enhance their own enjoyment. Making sex an act of shared, mutual pleasure is an essential part of creating true gender equality.

Four Myths

In order to begin rethinking sex, it is useful to first consider several taken-for-granted assumptions or myths that are the foundation of the sexual culture.

Myth #1: Women = Sex

In our society, the body of a woman—a young, beautiful, revealingly dressed woman—is the symbol for sex. More precisely, certain parts of a woman's body stand for sex because they are a turn-on for heterosexual men. A woman's breasts and buttocks are probably the prime icons of sex, but long legs, high heels, big hair, and a round, red mouth are also widespread cultural symbols that set up the sexual equation. The woman, like the car, the beer, or the magazine her body advertises, is an object of desire. A sexy woman is an item of consumption, and man is her consumer.

Equating sex with an idealized female image puts real women in a sexual no-person's land. The vast majority of women neither meet the criteria of what is sexy nor fit the profile of the consumer. Most women know that our sexual culture does not have them in mind when, for example, a magazine article entitled "Sex" is illustrated by a nineteen-year-old blonde in a Wonderbra, garter belt, and spike heels.

Every woman knows what it is to struggle with what one friend calls "the body thing." Women learn from the time they are young to treat their own bodies as perpetual improvement projects as they strive to emulate an externally imposed image of what is sexy. A woman's growth as a sexual person is compromised by the goal of looking sexy on the outside, and eventually a woman becomes estranged from what her body feels on the inside.

One woman told us that from the time she was a teenager, she felt she was expected to look *sexy* but never to be or feel *sexual*.

She often dressed in provocative ways. "But if I went beyond a certain point," she says, "my father would call me awful names. I never had it right, and I still don't." A woman is made to feel like a performer on a tightrope who walks a fine line imposed by the demands of the audience below—an audience that eggs her on while simultaneously criticizing her as shameless for performing in the first place. Despite its perils, this performance is one that many women feel compelled to carry out.

In a sexual culture that equates sex with the female body, a woman is told that she deserves sexual pleasure only if she looks attractive. Many women get great satisfaction from dressing up, but focusing on being attractive on the outside can interfere with sexual satisfaction within. A woman may never cultivate or respond to her own feelings or desires because she develops her sexuality based on the way others see, touch, and treat her.

The sexual culture's emphasis on a woman's exterior makes it difficult for her to develop a healthy sexual self. In reinventing sex, women can turn the focus of sex to their own experience of their bodies. They can have sex on their own terms, a privilege most men take for granted. Instead of handing her sexuality over to others, a woman controls and possesses it herself. She can enjoy orgasm when and if she wants to—she is neither pressured into coming to boost her partner's ego, nor denied orgasm because of neglect. When women reinvent sex, a woman will not earn good sex because she fits a sexy physical ideal. Instead, she will deserve good sex because she is a human being.

Myth #2: Sex = Intercourse

When heterosexuals refer to "sex," they usually mean vaginal intercourse. Whether euphemism ("the sex act"), slang ("getting laid"), or profanity ("fucking"), most words for *sex* are actually words for *intercourse*. Even many women get in the habit of thinking of intercourse as the only *real* sex. A woman recently told us that she likes to use a vibrator to have an orgasm before she has "sex." Apparently, sex does not begin until a penis gets into the act.

Vaginal penetration by the penis is the defining act of sex for most heterosexuals. A recent survey found that 95 percent of heterosexuals usually or always have intercourse when they have sex. Other sexual activities, such as manual or oral sex, sometimes serve only as either a warm-up for intercourse or an imitation of it. French kissing and finger penetration are sometimes performed to mimic it more than for their own intrinsic pleasures. Even though intercourse is the way women are least likely to come, the sexual culture places the greatest value on orgasm that results from intercourse. Clitoral stimulation is overlooked in favor of penetration, and the stereotype is that women want a man who is "long, hard, and can go all night long." Even many vibrators are shaped like a penis because it is assumed that a man's source of pleasure—the penis—should also sexually satisfy a woman.

Vaginal penetration is a rite of passage in our sexual culture. It is the only sex act that can validate marriage. (Lesbians are not granted any comparable rite to validate a partnership.) It is a testament to the crucial meaning of intercourse that a woman can engage in masturbation or in manual, oral, or anal sex with a partner and have an orgasm, perhaps multiple orgasms, but she is still a "virgin" if her vagina has not been penetrated by a penis. A woman's virginity is something *only* a man's penis—and not his hands or mouth, much less the woman herself, or another woman—has the power to take away.

To "go all the way" means arriving at the ultimate destination: vaginal penetration. For most men, intercourse is the last stop on the sex train. His orgasm announces to the woman that the trip is over. Intercourse is where she should get off, too. But it leaves most women idling on the tracks, their engines still running.

It is little wonder that men come easily during vaginal penetration. Intercourse brings a man to orgasm because the male counterpart of the clitoris lies within the penis, and the penis is surrounded on all sides by massaging vaginal walls. A woman's clitoris lies mostly within her body separate from the vagina. Her clitoris is mostly untouched by intercourse. Only the exposed tip and clitoral shaft receive some stimulation from the tugs and strokes of the man's penis or from intermittent pressure from his pelvis. For some women, this is sufficient for orgasm, especially if they are "on top." Most of the time, however, expecting intercourse alone to result in a woman's orgasm is comparable to expecting Joe to be satisfied by a massage of his testicles. It feels good, but the longer Nikki does it, the more likely he is to feel annoyed than to have an orgasm.

The low rate of orgasm for women is correlated with the high rate of intercourse-oriented sex. Intercourse simply does not give enough direct stimulation to the clitoris for orgasm to occur in most women. The penis and the clitoris pass one another like ships in the night, but only the penis makes it to port. Yet amidst multiple messages that it is the high point of sex, a woman battles a lingering feeling that she *should* be able to achieve orgasm during coitus.

A woman gets caught in a catch-22. Sex consists of intercourse, which does not make her come. Oral and manual sex do make her come, but they are seen as remedial or even "deviant" forms of sex. Oral sex is only a rare offering and manual sex is confined to foreplay, if done at all.

To some, intercourse may seem an imperative of nature. The vagina and the penis appear destined for each other, or rather, the vagina is made for the penis. The penis slips so easily into the vagina, like a sword into its sheath. Indeed, vagina *means* sheath. Its very name implies that the vagina has no sexual identity of its own but only becomes a sexual organ when the penis enters it.

The act of intercourse reflects the larger cultural notion that sex is something that men do *to* women. Even women's active role in reproduction is made to seem passive. The penis in intercourse is likened to a plow that prepares the soil and presses the seed into a receptive earth. Because of its role in reproduction, intercourse is seen as the natural way to have sex. People often point to other animals: Birds "do it," bees "do it," and so do cats and dogs. Sexual intercourse is indeed the typical and optimal means for egg to meet sperm in humans. But people engage in sex for conception only a few times in their lives. Above all, they have sex for pleasure. And as anyone who masturbates knows, the most fun one can have in sex, hands down, is orgasm.

Myth #3: Women and Men Are Different and Unequal

Perhaps the most influential myth of our sexual culture is that women and men are opposite sexes. But rather than opposite and equal, men are taken as the norm, and women the deviation. Women are both men's opposites and their inferiors. The apparently greater size of men's genitals is sometimes read as evidence of their more powerful sex drive, while women's seemingly smaller genitals reflect a lesser interest in sex. Seen as inferior in so many ways, it is not surprising that women tend to come out "on the bottom" in sex.

The myth that women are sexually inferior to men is supported by three beliefs: (1) that women have a lesser sex drive than men; (2) that women do not need orgasm as men do; and (3) that women have lesser genitals than men.

Women have a lesser sex drive than men. The sex drive is not considered the result of social conditioning or experience but as an inborn or natural gender trait. In our sexual culture, it is believed that "female hormones" (actually, the excess of female and shortage of male hormones, especially testosterone) make women less sexual. Yet hormones and other biological processes used as evidence of sex difference are always interpreted according to the terms of the culture. Women's lower levels of testosterone are said to explain why women initiate sex less often than men, but this ignores how women get decades of training to please others and are told that they are "bad" if they act on their own sexual desires. Women can be so busy responding to desires of men and the sexual culture that they hardly get a chance to cultivate their own. Women's capacity for multiple orgasms, for example, rarely gets nurtured, while the qualities that contribute to men's pleasure—beauty and sexual acquiescence—are rewarded and emphasized.

The notion of a natural sex drive helps to validate men's sexual priority. It is believed that women simply never experience the same urge to have sex "right now" that men do. Indeed, some men blame their uncontrollable sex drive when they pressure women for sex ("You got me so turned on"). It explains why men visit prostitutes or cheat on their wives or girlfriends ("Men have sexual needs"). It is even used to absolve the man and blame the woman for her own rape ("He was so turned on by her, he couldn't stop"). It seems that men simply cannot help themselves when sex goes into overdrive. For a woman to express a strong sex drive, in contrast, is seen as unnatural, even immoral. A woman who expresses an urgent desire for sex risks being seen as a "slut."

That our society considers sex a "drive" at all renders it a force beyond human control. It supports the notion that there is little an individual can do to control nature's engine. But neither men's so-called sex drive nor women's apparent indifference to sex is the product of biology and hormones, for sex unfolds in a social context. In a society that organizes sex around achieving men's orgasm and that caters to men's sexual pleasure in countless other ways, it is not surprising that a woman might show less interest in sex. But it is not because they are born that way. When sex lacks the direct clitoral stimulation that most women need to reach orgasm, it becomes a self-fulfilling prophecy that women are the less sexual half of the population. Yet when men have orgasms and women do not, the difference is treated as the playing out of the distinct sexual natures of females and males, rather than as the result of sex socialization by gender and the sexual culture's definition of sex as intercourse to the man's orgasm.

Women do not need orgasm as men do. Orgasm is practically a medical Rx for a man. If he becomes sexually aroused and does not reach orgasm and ejaculate, it is said he will suffer "blue balls." The man's visually obvious erection makes penetration (or, as many women well know, a hand job or a blow job) seem imperative. Even though a woman also experiences the equivalent of an erection, our sexual culture neither names nor recognizes this event. A woman is not described as suffering from "blue clit" if her sexual arousal does not culminate in orgasm—even though the frustration of sex that ends before orgasm is a much more common experience for women than it is for men.

To acknowledge that women need orgasms as much as men do is to suggest that women and men are much more alike sexually than different. This idea challenges the sexual culture because it implies that women are capable of and deserve pleasure no less than men.

> There are very few absolute sex differences and . . . without complete social equality we cannot know for sure what they are.
>
> —ANNE FAUSTO-STERLING, *MYTHS OF GENDER*

Women have lesser genitals than men. The sexual culture focuses on the towering erection of the man's penis while it ignores the fact that the erectile tissues of a woman's clitoris and bulbs are the same size and also respond to stimulation. The organs of both sexes expand and become firm during sexual arousal, yet the event that is so significant in men, erection, is not even acknowledged in women.

YOUR (SOCIETY'S) SEXUAL IQ TEST

1. What sexual activity is most likely to bring a woman to orgasm?

   a. intercourse

   b. clitoral stimulation

   c. sex with a partner she loves

2. What shape does the female clitoris most resemble?

   a. a four-inch wishbone

   b. a pea

   c. a miniature penis

3. When is sex between a woman and a man usually considered over?

   a. when the woman has an orgasm

   b. when each partner is sexually satisfied

   c. when the man ejaculates

4. What is the most common sign that a woman is having an orgasm?

   a. her pelvic muscle contracts

   b. her chest flushes red

   c. she moans

5. Some women ejaculate a fluid in sex that is chemically closest to

   a. urine

   b. vaginal secretions

   c. prostatic fluid similar to men's

6. What is the average duration of heterosexual vaginal intercourse?

    a. one hour

    b. two to three minutes

    c. fifteen minutes

7. Who can masturbate to orgasm faster?

    a. men

    b. women

    c. women and men can be equally fast

8. Only some women have a G spot.

    T

    F

9. A woman's vagina always lubricates or gets "wet" when she is sexually excited.

    T

    F

10. When sexually excited, women experience the same engorgement and increased muscle tension that is known as "erection" in men.

    T

    F

ANSWERS AT THE END OF THE CHAPTER.

The sexual culture defines erection as a purely male phenomenon and spotlights vaginal "wetness" in women. Vaginal lubrication is interpreted as a sign of female readiness for penetration (and the man's pleasure). It ignores how a woman's genitals become erect in the same process of blood engorgement and muscle tension that a man experiences.

Our sexual culture evaluates genitals based not on how people experience pleasure, but on how well they fit into a model of sex that features the penis in a starring role. When the stage is set for sex, the man's large, assertive organ appears at center stage and the vagina plays the part of its accommodating sidekick. The woman's clitoris acts only as a puny, uncredited extra who barely emerges from the wings.

Myth #4: Women Want Intimacy; Men Want Sex

An extension of the myth of gender difference is the belief that women and men want different things when they have sex: Women want decor (wine and candlelight), while men want hard core (genital sex and orgasm). Men want to penetrate and come; women want to cuddle and talk. Intimacy and genital sex are presented as opposite and irreconcilable goals. Women complain of not getting enough intimacy and attention, while men complain of not getting enough "sex." Women and men have indeed been taught to eat different halves of the sexual pie. But even after she gets her slice of closeness, and he gets his serving of orgasm, they both may be left feeling hungry. Perhaps the reason men get sex less often than they want is because women are not sexually satisfied. And women who are sexually unsatisfied turn their interests elsewhere. Susan Quilliam, who surveyed British women on sex, suggests that women may focus on intimacy to compensate for the lack of orgasms. A woman who regularly has sex without orgasms would indeed begin to think that pleasure must lie elsewhere.

WHAT WOMEN (DO NOT) WANT

What do women want, Freud asked. The old fool, the charlatan. He knew what women wanted. They wanted nothing. Nothing was good enough. Everyone knew that.
—A WOMAN REFLECTING ON SEX IN CAROL SHIELDS'S
NOVEL, *THE STONE DIARIES*

With the mantra "Women want intimacy and men want sex," sexuality splits into two parts, each assigned to one gender. Author and relationship guru John Gray goes even further. He argues in his books *Men Are from Mars, Women Are from Venus* and *Mars and Venus in the Bedroom* that, when it comes to relationships and sex, women and men are from different planets. This view is popular because it reassures heterosexual couples that there is nothing wrong with them. If they feel alienated from their partner, it is because she or he truly *is* an alien. Gray's view encourages people to believe that the problems between women and men are a result of innate differences that cannot be changed. Gray completely ignores how the sexual culture teaches women to focus on intimacy and men to focus on sex. By characterizing women as an emotional "planet" and men as a sexual "planet," he dresses up the sexual culture's oldest stereotypes in New Age garb. In bed, the two planets remain separated by the orgasm gap.

Rather than assigning intimacy to women and sex to men, sex could be better for everyone if it included both experiences. The last time we looked, women and men both lived on Earth, a planet located midway between Venus and Mars. Here on Earth, both women and men are capable of enjoying intimacy along with orgasmic sex. In fact, instead of conflicting, the two pleasures enhance one another. Orgasmic sex and intimacy are part of a single continuum of sexual, emotional, mental, and physical expression. When women reinvent sex, both women and men will have equal access to all the fruits in the same garden of earthly delights.

In this book, we gather together ideas and resources women can use to reinvent sex. We focus on the body and begin by rethinking women's bodies and sexuality; but a similar process for men is also needed. By considering the pleasures and desires women and men share, both can work together to debunk the myths and develop alternative, more inclusive, and more equal attitudes and activities that will make sex not just male fun, but mutual fun.

In Orgasm Denial

Reinventing sex requires that women recognize the problems of the sexual culture. Yet many women are in denial about the orgasm gap. Some ignore the problem because they have great, orgasmic sex with their partners. They say they feel no need to rethink sex, thank you very much. "Is there a problem?" asked one twentysomething college graduate who told us she has three orgasms every time she has sex. Some thirty-, forty- and fiftysomething urban professional women ask us: "Didn't we already do this in the 1970s?" And our mother tells us that she and all her World War II–generation friends figured out orgasmic sex without a hitch.

The key phrase here is "figured out." Many of these women just stumbled upon orgasm by accident or they were lucky enough to have a knowledgeable partner. Others became orgasmic in solo sex by violating the taboo against masturbation. All of them figured out how to enjoy sex not through the sexual culture, but *in spite of it*. One by one, each woman had to reinvent the sexual wheel.

There are other women, however, who are either unable or not inspired to make this effort. In a sexual culture in denial about women's orgasms, it can take a substantial effort to make partner sex satisfying. Since women's pleasure is not a topic either among women, in sex education, or even in the media, only a woman who goes out of her way to learn about sex is likely to become orgasmic. The silence surrounding female sexuality hurts even orgasmic women because it fails to acknowledge or give authority to their experiences of sex. A woman who comes with oral sex, for example, may enjoy sex less because she is wondering, "Am I coming the 'right' way?" A woman who has orgasms now and then may lack the information, opportunity, and encouragement to ask why sex is not always orgasmic. She may prefer to keep the peace rather than stir up trouble, especially when the solution challenges not only her taken-for-granted assumptions about sex, but also her relations with men.

Many women are aware of the orgasm gap but prefer not to confront it. We know women who have been married for decades, with grown children and sexually satisfied husbands, who have never had an orgasm. When they have sex they focus on the man's pleasure. Some have orgasms when they masturbate, but have not mustered the courage or developed the communication skills to talk to their partner about making orgasm a mutual part of sex together. A few have partners who refuse to change the way they have sex. For these women, orgasm looms as a daunting challenge rather than being something they look forward to enjoying.

Attaining orgasmic sex is sometimes so bewildering that, when a woman finally does have orgasms regularly with a partner, she may confuse what she feels with love. Or, she may stay in a relationship because she is afraid she will not find another partner who "gives" her orgasms. Good sex may enhance love, and love often enhances sex, but they are not the same thing.

Some feminists and sex therapists fear that encouraging women to strive for orgasm only adds to the women's feelings of sexual inadequacy. But in the name of protecting women's feelings, this view may inadvertently make orgasm all the more elusive for women. It implies that it is a woman's own fault that she does not have orgasms, rather than the fault of the way sex is defined. Others downplay the importance of orgasm because they believe that to celebrate orgasm is to succumb to male values. In a more female-oriented sexuality, they suggest, sensual pleasures such as caressing, kissing, and holding would supersede genital sex and orgasm. Women can enjoy what a special 1995 issue of *Ms.* magazine referred to as "hot unscripted sex," that is, "whatever turns you on."

Widening women's options for sexual pleasure is important, but to dismiss orgasm is to throw out the baby with the bathwater. This view also falls into the gender-stereotyped orgasm-versus-intimacy trap. Leaving women's physical pleasure vaguely defined as "whatever" makes it more likely that women's natural capacity for orgasm will remain undeveloped. A woman can always choose *not* to come, but it only truly becomes a choice for her when orgasm becomes a readily available option.

Dismantling the Sex Machine

Most observers of the 1960s now agree that the sexual revolution was a boon for sex—that is, if you were a heterosexual male. Many women expected that all the commotion would revolutionize sex for them, too. Some of them believed that by simply having *more* sex, with *more* partners, in *more* intercourse positions, on *more* days of the week, sex would become as good for them as it seemed to be for men. But more sex did not necessarily mean better sex for women, because the balance of pleasure did not change. Even when oral sex came into fashion, and more men were willing to give women cunnilingus (oral sex on a woman) than ever before, rates of fellatio (oral sex on a man) rose, too, and always remained higher. The so-called sexual revolution failed women because it did not change sex in the fundamental ways necessary to make it more *equal* fun. Ultimately, the revolution only revved up the existing sex machine. It oiled the gears, when what was needed was to dismantle the engine, melt down the parts, and completely rebuild sex from the inside out of women's experience. This has not yet happened and, as a result, at the turn of a new century, many women are still stuck in the missionary position wondering, "Did the sexual revolution come yet? . . . because I haven't!"

It is now time to rethink sex in fundamental ways. Feminists and lesbian, gay, and bisexual activists of recent decades form the vanguard of a contemporary rethinking that promises a *real* revolution in sex. Like the little girl in the village crowd who announced that the emperor had no clothes, these groups are revealing the secret that women habitually keep to themselves: Sex as it is currently defined does not satisfy women.

Crucial ingredients for reinventing sex have been contributed by people such as Shere Hite, who published a study reporting what thousands of women themselves said about sex. *The Hite Report: A Nationwide Study of Female Sexuality* was a highly controversial book that revealed the discrepancy between what women were supposed to experience in sex and what they actually felt. Critics found fault with its lack of statistical method (even though the gist of Hite's findings has been borne out by other, more "scientific" studies). Some bristled at its radical views of both sex and society. But many women found that what Hite was saying rang true to their own experience. The sexual culture was not ready to hear that sex (essentially, intercourse) was not as satisfying for women as it was for men.

Out of the grass-roots women's health movement came a new view of women's bodies. Organized through community clinics and epitomized by books such as The Boston Women's Health Book Collective's *Our Bodies, Ourselves,* first published in 1969, this movement encouraged women to take charge of their own health, including their sexual health, and to resist the alienating messages of the media and the medical establishment that treated women as either objects *for* or imperfect versions *of* men. By advocating that each woman learn to examine her own cervix and breasts and to take responsibility for her own sexual pleasure, the movement helped women to gain a greater measure of control over their bodies and lives.

The rethinking of female sexual well-being continues with books such as *A New View of a Woman's Body,* by a collective known as the Federation of Feminist Women's Health Centers, which replaces the male model of sex with one based on women's own experiences, observations, and self-examinations.

Lesbians and bisexual women are among the feminists who have challenged many facets of women's role in the sexual culture. With their critique of what Adrienne Rich called compulsory heterosexuality, activists in the lesbian, gay, bisexual, and transgender movement have helped imagine a new sexual culture for both themselves and others. Their work has made it easier for young women to avoid settling into sexual roles and ways of having sex that do not have women's best interest in mind. In their assertion that "we are here," lesbians, bisexual women and men, gay men, and transgendered people have forced the whole society to question traditional assumptions about sex and sexual categories. Bisexual visibility has put flesh on sex researcher Alfred Kinsey's view of sexual orientation as a continuum by suggesting that sexuality is more fluid and open than the categories of "heterosexual" or "homosexual" allow. Mainstream popular culture now acclaims gender-bending performers, such as the androgynous k.d. lang and flamboyant drag queen Ru Paul, who undermine the sexual culture's insistence that "femininity" and "masculinity" are inherent to people who have the genitals of women and men respectively. Books such as Martine Rothblatt's *The Apartheid of Sex,* Leslie Feinberg's *Transgender Warriors,* appearances by transsexuals on TV talk shows, and public writings by feminist scientists such as biologist Anne Fausto-Sterling (who asserts that there are five sexes at least) have created greater awareness that neither the genitals nor gender come in two neatly separated types.

The impact of these challenges on the sexual culture has been heightened by the AIDS epidemic. The need for a conscious and radical change in the way people engage in sex has rarely been more urgent than it is today when the questions are no longer simply whether to say yes or no. The questions people now face confront the very purpose and definition of sex. What is sex? Why have sex? Who is sex for? These questions force everyone to scrutinize and rethink the most taken-for-granted and fundamental aspects of sex. They unsettle sexual complacency and prepare the ground for reinventing sex for women's pleasure.

A clear alternative framework for sex has yet to be established, but it is in the process of emerging. Women are at the vanguard of this change, one that will transform not only how people have sex, but how the genitals themselves are envisioned.

It's the Clitoris, Stupid

Reinventing sex for women and men starts with outing the clitoris. The clitoris is absent from most talk about sex, especially compared to its high-profile acquaintance and alleged counterpart, the penis. References to the penis so often go without mention of its orgasm-producing counterpart in women that it sometimes seems as if the sexual culture had undergone a clitoridectomy. The vagina gets far more attention than the clitoris, and not just because it is the pathway to the uterus and conception. The vagina matters because it provides pleasure to the penis. The clitoris sometimes receives perfunctory attention as a prelude to intercourse, but that stimulation is usually neither sufficient nor appropriate for setting off a woman's orgasm.

Given its low profile, it is not surprising that the location, size, and behavior of the clitoris is a mystery for some men. One woman told us that she has considered pinning up a picture over her bed with a diagram of her genitals with arrows pointing to her clitoris and a label "Touch here."

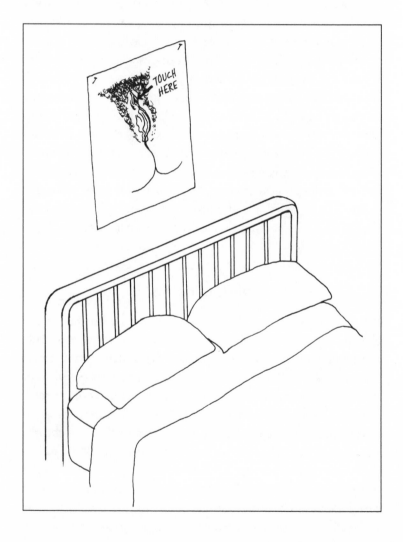

Even men who earnestly search out the clitoris in order to pleasure their partner often have trouble finding or keeping track of it. Others have difficulty staying with it long enough to allow the woman to come, or they are not sure how to stimulate it to their partner's satisfaction. When men realize that they have a clitoris too (which, as we will show, is inside their penis), they may be better able to appreciate why it is worth finding on a woman.

Women themselves may often be unable to instruct their partner because their own familiarity with female anatomy is limited. Many women avoid touching their genitals, and few are on the same first-name basis with their own clitoris that they are with their partner's penis. Boys grow up hearing jokes and stories about the exploits of the penis, but girls hear the word clitoris so infrequently that many are not even sure where the accent falls (cli´-to-ris and cli-tor´-is are both acceptable). A boy often learns from other boys what his penis can do, but a girl rarely talks about her clitoris with other girls and few get acquainted with it on their own. Indeed a woman can reach adulthood without even being aware that she has a clitoris. If a girl discovers clitoral pleasure, she often does so only by accident. The exact location of the good feeling between her legs remains a mystery to her.

Contributing to the clitoris's anonymity are sex education texts that portray it as a tiny organ that "hides" beneath its hood when erect, invoking the stereotype that women are sexually shy. Even when the sexual culture does acknowledge the clitoris, it cuts the organ down to a smaller size. Few women or men are aware that the clitoris is not a pea-sized penis, but is more than four inches long and extends inside the body.

It was decades ago that laboratory studies confirmed millions of women's own experience that the clitoris was the trigger for orgasm. Every sexologist from Hite to Masters and Johnson to

Dr. Ruth has made it clear that the clitoris is the place to stimulate a woman to orgasm. Yet the sexual culture's focus on intercourse continues undeterred. Freud's contention that women
who came only via clitoral stimulation suffered from a "sexual
dysfunction" still infects how people talk about sex, and there
is a lingering sentiment that the "vaginal orgasm" should be a
mature woman's goal.

Other misconceptions haunt the clitoris as well. Updated sex
manuals such as *Sex: A Man's Guide* by Stefan Bechtel, Laurence
Roy Stains, and the editors of Men's Health Books and *Mindblowing Sex in the Real World: Hot Tips for Doing It in the Age
of Anxiety* by Sari Locker describe the woman's clitoris as "the
only organ designed solely for pleasure." But even their inaccurate hyperbole (since men have this sensitive organ, too) does
not raise the clitoris to the stature of the penis. Sex remains focused on penis-in-vagina intercourse, often to the exclusion of
the kinds of sexual activity that directly stimulate the clitoris. In
women's magazines, for example, articles on sex dutifully mention the importance of clitoral stimulation for women's orgasm,
but rather than encouraging women to stimulate the clitoris directly, they frequently end up advising women to get on top in
intercourse and hope for the best.

There are signs that the clitoris is beginning to get noticed.
Many sex educators, activists, and researchers are trying to bring
the clitoris out into public discussion. Humor books such as
Holly Hughes's *Clit Notes* put the word on the front table of
some bookstores and woman-friendly sex outlets such as Good
Vibrations and Eve's Garden advertise vibrators and other sex
toys in mainstream magazines. But in a sexual culture either
afraid or disinclined to examine women's genitals too closely,
there are still millions of women and men who remain unaware
of the clitoris's orgasmic power.

It's the G Spot, Too

In 1982, a book called *The G Spot* by Alice Kahn Ladas, Beverly Whipple, and John D. Perry brought attention to another source of female sexual pleasure at a spot that can be reached through the vagina a few inches inside on the front wall. With the book, women familiar with pleasurable sensations from that area finally had their experience validated. But some feminists believed that the G spot was just a craze or a fad. Worst of all, it seemed to revive Freud's notion of the vaginal orgasm. Many women never even bothered to look for the G spot because they considered it a hoax, while others saw it as just one more sexual goal women were expected to achieve. Despite the controversy, the book helped women who were willing to explore to find their G spot. (Using the fingers works better than searching with their partner's penis.) A woman we know in her forties who never read the earlier book only found her G spot recently after reading Chapter 6 of this book. "I can't believe I've been having sex all these years and didn't know about this!" she told us.

Some researchers hypothesize that the G spot is the female prostate gland, similar to the male prostate gland. Men's prostate gland is also sexually sensitive and can be stimulated along the front anal wall, while the woman's G spot can be stimulated along the front vaginal wall. (Women can get "prostate" cancer, too, although it is less common and usually not life-threatening.) Although it is stimulated through the vagina, the G spot surrounds the urethra. Stimulating the G spot with the fingers, what we call G spotting, creates pleasurable feelings and can lead to orgasm.

G spotting also makes some women ejaculate. Like male ejaculation, female ejaculation is a pleasurable sexual experience in which fluid spurts out of the urethra. Yet women who ejaculate are often told they are "urinating." If they look female ejaculation up in books, they will find either no reference to it at all or contradictory opinions about what it is and doubts about whether it occurs. Those who have experienced or observed female ejaculation know that it occurs, and that ejaculate does not smell or look like urine. It is thought to be prostatic fluid similar to male ejaculate without the sperm. But debate persists among researchers about where it comes from and why only some women ejaculate.

The current sexual culture takes little account of either female ejaculation or the G spot because they do not fit into the existing framework for female sexuality. The current model of sex also keeps the clitoris a secret, depriving women of the information they need to enjoy orgasm. All of these secrets and misconceptions can be cleared away by reinventing sex from the inside of women's own experiences of pleasure.

Sex Transformed

Reinventing sex requires a new framework for understanding the body and sexual activity. Because the sexual culture has focused on men, and even sees women's bodies in terms of male (and, only secondarily, female) pleasure, women currently lack the concepts and words with which to talk about their sexuality. Women have neither names for genital parts nor words to describe the sexual techniques that make sex orgasmic. New words and a new language for sex will allow women to talk with and learn from one another. A new vocabulary will help women to communicate with a partner and will fundamentally change how women and men have sex.

Some new terms for *women's genitals* we develop in this book include:

- Orgasmic Crescent—This is our term for the crescent-shaped area that is women's pleasure center. The orgasmic crescent begins at the clitoris and extends back across the opening of the urethra (another sexual area) and up inside the vagina behind the pubic bone to the G spot. The labia swell when a woman is erect. Stimulating all the areas along the orgasmic crescent at the same time can give a woman a powerful orgasm. Some women also ejaculate.

- Cligeva (cli-GEE-va)—This is our name for women's genitals as a whole. No word now exists that includes all of women's sexual parts. The word combines the most important sexual parts for women's pleasure. The word combines the first syllable of each sexual part—the clitoris, the G spot, and the vagina. The final "a" also refers to the anus, an often overlooked site of pleasure. The word also has the advantage of listing the parts in the order in which many women like to be genitally stimulated.

We also use new words for *sexual techniques* that focus on women's pleasure including:

- Manual Sex—Many people use their hands in partner sex to great effect, yet they rarely use the name for it, manual sex. Manual sex is a widely practiced and highly pleasurable sexual art that has been trivialized as "foreplay" or "petting." As one of the most direct routes to orgasm for women, it deserves being promoted to a category of sex on a par with intercourse and oral sex.

- Clittage (cli-TAZH)—This is our word for the most basic kind of manual sex—manual stimulation of the clitoris. It combines clitoris and massage. Clittage or clitoral massage is the most common way women reach orgasm, yet this sexual act has no name. Fingers—one's own or a partner's—can provide orgasmic pleasure at any time, including during intercourse or in a mutually orgasmic quickie. Clittage can also be effectively performed with a vibrator.

- G spotting—Another kind of manual sex involves stroking the G spot with the fingers. G spotting can also be done with a dildo or performed by a man with his erect penis.

- Forget Foreplay—In a sexual culture that includes women's pleasure, "foreplay" will disappear. Instead of being treated as a prelude to sex, the manual and oral sex that now make up foreplay would become the central features of sex.

- Ladies First—This rule of orgasmic etiquette appears in many sex manuals but is frequently ignored in practice. Ladies first reminds a man that a woman's orgasm (at least her first one) ideally comes before intercourse and always before the man ejaculates. This ensures a woman of orgasm every time she has sex with a man.

- Mutual Erection—The genitals of both women and men become erect when sexually aroused. Even though women's genitals become engorged (and therefore erect), women's erections have been ignored. Erection is as conducive to a woman's orgasm as it is to a man's. Similarly, a woman's erection is as essential for intercourse as a man's penis. Vaginal penetration is far more pleasurable for a woman when she is erect. Mutual erection makes intercourse an orgasmic experience for *both* partners.

New words and concepts for sex will enable women to bridge the orgasm gap. Sex will no longer take place solely on men's terms. Instead, it will unfold according to a new sexuality that is equally oriented toward women's pleasure.

YOUR (SOCIETY'S) SEXUAL IQ TEST ANSWERS

1. b

Most women reach orgasm from direct clitoral stimulation, not from vaginal intercourse. Women who have orgasms during intercourse are probably doing so primarily because of clitoral stimulation, either from indirect pressure or from direct manual stimulation. While feelings of love certainly can enhance sexual pleasure, love does not provide the genital stimulation needed for orgasm.

2. a

The shape of the entire clitoris resembles a four-inch wishbone. It extends from the external and visible pea-sized tip, up the shaft and into the body. The legs of the clitoris inside the body split off like those of a wishbone onto either side of the vaginal walls. Men also have a clitoris inside the penis that is the same size as women's (relative to body size), but its legs are shorter. The tip of the man's clitoris cannot be touched directly because it lies underneath the head of the penis. The tip of the woman's clitoris is usually compared to the whole penis, but this is like comparing a part to a whole. The more accurate comparison is between the entire female and the entire male clitoris, from tip to legs.

3. c

Sex between a woman and a man is usually considered over when the man ejaculates (it is assumed he has had an orgasm, too). The woman's orgasm (and certainly not her ejaculation) is not a required part of sex as currently defined.

4. a

The pelvic muscle (specifically the PC or pubococcygeus muscle) usually contracts during orgasm in both women and men. Masters and Johnson observed a red flush on some women's chests during orgasm, but most women do not experience or observe this. A woman and a man can tell when a woman is having an orgasm by the buildup of her erection, her PC muscle contractions, and the subsequent release of muscle tension and blood in her genitals.

Many men expect women to make the same synthesized moans during orgasm that women perform in pornographic movies and on records. Instead, when her attention is truly riveted on the pleasure in her body, a woman may let out a scream or make no sound at all. There is no standard performance for orgasm.

5. c

It is not known what percentage of women ejaculate. It is possible that all women ejaculate but the amount of fluid is very small, so they are not aware of it. All women have a prostate gland or G spot and a urethra and therefore all are potentially capable of ejaculating. Yet because the sexual culture rarely acknowledges female ejaculation, most neither find their G spot nor learn how to ejaculate. Women who do ejaculate are sometimes told they are urinating and some women stifle their ejaculations. Others mistake the fluid as an abundance of vaginal juices. But female ejaculate comes out of the urethra, just as it does in men, and is a watery fluid chemically similar to prostatic fluid in men.

6. b

Vaginal intercourse lasts an average of two to three minutes. The average length of the whole sexual encounter is typically just fifteen minutes. Sex that begins with the man's erection and ends when he comes rarely lasts more than an hour.

7. c

It takes women and men about the same amount of time—about four to five minutes, on average—to reach orgasm. When women take longer to come than men or do not come at all, it is usually because they are not getting adequate clitoral stimulation.

8. F

Most body parts are not optional. If some women have a G spot, it is likely that all women do. Many women have never looked for their G spot because they are either unaware of it or doubt it exists. Rather than asking whether or not all women have a G spot, women should be asking why it remains a mystery instead of being treated as a pleasurable fact of a woman's sexual experience.

9. F

Some women get wet when they are sexually excited, yet all women are made to feel that vaginal lubrication is a measure of their sexual "responsiveness." Vaginal wetness is not always an accurate way to evaluate a woman's state of arousal. The more useful indicator in both women and men is the genital engorgement and muscle tension that occurs with erection.

10. T

When a woman is aroused, her genitals, including the clitoris and G spot, engorge with blood and the PC muscle becomes taut. This same process is called an *erection* in men. Women's genital erections have so far gone ignored and unnamed.

Sex
Undressed

Dressing for Sex

For many women, sex begins with *looking* sexy. If a woman knows that an evening out is likely to be followed by sex, she gets prepared to look good both in and out of her clothes. Nikki works on her body regularly to stay fit and healthy, but still worries about how her body looks. When getting ready for an evening that may end in sex, she goes through an especially detailed series of grooming and fashion rituals. These rituals contain both pleasures and stresses. The day before Nikki goes out with Joe, she climbs aboard a roller-coaster ride that takes her over steep hills of doubt, through tunnels of stress, and around loops of physical challenges until she gets off, breathless, ready to meet her man.

A day or two before their date, Nikki pays a visit to the beauty shop for a trim ($18). She goes to another salon to have her nails done ($12). Then she shops at three different boutiques for just the right top to go with the skirt she wants to wear ($42). When she returns home from work on the evening she plans to see Joe, Nikki hurriedly irons the skirt and new top. She gets in the shower, washes her hair—*lingering salon hairspray, yuck!*—and wonders how she will ever be able to re-create what her hairdresser did. Nikki washes carefully "down there"—twice to make sure the soap's fragrance replaces any telltale vaginal smells. She pumices her elbows and feet and shaves her underarms and legs. She steps out of the shower and carefully pats her-self dry (beauty magazines advise women never to rub the skin, especially the face). Nikki applies deodorant to her underarms, body lotion to her legs and arms, and for good measure, femi-nine hygiene spray. *Thank God I'm not having my period.* She picks out her favorite pink silk underwear and puts on her new black Wonderbra—*oops, pink doesn't go.* She changes to a pair of black cotton bikini briefs.

At the bathroom mirror, she plucks her eyebrows and applies moisturizing cream, foundation, blush, mascara, and lipstick. She spreads gel through her wet hair and blows it dry. She rolls up a panty hose leg and hops on one foot, then flops on her bed to finish encasing her legs and hips in tight, sheer nylon. Nikki gets up and slips on the new top—*no, too revealing for tonight. But nothing else goes with this skirt!* She takes off the panty hose—*good thing, hadn't noticed that run in the back*—and strug-gles into her best-looking jeans. She pulls on a favorite old sweater, then, to dress up the outfit, Nikki climbs into a pair of high-heeled boots. She decides on jewelry. *Silver? No, gold.* Ear-rings hung, necklace clasped, and rings in place, Nikki stands in front of the mirror. She sighs as she adjusts her earrings and fixes her hair. *It'll have to do.* She dots perfume on her wrist and behind her ears. The doorbell should ring any minute now. She quickly tidies her bedroom, checks that the sheets are clean, runs the vacuum hastily over the carpet, puts condoms discreetly be-hind the lamp on the nightstand, and sets some fresh flowers in a vase on her dresser.

After dinner, a movie, and a short stroll, Nikki and Joe get back to her place. They mix conversation with exploratory touches and eventually reach the bedroom. As they venture kisses and explore one another's bodies, they undress down to their underwear—she in her black lingerie, he in his gray, torn Fruit of the Looms. Joe is a well-groomed man; he routinely showers and cuts his nails and sees the dentist once a year. But he does not spend nearly as much time, effort, or money on the details of bodily refinement as Nikki or most other women do. Not all women go through elaborate beauty rituals, but all are held to a higher physical standard than men. A woman puts a great deal of thought and effort into being clean, smelling fresh, and looking good for her partner. As one woman observes, "All a man has to do in preparation for a night of sex is show up."

Many women enjoy sensual pleasures in caring for the body— the energized but relaxed feel after exercise, the warmth of a bath with fragrant oil, the smell of skin lotion, the feel of a silky slip on the skin—and the satisfactions that come with looking good. Dressing well, and even applying makeup, involve creativity and artistry. At the same time, every woman has known moments of panic about her body or about dressing up—the ill-timed blemish, the bad-hair day, the extra three pounds that settled on her thighs. Whether a woman enjoys dressing and making herself up or finds it depressing, one thing is certain: It is never enough. Most women know they fail to live up to the ideal "sexy" look, and even women who like what they see in the mirror know it is only temporary. Beauty takes persistence and women's work to achieve it is never done.

Most women have a lot at stake in their beauty ritual because the sexual culture measures a woman's sexual worth according to a brutally narrow ideal. Many women believe that they deserve sexual pleasure only if they look "sexy." If a woman's mirror, or her man, hints that she has failed, she may feel so deflated that she gets turned off to sex. As more than one woman has said to us, "When I feel fat and ugly, I'm not in the mood for sex." If a woman decides to have sex anyway, self-doubt may distract her to the point that she cannot enjoy herself. Fearful that her partner will see her "fat thighs," she refuses cunnilingus. Afraid her partner will see her breasts or her stomach, she does not get on top in intercourse. She even avoids the activities and positions that are reliably orgasmic for her.

Women are told by the sexual culture that their efforts to look good will be rewarded with good sex. But even a woman who feels good about how she looks discovers that beauty does not necessarily bring sexual happiness. Nikki spent hours dressing up for Joe, but at the end of the night, as she lay undressed next to her slumbering partner, she found that she had gotten all dressed up with no place to go—her pleasure was stood up.

A woman's efforts to look sexy mostly benefit the man. Her "sexiness" provides him visual arousal and enhances his status in the eyes of other men and women. Her looks reflect *his* power, not hers. In dressing for sex, a woman places sexual pleasure at the man's feet (or rather, his genitals). She acts as a beautiful backdrop to a man's solo performance. Her partner may not intend to play the prima donna. In fact, he may prefer to share the sexual limelight with his partner. The problem is, neither of them knows how to go about making their roles in sex more equal.

Redressing the pleasure imbalance involves undressing sex as we know it. It means posing fundamental questions about why women and men behave as they do in sex (and get different results). Undressing sex helps reveal the subtle obstacles that keep many women from having orgasms. By rethinking each stage of what Nikki and Joe actually do in bed, we can see how they can make sex more mutually fun.

Jumping Hurdles into Bed

After preparing her body and creating the atmosphere for sex, a woman may still be unable to leap headlong into bed with the same eagerness as a man. She has other hurdles to jump. If she is from a religious background, she may have to battle layers of guilt about having sex at all. *If I want sex, am I a "bad woman"?* With a new partner, a woman may worry about her reputation.

Will he think I'm too easy? The feelings of guilt and shame that she learned as a child about her body and about sex may resurface. Some women respond to these feelings by voraciously acting out every sexual fantasy they can imagine. More often, a woman reacts in the opposite way, by holding back. She may find it so difficult to overcome the hurdles that separate her from pleasure that she gives up on sex altogether. Getting to the pleasure in sex is rarely this complicated for men.

Of course, men experience anxiety about sex, too. Some men are self-conscious about their bodies, especially penis size. Many share women's concern about safer sex and even contraception. A lot of men's anxiety focuses on the "event" itself. A man may rush to intercourse and ejaculation because he fears losing his erection and being unable to "perform." At the same time he worries about coming *too* fast, before his partner is satisfied.

Meanwhile, the woman worries about whether she will come at all.

For women, sexual hurdles pop up before, during, and after sex. In addition, a woman faces consequences of heterosexual sex that can seriously affect her health and well-being. A premenopausal woman has to think about birth control. *Did I take my pill today? Do I have enough contraceptive gel?* A woman tends to be at higher risk than men for sexually transmitted diseases. She has to make sure her partner will wear a condom. *What if he gets angry and refuses?* If she has not had sex with this partner before, she does not know whether he has a tendency to become aggressive or violent in relation to sex. *What if he wants to do something I don't want to do?* A woman considers whether the place where they will have sex is safe and comfortable. *Gee, I don't like the looks of this motel.* If they are at home, both she and her partner may be concerned about being interrupted. *Will the kids knock on the door?*

Finally, the woman is alone with her partner. The door is locked, the phone unplugged, the shades are drawn. But as they start to undress, new hurdles appear. When she reveals her body, a woman exposes her Achilles' heel: *Will he think I'm fat? Will he notice how my breasts droop?* Seeking to escape these thoughts, she hurries out of her clothes and slips under the bedcovers. As she and her partner embrace, she wonders about how he will react to her body. *Will he be turned off by my love handles? Will he notice my stretch marks?* If he seems undeterred, they may get to the point where the woman's attention is finally drawn to her own experience. She enjoys the warmth of his skin against hers. She loves how he smells. As her body relaxes in his arms, she reproaches herself for not doing this more often. Her clitoris tingles with pleasure at his touch. Her nipples come to attention in response to his kiss. As she begins to focus on a building orgasm, the negative body concerns that loomed so large just a few moments before evaporate.

Don't Ask, Don't Tell

The feel of their bodies together delights Nikki. As she starts to sweat, however, new worries appear. When Joe moves down to her clitoris, she feels herself tighten up. Instead of lying back and enjoying his stroking tongue on her clitoris, she becomes concerned that he will be turned off by her genitals. *Do I still smell OK?* She tries to concentrate on what her body is feeling, but then Joe's tongue wanders and is not quite on the right spot. *If he would just move a little to the left . . . Should I say something?* After a few minutes, she knows she will never reach orgasm unless he moves his tongue over. But instead of telling him, she begins to worry about the orgasm that is slipping away. *I'm taking too long. He's getting bored. It's time to move on.*

Nikki stops Joe and pulls him on top of her. He takes this gesture as a vaginal invitation and, after quickly rolling on a condom, he begins penetration. It feels uncomfortable at first, but Nikki moves her body to direct his penis inside. She feels a pleasant pressure against her clitoris when he presses against her. When he pulls back, her G spot responds. She enjoys having his full body weight on top of her. She lifts her legs over his shoulders and his penis reaches the cul-de-sac. She tightens her PC muscle around his penis and her excitement heightens. He responds to her pleasure by thrusting faster and deeper. Suddenly, Joe cries out, "Aaagh!" and slumps on top of her. Joe revives briefly to give her a kiss and whisper, "Did you come?" Nikki evades the question and says, "It was great." Or, more honestly, "No, but it felt so good to have you inside." Usually, he doesn't ask and she doesn't tell.

Once again orgasm has slipped beyond Nikki's reach. She envies how easy it is for Joe to reach orgasm. *Oh, well,* she thinks. *Women don't come as easily as men. Besides, people make too big of a deal out of orgasm.* As he slips into slumber, Nikki looks at his closed eyes and strokes his unresponsive face. She reminds herself: *The most important thing about sex is not orgasm, but just being close.*

Indeed, for most women, sex is definitely *not* about orgasm. But the intimacy many women seek eludes a couple when, in ways both obvious and subtle, the man's pleasure takes precedence over the woman's. This pleasure gap creates anxiety and stress that is not conducive to the free flow of blood to the genitals of either partner. Nikki feels pressure to reach orgasm during intercourse, but it never happens. Joe feels on the spot to perform by giving Nikki an orgasm with his penis alone. Under this performance pressure, a man may suffer erection difficulties or come too soon (premature ejaculation).

A woman's orgasm would be assured and a man's performance worries would likely disappear if sex included manual and oral sex—more specifically clittage, G spotting, and cunnilingus—rather than intercourse alone. When a man uses his fingers or tongue to bring a woman to orgasm, it does not matter whether his penis is erect or not. Using hands and mouths rather than only the penis shifts the focus and pressure off the man to perform and ensures the woman's orgasm. Each partner is freed from the rush to reach the goal of intercourse and the man's ejaculation. Both the woman and the man can relax and take the time to have multiple orgasms. Oral and manual sex ignite the arousal of both partners for as long as either partner likes. When sex no longer revolves around intercourse but instead focuses on manual and oral sex, the very notion of "foreplay" becomes meaningless.

Forget Foreplay

Many people believe that women are slower than men to become aroused and to reach orgasm. As one man said to us, "Women are like an old Chevy; they take a long time to warm up." The man is the driver pumping on the gas pedal, while the woman is an old engine that refuses to turn over. If women got into the driver's seat, however, sex would probably not even be compared to old engines, much less behave like one.

Women do not take longer to get aroused and come than men; they simply get too little and the wrong kind of stimulation. The sexual activities that most easily bring women to orgasm are now called "foreplay." Foreplay is a dumping ground for everything—kissing, touching, and oral and manual sex—that is not intercourse. Shere Hite observed that the term itself reinforces the intercourse imperative. The suffix, "fore-," denotes an activity done before intercourse as the main event. "Play" implies that manual and oral sex are not serious sex, just fooling around.

Most heterosexuals engage in oral and manual sex as warm-ups for intercourse rather than as sex that leads to orgasm. Just when a woman nears orgasm, the stimulation suddenly stops. The man—or, like Nikki, the woman herself—interrupts cunnilingus, clittage, or G spotting to begin intercourse. As if responding to a schoolyard bell, the woman knows it is time for play to stop and the real work of sex to begin. She does not say, Hey, what happened? She knows the script for sex as well as any man.

Men often view foreplay as a hurdle they have to jump over in order to get "sex." One man repeated the joke to us, "Foreplay is three hours of begging." (Of course, foreplay rarely lasts that long, and if it did, men would not have to beg for sex in the first place).

A lot of men simply do not know what makes a woman come. They know the clitoris needs attention, but they do not know how it should be touched or kissed. Some men go through the motions of stimulating the woman's clitoris, performing clittage or cunnilingus in a perfunctory way. It is as if foreplay, like the flowers, dinner, and show that led up to it, were simply the price men had to pay for admission.

Clitoral stimulation, like the other gifts a man gives a woman, are offered only on special occasions. In contrast, stimulating the penis in sex is a standard offering of sex. What would be the point of sex without (his) orgasm? Sex without a man's ejaculation is considered incomplete. Yet heterosexuals regularly leave out the woman's clitoris and, as a consequence, her orgasm, and they still call it sex. In reinvented sex, "foreplay" would be forgotten, intercourse optional, and manual and oral sex done to the woman's satisfaction.

Caught in the Act

Along with forgetting foreplay, intercourse needs to be brought down from its high tower as the way for women to have orgasms. Women learn that orgasm should result from intercourse; yet this requires being sexually sensitive in ways that defy common sense. Like the princess who must feel a tiny pea through forty mattresses, a "real" woman is expected to reach sexual frenzy from the distant thrusts of her partner's penis. If she feels little or nothing, she concludes she is deserving of neither the prince nor sexual pleasure. And it is her own fault: She is no princess.

The sexual culture teaches women to undervalue the orgasms they have from manual and oral sex. The only orgasm that counts comes from intercourse. Apologetically, a woman says, "I have orgasms, but I am still unable to have them during intercourse." The ideal of "vaginal" orgasms even keeps some women from masturbating. One long-married woman who has never had an orgasm tells us that she does not even try to masturbate to orgasm because she wants her first one to come from intercourse with her husband. As if in a fairy tale some women believe that if they just try hard enough they will miraculously feel that pea one day.

All forms of women's orgasmic pleasure are considered inferior to orgasm from intercourse. Orgasm from fingers, a tongue, a vibrator, and especially from masturbation is seen as lacking the romance and magic of an orgasm bestowed upon a woman by a man's penis. Undeniably, orgasm during intercourse can be sensational. But it is most likely to occur when a woman's cligeva, the whole of a woman's genitals, is erect, usually after orgasm from clittage, cunnilingus, or G spotting. Even without orgasm, intercourse is a powerful means of expressing love, intimacy, and desire. It allows a woman and man to become as physically close as is humanly possible so that two can feel as one. But when intercourse brings the man but not the woman to orgasm, intimacy can evaporate and a huge gulf separates the two partners: The man is sexually satisfied while the woman is left either untouched by sexual pleasure or turned on but frustrated. While he relaxes into sleep, she lies awake. She has so much pent-up sexual energy, she considers getting up and cleaning the kitchen. Maybe eating some chocolate cake will feel good, she thinks. She seeks out some other pleasures to distract her from her emotional and mental arousal and from the tension and engorgement between her legs.

Putting Intercourse in Its Place

In heterosexual sex, all roads lead to intercourse. Some men model much of their foreplay on the act of penetration. What is sometimes known as French kissing can be an appealing interplay of tongues. But some men perform it in a way that not-so-subtly suggests that they hope vaginal penetration will soon follow. Done forcefully rather than sensitively, a man's kisses may feel more like an oral assault than a sexual engagement.

When women reinvent sex, the basic practice of sex will not be intercourse, but manual sex. Intercourse is inappropriate as the central act of sex because by itself it is usually not equally satisfying to both partners. A man easily comes to orgasm with intercourse because his penis, including his clitoris inside the penis, receives an overall massage from the woman's vaginal walls and muscles. The woman's clitoris, in contrast, receives no comparable stimulus because the penis bypasses its sensitive tip when it enters the vagina. In order for a woman to come during penetration, clitoral stimulation has to accompany intercourse in some way. Yet women are expected to enjoy what little clitoral stimulation they can get during penetration. Some women have orgasm during intercourse, primarily because they gain enough stimulation from the pressure of the man's body against their clitoris. For most women, however, indirect clitoral rubbing or pressure is usually not continuous or direct enough for orgasm to occur, especially when their genitals are not erect.

Reinventing sex does not mean renouncing intercourse. Rather, it means including intercourse among a wider array of pleasures. Intercourse is infinitely better when preceded, accompanied, followed (and sometimes replaced) by manual sex. By insisting that intercourse move over and make room for a wider repertoire of sexual pleasures, heterosexuals can make all of sex—including intercourse—more exciting. The erotic enjoyment of intercourse takes a quantum leap when intercourse occurs *after* the woman's orgasm. At that point, she often craves the feeling of a man's penis pressing against her engorged vaginal walls, G spot, and cul-de-sac. If Nikki and Joe had continued what we call clittage during intercourse, Nikki could share the same intense sensations that Joe feels during penetration. With clittage intercourse, they could both have orgasms.

Why should a woman struggle to make orgasm happen with intercourse alone when other things do it better? A woman goes to great lengths (sometimes performing great contortions) as she endeavors to have orgasms solely from the stimulus of her partner's penis inside her vagina. Even when a woman knows that what always works is manual or oral sex, she feels compelled to observe the rule that in partner sex, orgasm should come from a penetrating penis alone and not from his hand, her hand, his tongue, or the head of a vibrator.

The Orgasm Hierarchy

The sexual culture treats masturbation and oral and manual sex as second-rate forms of sex—even though women's orgasms are more likely to come from these activities than from intercourse. The sexual culture makes them seem to be remedial efforts to make up for intercourse that has "failed." Sex experts often treat manual stimulation of the clitoris as a substitute for orgasmless penetration. Barbara Keesling, for example, in her book *Sexual Pleasure,* recommends it to women only at the end of her book of sexual exercises. "What if you have tried every exercise at least three times and you still have not been able to have an orgasm during intercourse? Don't give up—I have another suggestion: manually stimulate your clitoris during intercourse." Yet some men resent manual sex, whether using the woman's or their own hands. One woman remembers a lover who was angry about being asked to manually stimulate her clitoris after intercourse so she could come. Clearly a believer in the orgasm hierarchy, he expected his penis alone to do the trick. When it did not, he deflected his own embarrassment by blaming her. She, in turn, felt inadequate. Neither of them blamed the real culprit: the ideal of orgasmic intercourse.

Even though it goes against many women's own experience of their bodies, they learn that there are right ways and wrong ways to orgasm. Many women strive for orgasm from intercourse because they consider it more romantic or meaningful. In her survey of British women, Susan Quilliam found that most women accepted what she calls an "orgasm hierarchy." Orgasm from no-hands intercourse that occurs simultaneously to the man's is at the top of the orgasm list. Orgasm from oral and manual sex are in the middle, and orgasm from solo sex is at the bottom. The ways most women have orgasm are the least valued.

Women can move the sexual culture beyond the orgasm hierarchy by recognizing that the way most women come during intercourse is from clittage, not from penetration alone. Intercourse is better seen as an accompaniment to clittage rather than the other way around. One woman says that either she or her boyfriend brings her to orgasm by manually stimulating her clitoris before and during intercourse. Another woman reports that she began to always have an orgasm with intercourse ever since a lover suggested she give herself clittage during penetration. People who have their finger on the clitoris are pointing to something important.

Naming Manual Sex

Many people use their hands to masturbate, yet refuse to touch their own genitals in the presence of a partner. Some people, however, are comfortable enough to enjoy what is known as "mutual masturbation," the term for self-stimulation in the presence of a partner. (It is also sometimes used to mean giving manual sex to a partner.) However, the verb *to masturbate*—literally, "to defile with the hand"—is primarily associated with solo sex. The use of hands in partner sex is extremely common, too, yet because sex is equated with intercourse, this important set of techniques does not even merit a specific name.

Sex with the hands needs its own name and deserves to be treated as a category of sexual activity on a par with oral sex and intercourse. Even anal sex, though often maligned, at least has a name. Most people regularly use their hands to stimulate their partner's genitals, yet they do not acknowledge this activity as manual sex. When manual sex moves from the margins to the center of partner sex, most women will be able to reach orgasm easily, as often and as quickly (or as slowly) as they like. Men, too, benefit from exploring manual sex. They can use manual sex to prolong sex and to heighten a partner's arousal, and by making sex more pleasurable for their partner, men can increase their own pleasure. Already, men's partners use their hands on and off throughout a sexual encounter to stimulate their penis and testicles and to keep them erect. Now it is time for men to reciprocate.

Like oral sex and intercourse, manual sex deserves a place in everyone's sexual vocabulary. Lesbians almost always use their hands in sex, recognizing that, as the most reliable source of women's orgasm, the fingers are fine instruments of pleasure. In "Dyke Hands," SDiane Bogus writes that "hands are the sexual organ of lesbian love." Women who make love with other women learn the effectiveness of manual sex for female pleasure. In one survey, 75 percent of lesbians said that they liked both touching a woman's genitals and having their own stroked, and there is a correspondingly high rate of orgasm in partner sex among lesbians. The word is beginning to get out to heterosexuals. Recently, an article in *Details* magazine advised men to take a lesson in loving a woman from lesbians. In her *Sexwise* chapter entitled "How to Make Love to a Woman: Hands-on Advice from a Woman Who Does," writer Susie Bright advises a woman's partner to "Use your hands like they're your tenderest parts."

Yet manual sex is rarely named even in lesbian sex. The names for manual sex that do exist deal with sex for men. There are slang terms for manual stimulation of the penis—men "jerk off" or "jack off," or receive a "hand job" or a "local"—but there are no widely accepted terms, slang or otherwise, for manual sex on a woman. Some women use "finger fucking" to refer to finger penetration and "jilling" to refer to manual stimulation of the clitoris, but these are, respectively, based on the intercourse model of sex and a derivative of a male term. Other terms, like "fisting," or penetration with a clenched hand, is a unisex term but it describes a fairly uncommon sexual activity. It is time that the activity that *most* women use *most* of the time to reach orgasm—finger stimulation of the clitoris—had a name of its own.

Clittage

Manual stimulation of the clitoris can make a woman come faster than the time it takes to say this awkward phrase. Without a precise name, manual-clitoral stimulation might remain no more than a ghostly presence in heterosexual partner sex. This most important sexual activity deserves a name that will call attention to it and give it authority and legitimacy. By combining clitoris

---

CLITTAGE BY ANY OTHER MEANS . . .

Clittage quickly makes the cligeva erect and leads to a woman's orgasm. Although it is usually performed with the fingers, vibrators provide an electrifyingly powerful form of clittage. A vibrator on the clitoris is like a fast, powerful finger that never tires. Plug-in vibrators provide especially long-lasting and strong stimulation. (Some vibrators can seem too intense at first, but after getting used to their unique stimulation, a woman may want an even stronger one.) In addition to the fingers and a vibrator, an erect penis (plied with lots of lubricant and a condom), a tongue, or even a firm body part like the thigh can also provide clittage with superb effects. Clittage can also be done with clothes on or through underwear. The variety of sources and contexts for clittage is limited only by the imagination.

with massage, we invented clittage. To name clittage is to enhance its role in sex. A name allows people to talk and think about, ask for, and offer this pleasure. Clittage (with lots of waterbased lubricant) is critical to making sex good for women because, no matter what other activities go on with a partner, the continuous clitoral stimulation of clittage assures that sex will include the woman's orgasm.

Clittage can bring women to orgasm so easily and rapidly, it redefines the "quickie." Clittage can make a woman's cligeva erect in seconds and bring her to orgasm in minutes. When clittage is combined with G spotting, a woman's partner can engage the whole orgasmic crescent. A woman who receives this kind of manual sex is likely to experience powerfully satisfying orgasms. Clittage and G-spotting combined, or what we call caressing the crescent, is also the way some women ejaculate.

Going for the G Spot

Manual sex opens up another overlooked but important area of sexual pleasure: the G spot. Most women do not even bother to look for the G spot because the sexual culture does not yet fully recognize it. Even doctors do not always learn about it. One woman told us about a pelvic exam in which the male doctor pressed against her G spot again and again, confused about what the lump he felt could be. She could hardly hold back from laughing, because he obviously had no idea that his fingers were on her G spot or that pressing there created a pleasurable sensation.

A few women discover the G spot inadvertently, but most find it by seeking it out on their own or with a partner (see box). The G spot is easiest to find using the fingers. Although a woman may have noticed a good sensation in that area during intercourse, finger stimulation of the G spot is much more direct and can

HOW TO FIND THE G SPOT

Some women have looked for their G spot without success. Instead of giving up and concluding that there is nothing to be found, the solution is to gain experience with manual sex. Although a partner's fingers may be able to find the G spot more easily, a woman can discover it on her own. She needs to reach behind the pubic bone with her fingers, a curved dildo, or a vibrator attachment ("G-spotter"). It is easiest to feel after making the cligeva erect using clittage or a vibrator. Once erect, a woman can reach the G spot by inserting two fingers inside her vagina and curving them up and behind the pubic bone along the front vaginal wall. Crouching or sitting on the edge of a bed or a chair allows best access. The G spot bulges out slightly and has ridges (called ruggae) on its surface. When she strokes or presses against the G spot, there may be a moment when a woman feels like she needs to urinate because of pressure on the urethra. This feeling quickly gives way to pleasure.

rivet a woman's attention to this site of pleasure. Once a woman's G spot has been directly stimulated to erection, she is better able to feel it during intercourse. Continued G spotting can lead to orgasm and, in some women, to ejaculation (see Chapter 7).

Manual Sex and the Orgasmic Crescent

Dell Williams, owner of Eve's Garden in New York, says "I think that for many women the combination of clitoral and internal stimulation is the ultimate satisfaction." Williams refers to the pleasures of what we call the orgasmic crescent. Until recently, heterosexual women and lesbians have found themselves on opposite ends of the orgasmic crescent: Heterosexual women often got only the indirect G spot stimulation of intercourse with little clitoral stimulation. Lesbians, especially those who rejected penetration as too reminiscent of sex with a man, often focused solely on the clitoris. Recognizing the G spot and the power of the clitoris has brought straight, lesbian, and bisexual women to a new attitude about how both the internal and external genitals can be combined for pleasure.

Using one or both hands, a woman and her partner can caress the whole orgasmic crescent. One hand stimulates the clitoris and the urethral opening, while the other hand stimulates the G spot. Manually stimulating the orgasmic crescent offers the same intense pleasure as stimulating the penis, which holds inside both the clitoris and the urethra. The major difference is that a woman's G spot, or prostate, is part of the orgasmic crescent, while the man's prostate is separate from his penis.

To look at women's genitals in a way most conducive to pleasure involves going beyond the isolated parts and seeing women's genitals as a sexual whole. The pleasure of the orgasmic crescent is within every woman's reach, whether through caressing the crescent or by combining vaginal penetration with clittage.

Is There an Oral Sex Gap?

While manual sex works its wonders in the obscurity of namelessness, oral sex has recently gained popularity. Even the mainstream media give it lip service. Oral sex has both an identifying name and a sexy, slightly kinky reputation. Some people still consider oral sex taboo and refuse to engage in it, and it is outlawed under sodomy statutes in some states. Yet, its popularity has grown over the past three or four generations and an increasing percentage of adults say they have tried oral sex at least once. Most say they do not give or receive fellatio (oral sex on a man) or cunnilingus (oral sex on a woman) every time they have sex, but oral sex is an activity with which the majority of people are familiar.

Some people enjoy mutual oral sex ("69"), but most partners take turns giving and receiving oral stimulation. Fellatio and cunnilingus are both oral sex, but they are not given or received with equal gusto by women and men. In the National Opinion Research Center's random-sample sex survey of nearly 3,500 Americans, social scientists found that more men than women (34 percent of men to 29 percent of women) considered cunnilingus "very appealing." Forty-five percent of men were enthusiastic about fellatio, a practice far fewer women—only 17 percent—said they enjoyed to the same degree. Women nonetheless gave fellatio somewhat more often than they received cunnilingus. The sex survey found that 20 percent of women said they received cunnilingus the last time they had sex, while 28 percent of men reported receiving fellatio. The survey researchers point out that men tend to overreport and women to underreport sexual activity and that their overall findings suggest that "women do not appear to receive oral sex less frequently than men do." At the same time, they acknowledge that their data do not allow them to "draw any conclusions regarding the 'fairness' of the typical sexual event." Their data do not reveal, for example, whether oral sex is done more than once in a single encounter. Nor does it specify whether or not oral sex led to orgasm or if it was reciprocal.

The survey researchers' results lead them to observe that "fellatio may be viewed as an obligation for women in a way that cunnilingus is not for men." Indeed, they found that many women who do not find giving fellatio appealing perform it anyway. Furthermore, women are unlikely to insist on cunnilingus in return.

When sex is focused on men's satisfaction, a woman is unlikely to feel like a proactive partner in oral sex. She may perform fellatio only because she has been coaxed to do so or because she believes that she should. A woman may even perform fellatio several times during sex, as one woman described to us was her experience, to make or keep the man erect. (A man does not give a woman cunnilingus for the same purpose because there is no concept of female erection in the sexual culture.)

Some women, of course, perform oral sex with zeal. They find fellatio to be both an expression and an enhancement of their own excitement. Some say they sense a connection between the sensations in their mouth and their genitals. Others enjoy cre-

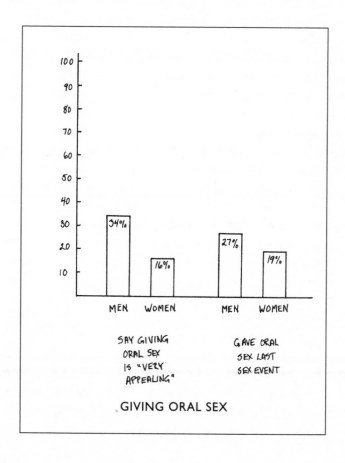

GIVING ORAL SEX

ating pleasure for their partner. Still others derive a sense of power from controlling what the man feels.

In any kind of penetrative sex, it is important that the receiving partner maintain the control. A woman who is a proactive rather than a passive partner can control the depth of penetration so that the penis does not press against the back of her throat, avoiding the gag reflex that can make her feel like throwing up. A proactive partner also insists that her partner use a condom. She avoids taking ejaculate or pre-ejaculate into her mouth and exposing herself to the risk of infection.

Young heterosexual women gain a remarkable familiarity with their partner's penis, even though their initial reaction to seeing a live, erect penis, with its odd shape and throbbing veins, is likely to be repugnance or concern. But learning to love the penis is part of women's initiation into heterosexuality. Many adult women remember spending hours on living room couches or in the backseats of cars giving boys "head." Sometimes a girl even performs fellatio while her partner is driving (a situation that is not conducive to either road safety or reciprocity). A gal often finds that a guy does not return the favor even after the car is stopped, and her pleasure is left in the parking lot dust.

Although oral sex may be performed frequently in the early stages of a teen relationship, once a couple starts having intercourse regularly, oral sex may recede in importance, despite the fact that cunnilingus can bring a woman to orgasm far more reliably than intercourse.

The pressure to give fellatio is driven by the belief in the sexual culture that men *need* sex to orgasm. A man's obvious erection may make his orgasm and ejaculation seem imperative in a way a woman's is not: A man is said to get "blue balls," a condition that currently has no recognized counterpart in women.

Although a woman may want or expect oral sex to be mutual, she may not feel comfortable asking for or receiving cunnilingus from her partner. Her reluctance may be because she shares the sexual culture's general distaste or ambivalence about the look, taste, or smell of the female genitals (sometimes compared to reeking fish). No matter how much a woman washes, she may never feel that her cligeva is sweet-smelling or clean enough to deserve her partner's attention. Even when safer sex practices prescribe that her vulva be covered with plastic wrap or other latex barrier to avoid the exchange of body fluids, some men may still be reticent about the practice. They are willing to kiss a desirable woman's body everywhere *except* "down there."

Twenty percent of all women included in the 1994 sex survey said they received cunnilingus in their last sexual encounter, but in a study of lesbian sex, 50 percent of lesbian partners reported both giving and receiving oral sex the last time they had sex. Lesbians' enthusiasm for cunnilingus suggests that they are much more at ease with women's genitals than heterosexual women and men are. They also know it makes women come.

In the sex scene between Nikki and Joe, Nikki loses touch with her own pleasure during cunnilingus because she feels embarrassed and vulnerable when her genitals are exposed. She enjoys the feeling of cunnilingus, but because she and Joe do not talk about sex, Nikki does not know how to tell him when he is not quite on the right spot. His efforts to please her do not result in orgasm, but she says nothing. Instead, they both pretend that sex is just fine. When a woman pleases her partner without pleasing herself, and when a man is at a loss about what to do in sex, it becomes clear that it is not only time to talk but to rethink sex at its most fundamental level.

All Wet

The signs of sexual arousal are said to differ by sex: Men get erections and women get wet. Vaginal wetness is a common theme in the media that, directly or obliquely, suggests female sexuality. In advertising, moist lips utter juicy words, encourage women to be "wet and wild," and entice men to "get your hands on a wet one." In stories and novels, when the heroine is sexually aroused, she feels moisture well at her vaginal opening.

The idea that wetness is the primary sign of a woman's arousal reinforces the sex-equals-intercourse equation. The lubrication of the vaginal walls is treated as a woman's primary (often, the only) physical response, as if making a smooth and cozy environment for the penis were a woman's sole sexual role. Many women do indeed get wet when they get sexually excited, but it has little or nothing to do with what makes sex orgasmic for them. Vaginal lubrication does nothing to excite the clitoris. Wetness or lubrication is not even a reliable sign of sexual arousal for every woman every time. Some women get abundantly wet when they get turned on; others lubricate very little or not at all. Vaginal lubrication also varies with hormonal fluctuations of the menstrual cycle and is reduced after menopause. It can be affected by medications. A woman's natural lubrication may dry up after having an orgasm—certainly not a sign of any lack of excitement. Yet women sometimes are made to feel as if insufficient lubrication were a personal inadequacy on their part, a sign of frigidity rather than a bodily process that can be sexually neutral.

In a world where artificial lubricant is available in bottles at the pharmacy or by mail order, whether or not a woman gets wet becomes moot. All women, even those who lubricate abundantly and continually, will benefit from sex that is accompanied by water-based lubrication. When applied in liberal amounts both inside *and* outside the vagina, lubricant is a boon to all manual sex, especially clittage. In vaginal intercourse, it enhances both partners' pleasure. In anal intercourse and anal-finger penetration, lubricant is a must. Water-based lubricant heightens sensitivity and facilitates the use of latex in safer sex. It prepares the cligeva for pleasure, not just intercourse. By applying plenty of lubricant as needed, a woman avoids the dry rubbing of sensitive tissues, and her enjoyment of clittage, G spotting, and intercourse is greatly intensified. Sex can also continue for longer periods of time without irritation.

When women reinvent sex, lubricant will be on everyone's night table. Once people try it, they will enthusiastically agree with the authors of *The Good Vibrations Guide to Sex* who say, "Lubricant [is] one of life's more enjoyable essentials, right up there with bread, wine and a decent cup of coffee."

A Woman's Erection

Rather than vaginal lubrication, the sign of every woman's (and man's) arousal is engorgement and the increased muscular tension of the genitals. Yet there is neither recognition nor a name for this state or condition. When a man's genitals become engorged and swell with arousal we call it an "erection." But when a woman's genitals become engorged and swell with arousal, we call it—*nothing*.

A woman's erection is not called an erection partly because it does not resemble an erect penis. Yet the only difference between a man's erection and a woman's is that hers is located mostly inside the body. A woman's erection involves the same engorgement process men experience, yet the concept is not a part of the sexual culture. However, once she and her partner know what to look and, especially, to feel for, a woman's erection becomes as apparent as a man's. A woman's genitals take on a flushed look and her labia swell. The labia and perineum puff up and press the vaginal opening closed. The entire clitoris swells and straightens out, making the tip protrude. The whole genital area, or cligeva, is transformed.

Women need an image of what happens to their genitals when aroused, so that they can feel it more fully and see it more easily. A friend says that when she is erect, her swollen genitals feel and look like a "baboon's ass." Similarly, another woman's male lover described her erect genitals as a "chimpanzee's ass." Although not as exaggerated as the female ape's genitals, a female human's erection can be perfectly obvious once people decide to look and feel for it.

A woman's erection is well worth exploring with both the eyes and the hands. With the fingers, the woman or her partner can easily feel her puffy labia and perineum, the erect tip of the clitoris and, inside the vagina, the aroused G spot. A woman can also direct her own pleasure and even make herself erect by simply flexing the PC muscle. Many women use the PC muscle to enhance their partner's pleasure by squeezing the penis during intercourse, but they can also use their PC muscle to increase their own erection and enjoyment.

Once a woman is erect, penetration becomes a far more exciting activity. A woman's erection transforms intercourse by making the engorged cligeva highly sensitive to touch, pressure, and friction. Erection allows the man's penis to stimulate the G spot more effectively and, if the man penetrates deeply (the angle, not the length, of his penetration is what matters), a woman may feel the cul-de-sac, a delicious space at the high end of the vagina that opens up or "tents" with erection. Erection also allows a woman to take a more active role in sex. A woman who is aware of her erection need never feel again that sex is happening *to* her. Instead, intercourse is transformed into a passionate genital hug.

Premature Intercourse

Penetration is difficult or impossible with a nonerect penis. Intercourse with a nonerect cligeva, in contrast, is done all the time even though it disregards female pleasure. We call having intercourse before a woman is erect and ready, "premature intercourse." Sexual intercourse often occurs prematurely because most people begin penetration before a woman is erect. Intercourse without erection can feel about as exciting to a woman as inserting a tampon. Worse, it can make a woman feel like a mere vehicle of a man's pleasure, or even as if she is having sex against her will. A married woman in her thirties describes how sex with her husband of thirteen years has never consisted of anything more than intercourse. She gets no direct clitoral stimulation at any point during sex and she is not erect when penetration begins. As a result, she says that intercourse makes her feel "imposed upon," even "violated."

Many couples have a chronic problem with premature intercourse because it bypasses a woman's pleasure. Yet premature intercourse is not acknowledged as a problem by the sexual culture since the only criterion for penetration is the man's erection. A woman sometimes even initiates intercourse herself in response to a man's insistent erection, as Nikki did with Joe. Neither of them considers that her readiness—erection rather than wetness—matters too. Just as a man's dozing penis comes alive in erection, a woman's cligeva awakens when erect and becomes primed for pleasure. By recognizing that both women and men have erections, partners can engage in intercourse that is not only more pleasurable for women but mutually orgasmic.

The Timing Problem

The sexual culture suggests that women and men are hormonally programmed to reach orgasm at different speeds. Women are seen as taking forever to come, while men take too little time. This timing problem seems to be a fact of nature that plagues sex between heterosexuals. Yet a woman can come within minutes when she masturbates, especially if she uses a vibrator. In partner sex that consists of intercourse and the man's orgasm, a woman is unlikely to come at all. Yet many men pump away, believing that their partner will come if they can just keep their penis erect long enough and penetrate deep and hard enough. It seems that no one stops to consider what exactly is being stimulated during intercourse. The sexual culture asserts that a woman's pleasure depends on the size and stamina of her partner's penis. This view ignores a woman's clitoris and leads men to misdirect their efforts. No matter how long a woman's elbow is being rubbed, she is not going to feel relief in her knee.

Calling women's genital excitement not just engorgement but an "erection" places women and men on a more equal playing field. It moves the goal of sex from penetration and the man's orgasm to the pleasure of both partners. It recognizes that a woman's erection is as much a prerequisite for intercourse as a man's. It provides a clear, specific precondition for a woman's orgasm.

Recognizing that women need to be erect for orgasm to occur can help dispel the notion that women take a long time to come. If sex begins with appropriate stimulation like clittage, however, a woman can enjoy herself from the start. Once she becomes erect, both she and her partner can embark toward orgasm together and keep apace of one another. Replacing premature intercourse with oral and manual sex can eliminate timing problems, including premature ejaculation. The goal is not for women to come quickly, as many men have learned to do. Rather, women and men alike can learn to enjoy orgasms on their own timing. Both partners can gain greater control in sex and together prolong and heighten the intensity of their mutual pleasure.

Ladies First

The notion of ladies first may no longer apply at doorways or on sinking ocean liners, but the rule still holds for sex. If ladies come first, partners can dramatically improve sex in three important ways: First, by coming before the man, a woman is assured of orgasm before her partner loses interest in sex, as many men do after they ejaculate and reach orgasm. Second, by coming before penetration, the woman establishes her erection. Her orgasm makes her vagina infinitely more sensitive so that she can enjoy intercourse if she wants it. Third, a woman is more likely to have the time and opportunity for multiple orgasms if she first comes before the man does.

Ensuring that ladies come first relieves both partners of a number of performance worries. Once the woman has her first orgasm, she and her partner can engage in intercourse without having to worry that the man will ejaculate before she is satisfied. With ladies first, the man can enjoy the woman's orgasm. As he learns to control his ejaculation, he may also have multiple orgasms.

When the emphasis in sex moves from intercourse to manual and oral sex, and from the man's erection to the equal and similar erection of both the woman and the man, whole new arenas of pleasure open up. With mutual erection, intercourse is transformed. The woman and the man both become proactive partners. Sexual encounters can last longer because of the heightened level of arousal created when both partners are erect. One encounter will link with the next because the exquisite feeling of orgasm will infuse a woman's body with memories of pleasure for hours and even days afterward.

Clittage Intercourse

Even the most traditional intercourse positions take on whole new dimensions when partners are aware of the power of manual sex and of the importance of women's erection and orgasm.

The Missionary Position

The man-on-top intercourse position continues to define the norm for heterosexual sex. On-your-back intercourse is burned into many women's sexual imaginations, even though many couples perform it in a way that hardly sets women's genitals on fire.

The man-on-top's nickname, "missionary" position, is attributed to Polynesian women who were amazed to learn that English missionaries and their wives had intercourse exclusively in this position. Sex for them was far more playful than for colonial wives, many of whom heeded Queen Victoria's advice to her own daughter to "close your eyes and think of England." Such counsel suggests that these women succumbed to intercourse out of duty, expecting (and often getting) little pleasure and even pain in the process.

The missionary position maintains its image as the more "civilized" intercourse position. In *Quest for Fire,* the popular movie about early humans, the missionary position was portrayed as an evolutionary step up from the rear-entry position practiced by our more primitive ancestors. Face-to-face sex marked an important divergence of human culture from the animal world. It supposedly enhanced human communication during sex, even though it did not enhance genital communication in a way conducive to female orgasm.

Today, this position is still the default position for intercourse, even though it has become a synonym for boring sex. This posture also places women under men in a way that reflects the social juxtaposition of the genders. However, the literal inferiority of the female posture in the missionary position need not mean that women cannot come out on top of their own pleasure. Some women enjoy the feeling of vulnerability, even submission, of letting the man be in control. They can lie back, concentrate on their own sensations, enjoy the skin-to-skin contact and the weight and warmth of their partner's body. But without the woman's erection, the work of even the most energetic lover will be for naught.

Man-on-top intercourse can be transformed by adding clittage. Clittage ensures that the woman becomes erect. With erection, a woman can enjoy having her G spot stimulated by the man's penis during intercourse (easiest if the man kneels or stands and the woman lies with pillows under her hips). With a finger on her clitoris and deep penetration that engages the woman's cul-de-sac, partners can transform man-on-top intercourse into an experience in which even atheists will cry out, "Oh, god!"

Woman on Top

Some people consider the woman-on-top position to be slightly subversive—and therefore exciting—because it inverts the sexual hierarchy in society. A woman can indeed enjoy the sense of power being on top offers, and a man may enjoy a break from his usual role as the doer in sex. This position is also highly conducive to orgasm for many women because they can control the clitoral pressure as well as the angle, rhythm, and depth of penetration.

Some women feel uncomfortable being on top, however, because it puts their body on display. They may be concerned that their partner will compare them to the perfect women in movies. They may even be reluctant to look down at their own body. When a woman or her partner add clittage, however, the immediacy and intensity of her pleasure will quickly distract her from these concerns. Clittage intercourse with the woman on top puts the woman fully in control of her own pleasure and transports her from the outside to the inside of her body.

Rear Entry

Rear-entry intercourse evokes strong feelings of both distaste and excitement in our sexual culture. Some people do not like it because it too closely resembles anal intercourse or sex between animals. Others say rear entry seems too impersonal because the two partners are not face-to-face. For yet others, the rear-entry position is erotically exciting precisely because it is animalistic and taboo. It is the favorite of some women who find it hits their G spot.

Rear entry is also the easiest position for clittage intercourse. The man's body is not up next to the clitoris and his hands are free. In this position, it is also easy for the woman to give herself clittage. The angles of the vagina and the penis in this position make it more likely for some that the penis can stroke the woman's G spot. They also enjoy the rhythmic force of the man's hips against their buttocks and the man's hands on their buttocks and hips.

Other Positions

Clittage and a woman's erection transform any intercourse position into an adventure. Partners can enjoy the slower pace of intercourse while lying side by side with legs intertwined or in the "spoons" position (both partners facing the same direction). In these positions, neither partner is on top and there is always a hand free for clittage.

Partners will find that adding clittage to any horizontal, standing, or sitting intercourse position can provide surprising sensations and new dimensions to sexual pleasure. Furniture is also a key ingredient to varying the way intercourse in any position feels. Toys in their infinite variety can also add to the fun of sex. For example, a small egg-shaped vibrator against the clitoris (held in place with a strap made for that purpose) can free the hands for other pleasures.

Anal Sex

The anus is an often overlooked area of heterosexual sex. Once it begins to be viewed as part of the cligeva, more people can appreciate its sexual role. Erection increases the sensitivity of the anal area. A woman whose cligeva is erect may enjoy the sensation of the partner's finger (or penis) caressing the sensitive nerve endings at the anal opening. She may enjoy penetration using a finger, penis, or dildo. To avoid discomfort or injury, anal penetration should take place *only* after the receiving partner's genitals (whether female or male) are erect. Care, patience, lubrication, and latex are also essential. Not all women like anal intercourse, but many women find that adding anal-finger penetration or anal touching to clitoral and vaginal stimulation sends them into the O zone.

Anal-finger penetration is also the best way to stimulate the man's prostate gland. But many heterosexual men never explore this pleasure because they associate it with gay sex. Enjoying anal sex has nothing to do with sexual orientation. Both women and men, heterosexual, bisexual, and gay, can enjoy anal sex when it is done with clitoral or penile stimulation, lubrication, and care. (A good resource on safe anal sex is Jack Morin's *Anal Pleasure and Health*.)

Other Stimulation

The pleasure a woman can derive from sex is constantly expanded and enriched by the touch of the partner's hand on nongenital parts of the body. A partner's kiss—on the lips, neck, under the arms, in the crook of the elbow, on the palm of the hand, on the fingers or toes—adds to the whole-body experience of sex. Many women find that a partner's kiss on their nipples is what takes them over the edge of orgasm. For other women, it can be a kiss on the ear, or a tug on the rear.

Shere Hite has asked why there is no word for "pressing together," or full body contact, one of the most satisfying sexual activities there is. (After all, it involves the largest sexual area of the body—the skin). Body rubbing, sometimes called frottage, adds delicious textures and deep gratification to a woman's orgasm. These gestures are much more than icing on the cake. They can be the touch that sends a person to an alternate state of being. Yet they will seem only empty gestures unless the basics of orgasm for women—clittage, erection, and lubrication—are first in place.

Redressing Sex

Making sex as good for Nikki as it is for Joe involves moving from a concern with her appearance and his pleasure to a focus on their mutual experience of pleasure. Nikki now spends hours making her body *look* good for sex, but she and her partner never give more than a few minutes of attention to making her body *feel* good. When sex becomes as good for Nikki as it is for Joe, she will focus less on dressing up and more on getting undressed. When sex includes her orgasm as surely as it does his, Nikki will not be thinking about the size of her thighs or be concerned that her hair is getting mussed. She will be too busy enjoying orgasmic sex. And as orgasm brings her closer to herself, the benefits of sexual pleasure will spill over into other parts of her life. Nikki's beauty will not be mere exterior dressing but a reflection of her inner joy. The hurdles Nikki once faced on her way to orgasm will drop away, clearing a path to the orgasms that no woman should have sex without.

CHAPTER THREE

Learning Desires

Nikki remembers her "first time." She was sixteen, a high-school junior, and Jason, her first serious boyfriend, was eighteen and a graduating senior. It was the night of his senior prom. After the dance, Jason and Nikki went home to change and then met two other couples at a favorite diner. Around 2 A.M., each couple drove off separately to be alone. Jason and Nikki headed up to a lookout over the city where they had gone many times before. Usually they got into the backseat and spent hours together, their lips and hands roaming all over each other's bodies. Jason had kissed and touched Nikki just about everywhere. She knew his body, too, how his penis responded to her touch and to her kisses. Each knew how to bring the other to orgasm.

They had planned to celebrate Jason's graduation by doing what they had not yet done: "going all the way" and having intercourse. As they kissed, Nikki first undid Jason's pants, then helped him remove her underwear. Nikki took Jason's penis in her hand as he reached between her legs and stroked her clitoris. Nikki closed her eyes to focus on the familiar tingling of her genitals, but as she neared orgasm, Jason abruptly stopped. He pulled the condom they had bought out of his pocket and, quickly rolling it on, he pressed his penis past her labia and into her vagina. It hurt a little at first but the slight burning sensation soon dissolved into pleasure. Nikki noticed that the feeling was different from clitoral stimulation—milder and more diffuse. As Jason, who seemed highly aroused, thrust and poked inside her, Nikki wondered why she wasn't feeling more. She tried adjusting the position of her body and she concentrated hard, telling herself, This is it, this is the real thing! *Then Jason's pace accelerated. Suddenly, he gasped, moaned, and stopped moving. It was over.*

Nikki stroked Jason's hair, thinking it was now her turn. But Jason lay depleted on top of her and did not respond. Nikki began to feel sad. She gently pushed him to one side and sat up. She had to hold back tears as she reached for her underwear. So that was "it"?

Learning to Please

The primary lesson a young woman learns the first time she has intercourse is that sex is not about her pleasure. The great majority of girls do not have orgasms while most boys do. This is an especially cruel lesson if a girl has enjoyed orgasms up to that point or if she has been led to believe that her "first time" would give her her first orgasm. First intercourse is treated as an important milestone in a girl's life. After years of anticipation, fear, postponement, and excitement, "it" finally happens. Despite all the fanfare, intercourse is almost always a letdown for a girl. Her underwear goes off, but she does not; there are no bells or fireworks.

There was little fun in Nikki's first intercourse. It included far less of the manual and oral sex she usually enjoyed with Jason. Although she was glad to give him the pleasure of having an orgasm inside her, she wondered why she had not come. Nikki had been led to believe that intercourse was the ultimate sexual experience, but it turned out to be far less pleasurable than the sex they had had before. She began to wonder whether there was something wrong with her. After that night, sex between Nikki and Jason consisted of manual and oral sex as foreplay to intercourse and to his orgasm. Nikki stopped having orgasms with Jason, but she did not feel that she could insist on going back to the way they had sex before. They had graduated to "real" sex—intercourse. Although both Nikki and Jason thought they were heading toward pleasure together, he ended up in the driver's seat and she became a passenger going along for *his* sexual joy ride.

It is widely believed that men reach their sexual peak at eighteen, while women only do so at thirty-five because they have different biological natures. The reason for this large gap between women's and men's sexual peaks (if, indeed, the notion of peaks is meaningful to begin with) is that our culture equates sex with intercourse. Vaginal intercourse provides the penis with all-around pleasure and is an extension of the pleasure boys learn from years of practice at masturbation. For boys, first intercourse marks the beginning of a lifetime of orgasmic partner sex. For many girls, in contrast, first intercourse marks a less clear-cut transition. Intercourse does not usually give a girl or-

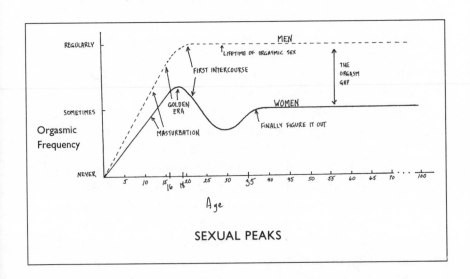

SEXUAL PEAKS

gasm because it bypasses the clitoris. A woman's sexuality is therefore unlikely to "peak" until years later (if at all) when sex is mostly penetration. Especially if having intercourse means dispensing with foreplay, a woman's first time may be the last time sex reflects her body's experience of pleasure.

The First Time

Anyone whose own first time was ecstatic, or who doubts that early sexual experiences are notably different for girls than for boys, can take a reality check by reading Karen Bouris's book, *The First Time: What Parents and Teenagers Should Know About "Losing Your Virginity."* The "first time" stories Bouris garnered from 150 American women, ranging in age from their twenties to their seventies, are shocking and sad. Only a handful of women remembered their first time as being good, and even fewer had orgasms. One woman who responded to Bouris's questionnaire explained how disappointing first intercourse was for her because she already knew the pleasures of orgasm:

> [First intercourse] was quick and not particularly satisfying or pleasurable for me. After he came, he said, "Well, that's it," and I thought, That's it? (I had been masturbating since age eleven or twelve and knew what it meant to have an orgasm!) I felt lonely and disappointed; he didn't speak to me or touch me lovingly. I broke off our relationship shortly thereafter. . . .

Some girls did not expect orgasm, having never had one. They were happy just to have had this special experience with a man they loved. For a majority of girls, first intercourse was so-so or mildly disappointing—not bad, but not great. Some women engaged in penetrative sex simply to "get it over with" because they did not want to graduate from high school a "virgin."

Typically, first intercourse occurs within a dating relationship, but the specific occasion is often spontaneous and unplanned. The 1994 National Opinion Research Center (NORC) sex survey reports that nearly one-fourth of all women queried "did not want to have intercourse the first time." Even when a girl is as eager as her partner to try intercourse, she loses control of the event if it occurs on the spur of the moment. Without the right equipment and preparation for birth control and safer sex, the "first time" can be an unsettling event that puts a girl unnecessarily at risk of pregnancy and infection. On top of that, first intercourse that is unwanted is traumatic.

Even when a girl initiates and orchestrates the setting and conditions for the big event, she may feel that intercourse is something that happens *to* her. Once sex begins, a girl is led by her partner as if it were a dance. She wears Ginger's shoes and, like the screen star, she not only dances to Fred's steps and timing, but, in the words of the feminist saying, she does it backward in high heels. Although first intercourse can be awkward for a boy, too, he is in the lead and choreographs a dance that culminates in a solo performance (the man's orgasm and ejaculation).

First intercourse delivers a clear message to girls: "This is sex. Sex is intercourse, and intercourse is really fun for your partner. If you can figure out a way to make intercourse fun for you, too—even orgasmic—fine. But don't expect special concessions (like direct clitoral stimulation). You'll have to make do with what your partner's penis gives you. . . . And, by the way, don't let your partner know you didn't come. It might hurt his feelings." So girls fake orgasms and keep quiet about wanting clitoral pleasure (that is, if they are even aware of having a clitoris). Some embark on a hunt for orgasm through intercourse because, as a girl soon discovers, once she and her boyfriend "advance" to penetration, the petting or foreplay that had made her orgasm now falls by the wayside. One woman tells us that before she and her first boyfriend ever had intercourse, she had enjoyed manual and oral sex that led to orgasm and ejaculation. When the two of them eventually managed to get birth control and started having intercourse, her orgasms and ejaculations stopped. She did not experience them regularly again until her late twenties, when she determined to put manual and oral sex back into sex.

For some women, first intercourse occurs not only without pleasure, but without their consent. Their first time is not sex at all, but rape. They experience penetrative sex that is either unwanted, involves coercion or violence, or occurs under conditions not under the woman's control. Bouris quotes one woman whose sexuality was forever clouded after being raped by her older boyfriend.

> I didn't tell anyone. It didn't seem like sex, but sex since then has seemed like that experience: a kind of resignation to the man's sex drive and tremendous confusion on my part. My body felt scorched. I think rape has defined my experience. I cannot turn away from it. I don't believe I know what sex is. What it's for.

When a girl's first experience of "sex" is abuse, incest, or date rape, the message she learns is that her sexuality is not her own, but instead belongs to men.

For most women, first intercourse is not without her consent, but it is without her physical pleasure (orgasm). The event can inhibit a woman's sexual growth because, instead of building upon what a girl learns from masturbation and manual and oral sex with a partner, it negates that knowledge and experience. It informs her that real sex is not something that she or her body defines. Instead, she is expected to do what gives the man pleasure. When a girl "loses her virginity," she does indeed lose.

Sacrificing Virginity

Many women around the world are introduced into sex at marriage with only the slightest idea about what it involves. One sixty-year-old Mexican woman told us about getting married at age fifteen to a man she loved, but being terrified when she awoke one night and found her husband thrusting away on top of her. She thought he was trying to kill her.

In other cultures, first intercourse is not only violent and devoid of pleasure for the girl or woman but part of a marriage ritual that symbolizes a girl's transfer of ownership from her own family to that of her husband. Writer Jane Kramer recalls attending the wedding of a fourteen-year-old Moroccan girl. Following the marriage, the girl was tied up so she would not struggle during her "deflowering." Two minutes after the event, Kramer found her "passed out on the dirt floor of her bridegroom's house." Her husband received congratulations from the men as his mother paraded the bride's bloody pants, "proof" that her son had gotten "his money's worth."

Proof of a woman's virginity is required in many societies at marriage to ensure that any children born to her are undeniably her husband's. Virginity was one of several reasons that Prince Charles married Diana Spencer, rather than Camilla Parker-Bowles, the woman he apparently loves. Unlike Camilla, Diana was not only single, but a virgin and therefore appropriate to become the mother of an heir to the throne. Her virginity assured the royal house that no sexual scandals from her past would surface to taint her (and their) image. It also left no question that her children would have their father's royal blood.

Even where pedigree is not an issue, some women "save themselves" so they can offer their virginity as a gift to a worthy man. The 1994 NORC sex survey found that, among people "who wanted their first vaginal intercourse to happen when it did," half of the women were motivated by affection for their partner. Half of the men said they sought intercourse out of curiosity. Some men also save their "first time" for the right woman or the right occasion. But virginity does not have the same meaning for women and men: *A man's virginity belongs to him, whereas a woman's belongs to men.* A woman "loses" her virginity to a man, while a man loses his virginity only to gain his manhood. He loses only his inexperience, and his status is enhanced by having intercourse. For a girl, her first time may make her feel that she is a woman, but it is at the cost of losing ownership and control of her sexual selfhood.

A woman's virginity is a guarantee to her partner that she is untouched by other males. Many men consider the prospect of being a woman's "first" lover as an honor and treat their inexperienced partner with care and respect. But there are other men who treat sex with a "virgin" like a dog treats the backyard of a new house, as territory to mark and claim possession of to the exclusion of all other dogs. No woman can mark a man in the same way.

Doing away with the concept of virginity altogether would give women more control over sex. It would also help both women and men focus on ways of having sex that are more mutually pleasurable. Instead of first intercourse being the defining act of a woman's sexual life, a woman could decide for herself which sexual event(s) or experience(s) she finds meaningful. For some, the first time might be first sex (of any kind) with a person they love. For a lesbian, the significant sexual life event may be her first physically intimate time with a woman. For others, it could be first masturbation, or first orgasm. Maybe sex would not even be marked by any kind of first at all, but would be seen instead as an ongoing process of sexual self-discovery and interpersonal expression.

The Missing Orgasm

It is striking how, even today, many sexually active women skip the all-important step of learning how to have an orgasm. It is often suggested that since the "post-feminist" 1990s women are now fully in charge of their sex lives. But studies, observation, and anecdotal evidence suggest that sexual awareness and self-determination for young women, while much ballyhooed, is still far from the norm. In her late-night cable talk show, sex educator Sari Locker, the author of *Mindblowing Sex in the Real World*, asks an assembled group of women in their twenties about orgasms. Do they have them? Locker asks. There is silence. One woman finally speaks up, explaining that she learned how to have an orgasm from a book she read as an adolescent. When she began to have sexual partners a few years later, she taught them what she had learned on her own. Ever since, she has enjoyed orgasmic, satisfying sex. The hands-on style and smooth development of this woman's sexuality is the exception, however. The other women who gathered to talk sex with Locker say nothing and shoot uncomfortable glances at one another.

Among heterosexuals, whether you have an orgasm or not with first intercourse can almost be predicted by your gender. College students surveyed by researchers Susan Sprecher, Anita Barbee, and Pepper Schwartz showed that 7 percent of the women and 79 percent of the men reported having an orgasm with first intercourse—quite a gap. The women and men who had orgasms expressed the most positive feelings about their first intercourse experience. Although partner sex does eventually improve for many women, their orgasm rates never catch up to those of men.

When sex is not orgasmic, women tend to blame themselves, as if it were some kind of psychological or personal weakness on their part. (Thus the silence among Locker's guests.) Most women do not feel angry, cheated, or resentful, even though they are missing out on pleasure, because they see orgasmless sex as their own failure. They are also reticent to mention the problem, much less complain, out of concern that their partners will feel inadequate. Some women keep quiet because they fear making the man angry.

Pretending that bad sex is good sex is practically a national pastime for women. In *Going All the Way: Teenage Girls' Tales of Sex, Romance & Pregnancy,* a ten-year-plus study of some four hundred girls' experiences, author Sharon Thompson quotes one young woman who described how she got into the habit of faking orgasm with a man who refused to talk about sex because he said, "Animals don't":

> He, instead of dealing with it like there was obviously something wrong that I didn't have one orgasm ever or even close to one, dealt with it by, "Oh, my god, there's something wrong with me," and reversed the whole thing around and made me feel really sorry for him to the point where I said, "Look it's not your fault. It doesn't matter anyway." And to the point where the next time we had sex afterward, he said, "Did you have an orgasm?" and I said, "Yes," which I really felt cheap about. . . .
>
> I had to say yes about three times after that and then it was sort of understood that I was having orgasms even though I never did and our sex started getting worse and worse and less and less frequent and our time together started getting more and more rushed.

Women fake orgasm to protect the man's ego. Other reasons a woman may fake orgasm are to get bad sex over with and to avoid the limelight—a woman wants to keep the pleasure focus in sex on her partner. Some women just avoid having sex so that they do not have to deal with the problem. The one thing they rarely do is confront the problem.

"IT'S OK, REALLY"

Girls learn that they should have orgasm from intercourse. When they do not, they do not complain, they explain.

In Sharon Thompson's study, one girl says that her boyfriend "tried very hard actually to give me an orgasm. And after a while I said, 'Well, don't worry about it, because I'm enjoying myself anyway. It doesn't really matter to me. Don't wear yourself out.' " Another told her boyfriend when she did not come from intercourse, " 'It's really okay. For now I'm really satisfied without having an orgasm, just being with you and everything. It's just fine. It's great for me.' " Bouris's first-time stories include similar justifications, such as the woman who said, "I didn't have an orgasm then—or for many times thereafter—but I felt loved. . . ." Many women accept love or romance as a substitute for, rather than a complement to, sex.

Spring Training and the Masturbation Gap

It is not surprising that women do not reach orgasm when the information about and the stimulation in sex that they receive is insufficient and/or inappropriate. In contrast, men are provided with the support and resources to have orgasmic sex from the first time they take their penis into their own hands. Although parents may either discourage or remain silent about their sons' masturbation, the sexual culture generally accepts it as a natural outlet for maturing boys' sex "drive."

Long before a young man has partner sex, he learns how to have an orgasm and ejaculate through masturbation. A majority of boys make a point of "becoming orgasmic" by age eighteen (and without the need for a how-to book), but only 40 percent of girls masturbate. For all ages, the gender split of people who masturbate regularly remains at roughly 60/40—a majority of men do, a majority of women do not.

A boy tends to develop his sexual appetite early in his teen years when he avidly begins exploring such magazines as *Playboy* and *Penthouse.* He talks and compares notes with male friends. He may even participate in a "circle jerk." Boys are subtly encouraged to cultivate a kind of clandestine eroticism that gives them a head start (so to speak) over girls in sexual self-knowledge. Masturbation itself is something that the sexual culture connects with boys. Girls are not thought to need sexual "release" in the way boys do. As a result, a girl who masturbates is likely to discover its pleasures by accident: rubbing against her clothing or bedding, rocking back and forth on a hobby horse, or bouncing up and down on a real horse. One friend remembers sliding down a pole as a kid and excitedly telling others, "Hey, try this—it's great!" Some girls get around the warning not to touch themselves "down there" by clasping a pillow or a favorite teddy bear between their legs. Others muster the courage to use their hands. But masturbation for girls never becomes the bustling industry that it is for boys.

A man goes into into adulthood with far greater familiarity with his genitals and sexual responses than does a woman. Besides years of masturbatory practice, he may have received private training from an older or more experienced woman or from a prostitute. In his sexual memoir called *Making Love: An Erotic Odyssey,* Richard Rhodes describes going as a seventeen-year-old college freshman to a "part-time prostitute at least forty years old" to lose his virginity. Rhodes was luckier than most since, in addition to her body, this knowledgeable woman, Gussie Clarke, also offered some instruction about clittage. " 'You need to make sure the girl comes first. . . . Feel here, this little button, see, put your finger here. . . . You rub this, see,' Gussie demonstrated, guiding my hand with her own, 'until she comes. Then you won't leave her hung up.' "

Men today who are uncomfortable about visiting a prostitute but who want the education an older woman can offer, sometimes seek out a mature friend or place an ad in the personals column for an "experienced lady." But many men never encounter a woman who is willing or able to give them lessons in sex, nor do they feel it is appropriate to ask a partner because the man is supposed to know more than the woman. They may never realize there is anything *to* ask unless their lover at some point stops the charade and tells them, "Look, try it this way." In order to be an instructor, of course, a woman has to know herself first.

In a sexual culture that discourages women from cultivating their sexuality, figuring out what to tell a man can take a woman years. By the time a woman knows herself sexually, she may have priced herself out of the market because men generally want a woman who is less experienced than they are. A man who, like Rhodes, gets a lesson from an expert before having sex with a lover, is making sure he can be the one in charge, the one who knows. Such a man neither expects nor wants to be in the position of having to receive instructions from his wife or girlfriend.

Women also expect the man to take the lead in sex and to know what to do. Few women embark on a sexual apprenticeship of their own, for there is little opportunity to do so. Having first sex with a prostitute is not a choice women have (or would be likely to take advantage of because the power dynamics of heterosexual sex forbid *her* from paying for *him*). And although some women consciously desire first sex with an older or more experienced man, even a well-meaning partner of this type may not know how to put a woman's pleasure before his own. Like Nikki, many young women have a first sex partner who is several years older than they. An age gap makes it more likely that sex will be on the man's terms or even be coercive. The study of college students by Sprecher, Barbee, and Schwartz found that girls had a better experience overall if they were older than sixteen and if their first partner was more or less their own age and of more or less equal sexual experience. Yet even a man who is a fellow virgin is likely to have both more self-knowledge from masturbation and a more pleasure-oriented perspective on sex. From childhood on, a man is trained to have sex for sex's sake, while a woman learns to have sex for the sake of a man.

The Golden Age of Partner Sex

When a young woman and man proceed gradually in sex together, and when they postpone intercourse in favor of lots of manual and oral sex, they enjoy what we call a golden age of partner sex. During that time, the heterosexual couple engages in "everything but" or what sex educators call "outercourse": every kind of sexual kissing and genital touching possible without having vaginal (or anal) intercourse. Most heterosexuals still consider intercourse to be the ultimate sex act, however, and they go through this golden age not by choice or intention, but by default. In a sexual culture that is simultaneously obsessed with and prudish about sex, there is a great deal of embarrassment, confusion, and difficulty involved in getting birth control. This hindrance can turn out to be an inadvertent boon to the sexual education of young people.

Several decades ago, anthropologist Margaret Mead suggested that Americans could benefit from adopting some of the less secretive and more playful sexual attitudes of the Samoans she studied, who did not shield young people from learning about sexual activities. Generations later, however, American young people still are discouraged from exploring their sexuality. The sexual culture leaves them to stumble into partner sex in the dark and to glorify and idealize vaginal intercourse. Yet this is an impoverished view of sex that can lead young women, especially, to have sex that is less fun than it could be and more risky than it needs to be.

Girls need the knowledge that can make sex both safer and more playful. They need support from families and from a sexual culture that is not afraid to talk about sex. They need access to good birth control. For girls, sex without the threat of an unintended pregnancy can be joyful rather than scary, carefree instead of traumatic, and mutually pleasurable instead of dull or demeaning for girls. They need an awareness of the advantages of noncoital sex, such as giving them the opportunity and time to explore sexual paths to female pleasure they might otherwise overlook. By having sex on a woman's terms—focusing especially on manual sex—rates of teen sexually transmitted disease and teen pregnancy would likely fall while the quality of sex for young people would surely rise. But instead of encouraging intelligent sexuality, many adults just close their eyes and hope their children will abstain altogether. While some parents and teachers work tirelessly to get information, birth control, and latex condoms within reach of sexually active teens, the sexual culture generally either looks the other way or is flatly condemning of sex for young people.

If young heterosexuals knew how to make noncoital sex good, they might postpone having vaginal or anal intercourse, the riskiest type of partner sex. Safer sex is any kind of genital contact that avoids the exchange of bodily fluids. According to that definition, manual sex (with latex) is the safest of all. Young couples who enjoy months or years of a golden age that centers on manual sex learn a lesson about how their own body experiences pleasure that is both lifesaving and of lifelong value.

Orgasm from the First

Heterosexual girls may have partner sex for years before encountering an orgasm. Lesbians are far more likely than straight girls to enjoy orgasm with first sex because it involves manual and oral sex, not intercourse. Studies suggest that women whose own first time was with a woman found the experience more revelatory than disappointing or traumatic. Sharon Thompson reports that many lesbian girls' first time provided relief, romance, and passion rolled into one. Sex for the young lesbians Thompson interviewed was both more physically satisfying and more lighthearted, fun, and funny than most male-female encounters. Thompson cautions, however, that, for some, the ordeal of coming out outweighs the pleasures of the relationship and of sex. For a young person, coming out can be scary, especially when she or he lacks the support of family and friends. Furthermore, lesbian girls do not have the same freedom heterosexuals enjoy to openly date or to explore their sexuality. In a sexual culture predicated on heterosexuality, a woman may realize that she is attracted to women only after a long, arduous, and painful journey.

Because there is so much pressure to *be* straight, some lesbian girls just assume they *are* straight. Many even have sex with boys. The sex is likely to be as disappointing physically as it is for heterosexual girls, but it can help a young woman recognize that she is not attracted to men. One woman tells us that the first time she kissed a boy was her last. She thought, "yuck," and could not figure out what other girls liked about it. When she finally kissed a girl, the lightbulb turned on.

Coming out is uniquely complicated for bisexual girls and women. They often have to come out twice, first when they recognize their attraction to women, and second when they recognize their attraction to women *and* men. They experience both homophobia from some heterosexuals and suspicion from some lesbians who believe bisexual women are simply "confused" and unable to accept themselves as lesbian. The sexual culture offers only two categories, "heterosexual" and "homosexual," one labeled "normal" and the other "abnormal." Bisexuals must struggle either to fit into or to change this dichotomy. Women and men who come out as bisexual are following their self-knowledge and awareness that, for them, sexual pleasure and love do not come in one gender only.

For girls whose first time is with a female partner, sex is far more likely to be orgasmic than those whose partner is male. Thompson writes: "Orgasms—as rare as hen's teeth in the heterosexual narratives—were reported in every lesbian account. Only girls who had been with men initially saw orgasm as a feat." This does not mean, as Pat Califia points out, that women automatically know how to "do" women. A woman has to learn to make love to a woman, too, something the sexual culture does not teach anyone.

Going All the Way to Orgasm

What if, instead of intercourse, a heterosexual woman's "first time" was first orgasm? When a girl told her friends or her diary that she "did it," she would mean she had an orgasm. "Going all the way" would mean going all the way to orgasm. No one would have partner sex before first getting to know their own body sexually. "Virginity" would be a meaningless concept because vaginal penetration would merely be one of many ways in which people might eventually enjoy sex with a partner.

If orgasm and not intercourse were the rite of passage into sexuality, the lesson to girls would be that their body is not the possession of a partner or of the sexual culture. Putting orgasm first would encourage women to get to know themselves first. Unfortunately, many women now masturbate only *after* they begin to have partner sex. They start exploring their sexuality only after it has come to their attention through a man. In contrast, a woman who knows herself sexually goes into partner sex from a position of strength. For her, partner sex can be a gain rather than a loss. She already knows that although sex may be *with* another person, it is not only *for* her or him: Sex is equally for oneself.

Typically, first intercourse teaches a young woman that sex is fundamentally about someone else's pleasure. First orgasm, in contrast, marks the onset of a woman's own sexual life. Every woman's first experience would be like that of a sexually contented friend in her thirties who told us, "I honestly cannot remember my first intercourse, but I do remember my first orgasm: where, when, how. And I remember thinking—so that is it! Oh, yes!" Another woman who experienced orgasm for the first time in her late twenties told us, "When I finally had an orgasm, I thought, 'Now I understand why men like sex so much.' " Still another woman said, "I didn't have an orgasm until I was thirty because I thought having intercourse with my husband was supposed to do it. What a lot of time I wasted!" The sexual culture has it backward when it claims intercourse as the apex of sex. Now women can put things right by putting orgasm first.

The women's health classic *Our Bodies, Ourselves* expresses concern that making orgasm a goal of sex will set up "one more performance pressure" for women already beleaguered by too many external standards and demands. It is a far greater problem, in our view, that women are agreeing to have what is literally *partner* sex with men: He gets the sex, and she gets (she hopes) the partner.

Love Lines

Instead of developing a sexual self, girls learn to focus on pleasing boys. Sexologist Naomi B. McCormick points out how adolescent boys learn *recreational* sexual scripts or styles of behavior, while girls learn *relational* ones. Books, movies, and glossy magazines for girls focus their attention on love and romance. Young people learn about sex in two separate worlds defined by gender. As researcher John H. Gagnon notes, "Boys learn about genital sexuality and masturbation, while girls learn about love and the importance of boys." What girls get from sex are its by-products: Romance, intimacy, and boys' attention. What boys get is orgasmic sex.

Heterosexual girls learn that sex is a part of a larger love project with a particular male, while boys are allowed, even encouraged, to distinguish between love and sex. Although they do not look to boys, lesbian girls also learn to see sex as part of being "in love" with another girl or woman. The difference is that, unlike with boys, the other girl may be more likely to feel the same way.

The sexual culture discourages boys from expressing romantic feelings while girls are taught to ignore or fail to cultivate their physical sexuality. Researcher Deborah L. Tolman reports that girls experience sexual desire, but react to it in different ways. She found that some girls talk passionately about their sexual feelings. One told of feeling like "every time I see him, I . . . just wanna go over and grab him and say, let's go, . . . 'Cause I just want him so bad . . . He just gives me a funny feeling. . . ." Another girl tells Tolman, "I wanna have sex so bad . . . you have this feeling, you just have to get rid of it." Other girls described how their body "says yes yes yes yes" and feels "ready to burst" with erotic excitement.

Instead of being encouraged to consider their own feelings, girls learn to stop themselves and wait for a boy to initiate. They may even resist advances they want. A girl's sexual desire is channeled into desire for a boy's attention and, ultimately, his love. Because a girl is less likely than a boy to be on familiar terms with her own body, her desire for a relationship and romance may be more of a factor in deciding to become sexual rather than for the pleasures of sex itself.

Most girls grow up learning to connect sex with romance instead of orgasms. Few girls are able to link sexual desire with their genitals and are not especially attuned to the physical sensations of sexual excitement. One girl was the exception when she told Tolman, "My vagina . . . kinda like quivers and stuff" when she is turned on. But most girls interpret physical desire in romantic, not sexual or genital, terms. The focus on romance can have consequences beyond being detrimental to sexual pleasure. Sharon Thompson concludes that girls who focused on romance got "lost" in love. They were more easily led to behavior with men that could "endanger themselves or foreclose the future" than girls who did not. Early love relationships also threatened to derail girls' lives into social, emotional, and financial dependence on a man or men.

Love could also lead to unsafe sexual behaviors. Girls had sex with a steady boyfriend as a sign of what Thompson calls "progress in love." They had sex to strengthen or maintain a relationship, not for pleasure. In contrast, girls who had sex for fun were in a better position to develop a sense of self. Some girls Thompson interviewed purposely sought out relationships with older men that were purely erotic. Sex with such men was still not necessarily orgasmic or particularly equal, however. Even a confident girl who goes into a sexual relationship with her eyes wide open, goes up against a sexual culture that defines sex—and even her own body—on a man's terms rather than on her own.

Learning the Body Through Men

Unlike boys who set out early on a course of sexual self-training, girls' first experiences of sex are likely to be with boyfriends. Instead of first becoming their own best lovers, most girls hand over their sexual training to a boy or man. They learn about sex from a male perspective and even become familiar with their own body through the eyes, hands, images, and words of men.

A heterosexual adult woman can think back and list the sequence of various boys' and men's intervention into her body as each one recorded himself into her sexual history. She remembers how these men's touches, their opinions, and even their leers molded her body's budding sexuality. She remembers boy-imposed firsts—first sexual comments, first kiss, first fondling, first time a man saw her naked breasts, first time he touched her genitals, etc. Her sexuality unfolds as a chronology of men's attentions.

The sexual culture permits a masculine eye to frame and his hand to define what is interesting about the female body. The primary focus of male attention in U.S. sexual culture is the breasts. A girl may play with her clitoris as a young child, but as she reaches puberty, men and boys make it obvious that what counts are her breasts. (A firm, round bottom runs a close second.) As an adolescent, a girl wonders what her breasts will grow to be like: round and soft like her mother's, or small and alert like her aunt's?

A girl knows that she will be sexy to men if she has large or perky breasts, but that boys will tease her if they are too big or if she is "flat." As her body matures, she thinks about how her breasts appear to others. How do they look from the side? How do they look in a low-cut blouse? From the time boys start snapping her first training bra (what does it train, anyway? her breasts? herself?), a girl becomes aware of her breasts as sexual capital. She learns to make them look bigger and rounder with push-up bras and, later in life, if she or her partner is unsatisfied with them, she may have them enhanced, reshaped, or reduced. (It is a poignant fact that, although women feel sexier when their breasts are surgically "improved," breast implants may reduce nipple sensitivity, not to mention being linked to illness and even death.)

A woman gets to know her breasts and how they look from the outside in, rather than learning about how they feel from the inside out. Except insofar as they attract men, a girl does not hear anything about the breasts as a site of her own sexual pleasure. It is the breast's contours and size that matter, she learns, not how her nipples sizzle when she comes, or how their stimulation can make her come. Indeed, a woman may not even discover the sensitivity of her nipples until a partner (or, in some cases, only when an infant) sucks on them. A woman is limited to the feelings others may or may not awaken in her.

A woman undergoes a similar learning process with her genitals, learning to appreciate the parts that create pleasure for men (the vagina) over the parts that make sex orgasmic for her (the G spot, cul-de-sac, and clitoris). Because a woman discovers her sexual body through a man (the reverse does not occur for boys), it may never occur to her to explore beyond the territory that he defines. If he never touches her clitoris, it doesn't get touched. It's all up to him and to the luck of the boyfriend draw.

Cultures of Sex

The sexual culture orients sexuality to the interests of boys, and girls follow their lead. Although every woman takes a distinct sexual path, coming-of-age stories tend to fall into patterns influenced by racial, ethnic, class, and religious backgrounds. They vary geographically and by generation. *Where* and *when* a girl learns about sex affects *what* she learns, as does the particular history and character of her family.

When we (the authors) were growing up, sex was cool—in theory, at least. Growing up as white upper-middle-class girls in the San Francisco Bay Area during the sexual revolution and before the age of AIDS, our local culture and our parents taught us, mostly indirectly, that sex was fun. (Our mother's word for something really wonderful was "sexy.") In contrast to the mainstream white culture's message that sex was bad, we got a different picture through witnessing the way she and our dad touched each other, how they responded to the sex in comedy and in movies, and how their friends joked and talked about sex at the parties where we were allowed to eavesdrop. To us, sex sounded intriguing and good.

Ours was a sex-friendly, but not totally open, subculture. Our parents did not actually *talk* to us about sex: What you do when you have sex, what it felt like, or where and how to get and use contraceptives. We did not talk about these things with our mother or our friends. We did not talk about it with one another—sisters close in age—until we were in our twenties. Looking back, we now know that many of the influences of our parents' era, such as copies of once-banned novels by Henry Miller and D. H. Lawrence lying around the house, depicted a sexual world that prioritized men. The formal sex education we all got in school was limited to one sex-segregated lecture by the gym teacher on menstruation (several months to a year after many of us had already started having periods) and another on what happens when egg meets sperm (without it ever being made clear how that sperm got inside).

Somehow, our family's generally positive attitude prevailed and we learned to see sex as basically healthy and good. We were also fortunate enough to have first boyfriends who were school peers and who were as eager and inexperienced as we were about sex. This meant we both enjoyed long golden ages.

Our family's generally positive attitude contrasted with that of the sexual culture at large and with a more shame-oriented attitude of some of our school friends. Rooted as it is in puritanism, the dominant European American culture in the United States encourages girls especially to repress sexual desires and to feel shame if they experience or express them. In our late

1960s-, early 1970s-high school community, however, even "good girls"—read "nice," heterosexual, middle-class girls—had sex. But they were at risk of immediately becoming "bad girls" if they "got caught" by getting pregnant.

The majority of our high school contemporaries were Mexican Americans who in their homes were exposed to a similar good girl/bad girl opposition in the form of madonna/whore classification of women from the Catholic Church. Telenovelas, Latin music, and pop culture promoted overtly sexy image of women that contrasted with the idealized image of a good wife and mother. Powerful images of the "good" virgin and the self-sacrificing mother (simultaneously embodied by the Virgin Mary) stood in opposition to the *puta.* A good daughter or wife knew which role she was expected to choose. Writer Ana Castillo notes how a "woman is taught by her religion and by her cultural mores to negate sexual desire." Psychotherapist Olivia M. Espín concurs, noting that "the honor of Latin families is strongly tied to the sexual purity of women. . . . To enjoy sexual pleasure, even in marriage, may indicate lack of virtue. . . . Some women even express pride at their own lack of sexual pleasure or desire."

One Latina told us that it took years before the sensual mood of the songs of love and lust that played endlessly in the family dining room finally carried over to her bedroom. She so took to heart the lesson that feeling good about sex was bad, that during the first few times she had intercourse with her husband she lay stock still. She vaguely expected to feel *something,* but she had not yet gathered the courage to explore the possibility of actually having fun in sex.

While Latin American cultures exult in romantic expression, the sexual values of many Asian American families are conveyed by silence. "You don't talk about sex in Asian culture," one Chinese American woman tells us. This silence may even be written into the language. A Vietnamese woman says she knows of no word for "masturbation" or even "sex" in her language. The silence about sex is its own message, and the message conveyed to girls and women is that sex is for the man's pleasure. Pamela H., an Asian American writer, says that there is an extreme sexual double standard in which "women have been indoctrinated to believe that anything dealing with sex is shameful and must be avoided. . . . Conversely, men are allowed to deal with sexual feelings as youths and are even encouraged by peers to be sexually active." Like many Latinas, Asian women may feel pressure to uphold family honor by avoiding or hiding sexual activity before marriage and showing only minimal enthusiasm afterward.

Many African American girls grow up surrounded by music, stories, and adult talk that recount positive tales of sexual pleasure with humor and wit. But these influences may compete with religious and family values that consider sex or some sexual acts a sin, especially for a good girl or woman. One African American woman who enjoys sex says that she has never talked about sex with her sisters or mother. They have never even mentioned the word. Studies repeatedly confirm that African American girls develop better body- and self-images growing up than do other U.S. women. African American women's resilient selfhood may conflict with men's attempts to control them and their sexuality, however. Poet and playwright Ntozake Shange writes, "If some of us are wont to touch ourselves to enhance our own pleasure, these very same fellas may demand to know what we are doing with their nipple, their clit, their bush, which apparently were appropriated without our knowledge or consent." While African American culture supports women's development of a sexual self, many African American men participate in the same mainstream sexual culture as other men.

Women do not learn their sexuality as either isolated individuals or in response to their hormones and gonads. Instead, family, cultural, and other factors combine with individual his-

INITIATION INTO THE SEXUAL CULTURE

Although a wide variety of social factors comes into play that influence how a woman experiences her "first time," there are aspects of a girl's coming of age in American sexual culture that are remarkably consistent across time and space. They include:

1. shame, prudery, and embarrassment about sex and the body

2. confusion about and lack of familiarity with the female body, especially the genitals

3. little or no experience with masturbation

4. relying on a boyfriend to make the first move and to guide sex

5. little, inadequate, or incorrect sexual information

6. insecurity about her body and her own attractiveness

7. emphasis on

   - intercourse over manual sex

   - reproduction over pleasure

   - his pleasure over her own

tories and the influence of mainstream sexual culture to make sex what it is for each person. But despite cultural and individual differences, all girls learn a strikingly similar lesson about sex.

Some women have life circumstances that, because the sexual culture is unwilling to accommodate them, present unique challenges. Young lesbians of color, for example, must confront racism and racial stereotypes as well as homophobia. Lesbians are coming out with greater ease and at younger ages than in previous generations due to more developed support networks. However, this process remains more difficult for lesbians of color. Pamela H. writes that her lesbianism is additionally problematic for her family because it is often seen by Asian American parents as a "white disease," and most Asian languages do not even have a word that means "lesbian." African American lesbians are sometimes accused of betraying their community and African American men. Latina lesbians may become alienated from families and communities because, unable to fulfill their roles as wives within heterosexual marriage, their families cannot always easily accommodate them. Community groups supporting lesbians, gays, bisexual, and transgendered people can often act like a family and have been crucial to helping young people come out.

Disabled women may have an especially difficult confrontation with the male-defined physical idea of a "sexy" woman. In her essay "You're Short, Besides!," Sucheng Chan writes about her sexual experience as a woman disabled by polio. Beyond feeling physical dependence upon others and chronic pain, she writes:

> The most difficult thing a handicapped person has to deal with, especially during puberty and early adulthood, is relating to potential sexual partners. Because American culture places so much emphasis on physical attractiveness, a person with a shriveled limb, or a tilt to the head, or the inability to speak clearly, experiences great uncertainty—indeed trauma—when interacting with someone to whom he or she is attracted. My problem was that I was not only physically handicapped, small, and short, but worse, I also wore glasses and was smarter than all the boys I knew! Alas, an insurmountable combination. Yet somehow I have managed to have intimate relationships, all of them with extraordinary men. Not surprisingly, there have also been countless men who broke my heart—men who enjoyed my company "as a friend," but who never found the courage to date or make

love with me, although I am sure my experience in this regard is not different from that of many able-bodied persons.

The day came when my backaches got in the way of having an active sex life. Surprisingly that development was liberating because I stopped worrying about being attractive to men. No matter how headstrong I had been, I, like most women of my generation, had had the desire to be alluring to men ingrained into me. And that longing had always worked like a brake on my behavior. When what men think of me ceased to be compelling, I gained greater freedom to be myself.

All women share one social status that is by far the most significant factor in their sexual life—female gender. Women are simply not given the same entitlement to sex as men. By making the effort to define themselves independently of a partner and of the sexual culture, however, women can begin a journey to re-create sex on their own terms. The process has to begin with young women so that they do not waste decades searching for the pleasure in sex or having sex for someone else.

The Sex Ed Gap

The separation between women and their sexual pleasure widens with poor or inadequate sex education. From hygiene-class textbooks and doctors' office pamphlets, all girls learn something about their reproductive capabilities but almost nothing about their capacity for pleasure. They see sketches only of the genital parts involved in reproduction. Most women can draw their vagina, uterus, and fallopian tubes from memory, but would have trouble depicting (and, perhaps, even finding) their clitoris. In health diagrams, the sexual parts are either de-emphasized, distorted, inaccurate, or left out altogether. Sex education texts may mention that stimulation of the clitoris can give a girl or woman orgasms, but how that is to be accomplished is unclear. They suggest that the woman's orgasm may occur during intercourse. The G spot and female ejaculation are discussed in college-level human sexuality texts as points of controversy.

Female ejaculation is never mentioned in high school sex education, leaving some girls who ejaculate to wonder if they are freaks of nature. They may hold back in sex in order to stop ejaculation from occurring. One woman who says she has ejaculated during manual sex from the time she was a teenager recalls asking her college human physiology professor, after he explained the process of ejaculation in men, if it was the same in women.

SEX ED 000: THE MISSING CLITORIS

- The 1994 edition of a textbook used for high school sophomore health classes includes an optional unit on sexual behavior and pregnancy prevention. Throughout the section, sex is implicitly assumed to be intercourse. The unit identifies the clitoris (along with the brain) as the source of women's orgasms without indicating how a girl is supposed to sexually stimulate either. There is no diagram showing where the clitoris is located or what it looks like. Although the woman's orgasm is mentioned, it is only to note that "it can occur prior to, along with, or after the man's," without saying how it might be done. But the text makes it clear that the central act of the heterosexual encounter is supposed to be intercourse.

- A 1992 pamphlet on contraception, published by a pharmaceutical company and approved by The American College of Obstetricians and Gynecologists, offers a diagram of women's genitals that excludes the clitoris. For a brochure

Her question was greeted with dead silence from the professor and students alike, who could not imagine what she was talking about. The girl had previously assumed that it was something that all women did, because it happened to her.

Female ejaculation is still not widely discussed, especially in sex education for girls, but there is more information available to young people today. By gathering bits and pieces from here and there, a young woman can fashion her own sex education. She must make an effort, however, to find sources of information that resonate with her own experiences. For many girls, what they know conflicts with what they learn from books, their parents, or their health teachers. Between theory and practice

intended to prevent pregnancy, it would seem appropriate to mention that noncoital sexual activities such as manual and oral sex have the advantage of avoiding conception. Instead, manual sex is reduced to "petting" and no mention at all is made of oral sex. The text of the pamphlet describes how conception occurs and suggests that orgasm may occur for either or both partners only during intercourse.

The pamphlet "Being a Teenager: You and Your Sexuality" states: In sexual intercourse, a man and a woman join their bodies together. The man's penis gets hard, or erect, and the tissues of the woman's vagina become moist. The man's penis enters the woman's vagina. During intercourse, the woman and man may have orgasms, or climaxes. The woman's orgasm is usually a pleasurable, rhythmic contraction of the muscles in the vagina and uterus. When the man climaxes, he ejaculates a fluid containing his sperm, which goes into the woman's vagina and travels through the cervix into the uterus and fallopian tubes.

lies a big and ragged information gap. Many girls find themselves unable to bridge the information gap and, as a result, fall into the chasm of sexual silence below.

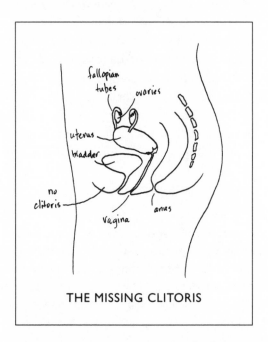

THE MISSING CLITORIS

Silence Is Not Golden

Young women need access to information about their bodies. They need settings where they can talk to female peers about sex, in all its controversial detail. For until women start to share information and compare experiences, they must rely on the few other sources of sexual knowledge available. Sex education in the schools is inadequate because, hard pressed to provide many other services to students, schools succumb to pressures from those who believe that silence leads to abstinence, and that ignorance is a deterrent to having sex.

Ignorance about sex does not stop teenagers from having

sex. In fact, the opposite is true. Ignorance increases the chance of unsafe sex and teenage pregnancy. Studies from Holland and other countries show that the more information young people have, the fewer teenage pregnancies occur, even with the same or higher rates of sexual activity. Many social conservatives believe that giving young people information about sex encourages them to have it. It is sexual morality and not sexual health or well-being that opponents have in mind when they repress sexual information. Yet girls and boys need accurate information that ensures that if they do decide to be sexually active, they will have access to contraception and safer-sex information, as well as the latex and lubricant that goes with it.

Many parents still find it notoriously difficult to talk about sex with their own kids, especially if their own vision of sex is clouded with shame, guilt, or confusion. Rather than keeping teenagers from having sex, silence about sex may actually encourage them to sneak around and have sex in ways that are more dangerous and less satisfying, particularly for girls. Instead of learning sexual responsibility, young people only hear an emphatic "Don't do it!" from adults, inspiring some to "go for it" all the more. The greater the silence at home and at school, the louder the sound of peers and of media messages that glamorize spontaneity—unsafe sex, sex in public places, sex with strangers—selfless "what-the-hell" sex. Messages to abstain also reinforce sex as intercourse, and keep young people from enjoying satisfying and safe manual sex.

Understanding how to minimize the dangers of sex and knowing how to use reliable, available, and affordable birth control can help a woman take control of her sex life. An additional tool for making sex safer is to learn about pleasure. Acknowledging the pleasures of sex can help young women to learn to have sex for themselves and not just for others. Instead of having sex because it is cool, to cement a relationship, or in order to fit in with peers, young women would do better to be outright *selfish* in sex. They would benefit from having sex on their own timing and with their own pleasure in mind.

By emphasizing sex for pleasure, young women will think of and protect themselves first. If they are also equipped with good information, self-esteem, and self-love, they are less likely to agree to intercourse they do not really want. A woman who knows her own body and how to have orgasms is more likely to be proactive rather than passive, and can act as a true *partner* in sex. With manual sex, especially, a woman can have all the orgasmic sex she wants and avoid intercourse until she is ready to take that risk.

Know Thyself

Partner sex is enhanced when each person comes to the encounter with self-knowledge. A person gains that self-knowledge through masturbation. Masturbation and partner sex can coexist in a kind of symbiosis, each one enhancing the other. Although it undoubtedly enhances sex with a partner, masturbation can also stand on its own (as it does for women who do not have or do not want a partner). Just as regular exercise and a good diet contribute to overall health, the baseline of healthy sexuality for many people is a regular regimen of pleasure for one. A person who is not partnered need not forego sex. As sex educator Betty Dodson says, "Lovers come and go, but you can have an ongoing love affair with yourself."

Masturbation prepares a young woman to be a wiser participant in sex with a man. The woman who has orgasms before she has intercourse is better able to make partner sex more fun and meaningful. She acts not as the man's apprentice, nor as his clay to be modeled, but as an equal sex partner. There is no reason, for example, why either a girl or a boy cannot make the first move. Girls who wait for boys to initiate physical intimacy may go more easily into sex on boys' terms. In a sexual culture where sex is a playful game rather than a competitive conquest, and where education, safer sex, and contraception are standard equipment for the young, desire, not gender, would determine who initiates.

Another part of making sex better is making it more playful. Around the world and throughout history people have cultivated the art of noncoital sex. Noncoital partner sex has long flourished among heterosexuals in the period prior to marriage. In nineteenth-century rural France, for example, young women and men used manual sex to enjoy one another's sexual company without the danger of pregnancy. Couples would gather with other friends in forest cabins at night to talk, sing, and tell jokes. The women sat on their partner's lap and engaged in *migaillage,* that is, they allowed their partner to dip his hand into the open, bottomless pocket (*migaille*) of their skirt to give them clittage.

Saying Yes to Good Sex

As a precocious girl of twelve, Mae West arranged with an older man she knew in the theater business to have intercourse for the first time. Throughout her life, West provided her own most powerful antidote to the sexual limitations placed on women by having sex on her own terms. She believed in having "an orgasm a day" and enjoyed sex with many different men. Her self-assured yet playful attitude provides a model that girls and women today might reflect upon and adapt for today's safer-sex climate.

Women cannot explore and enjoy sex fully, however, until the sexual culture makes it safe for them to do so. Pleasure and safety are inseparable. Girls and women need to gain the power in sex to help make the world safer for themselves and other women.

When teenagers can safely enjoy a golden age in which partners share pleasure equally, both sexes become better, more respectful lovers. Both learn to take equal responsibility for birth control and safer sex. In such a world, girls could be spared decades—or even whole lifetimes—of bad, demeaning, or injurious sex.

Learning desires does not therefore mean that girls should give an unqualified yes to sex. But it means more than just saying no. In conclusion to her collection of "first time" stories, Karen Bouris writes that "Teenage girls (and all of us!) have no sense of their worth, and haven't formed a strong voice—one that can say 'NO!' loud and clear when necessary, or one that can say, 'Yes, this is what I want and here's how I want it.' " Reinventing sex means learning to say yes—not to a man, but to pleasure. It means developing what Michelle Fine calls a "discourse of desire" for adolescent girls that is self-affirming because it is focused on pleasure. It means ensuring that girls and women have the authority and power to define the terms of partner sex. Most women, like Nikki, only discover this power after many years of being sexually active. Looking back, they realize that first intercourse was really not their first time at all. In fact, a woman never has sex—real sex—until she experiences sex on her own terms and for her own pleasure.

CHAPTER FOUR

Pop
Porn

Nikki sits in the darkened theater with Joe and watches as the camera closes in on the body of a woman. The camera looks over the shoulder of the approaching man, and brings Nikki, Joe, and the rest of the audience with it. This collective eye embraces the woman where she stands, taking all of her in. It follows the man's hands as he discovers and unveils her, body part by body part. As the man removes her clothes, the camera cuts between the woman's face, breasts, navel, and thighs. Then, in one corner of the screen, the man quickly disrobes. Nikki catches just a glimpse of his buttocks and his muscular back. Hey! Wait a minute! *But the camera is not interested.*

Nikki tosses popcorn into her mouth. She starts to chew, then freezes. The pace of the action suddenly picks up. The lovers fall to a couch and seem to be having intercourse. Some foreplay! *The camera offers a tight shot of the woman's face.* She is so beautiful, so perfect. I'll never look that good. *The woman's eyes are closed, her mouth open, her neck arched back. The camera cuts to her heaving breasts.* How about a shot of his chest? *The woman pants and moans. With a few short thrusts and one long groan, he comes. The scene—and the sex—is over.*

The woman on the screen smiles with apparent satisfaction, but Nikki is dubious. She didn't come. No way. *Later, as she and Joe leave the theater, he says excitedly,* "The sex was hot!" *Nikki knows that she is expected to agree, but instead she feels cold. Her*

*head is full of frozen images of the woman's anatomy and the
sound of the man's heated orgasm, and she can identify with neither. Nikki feels left out and angry. She is not so sure that, by the
time she and Joe get home, she will be in the mood for sex.*

Like Nikki and Joe, many couples go to the movies or rent a
video as an evening prelude to a night of sex. What they typically see on screen—the woman's exposed body and the man's
orgasm—is designed to appeal to heterosexual men, yet everyone learns to see this movie as "sexy." All moviegoers—who are
female and male, gay and straight, young and old—see sex depicted this way so often they hardly notice that they are only
shown *men's* orgasms (but rarely a male body) and *women's*
bodies (but rarely a believable female orgasm). Instead of hot
sex with her buttered popcorn, all Nikki (and every other
viewer) gets is "pop porn."

Pop Porn

Pop porn is the pervasive panorama of female flesh—the high-
heeled foot, breasts spilling out of a low-cut gown, the pouting
red lips, the sultry stare from under a thick mane—that is the
everyday stuff of popular media. Many people believe they can
escape pornography by ignoring X-rated movies, staying out of
"adult" (actually, straight men's) bookstores, and avoiding the
back room of their video store. But pornography is only pop
porn's more flamboyant, renegade cousin. Pop porn shuns the
images of an erect penis or a naked vulva that one sees in pornography, yet because it is impossible to escape, it ultimately has a
stronger impact. Pop porn is everywhere. Its images saturate the
movies and adorn billboards, video boxes, television ads, and
the covers of novels and magazines. It insinuates itself into tele-

vision and printed news reports, especially in the sensationalist press. It is even used to sell products that have no sexual content. Pop porn's most influential and far-reaching forms are television and the movies, which can actually show sexual action. Network television regularly features provocatively dressed women and occasionally presents mild forms of heterosexual play. On cable TV and, especially, at the movies, viewers can actually watch sex unfold "all the way" to intercourse.

Since the 1990s, pop porn's pervasive and insidious message seems to be getting louder, informing women that their bodies are a medium for other people's sexual consumption. Although starkly out of synch with what many women now think about themselves and about sexuality, a surprisingly 1950s *Playboy* image of the female body still prevails. Women who stand for sex—bunnies and centerfolds, swimsuit calendars and pinups—continue to adorn many a wall in workshops, offices, and homes. Their images fill lingerie catalogs and adorn tropical travel brochures. Provocatively dressed women appear in action on television beer ads, late-night movies, and MTV. Pop porn's retrograde images of women and sex are readily available in cyberspace.

Pop porn provides visual entertainment for an audience of straight men, yet insidiously imposes itself upon everyone. All women and gay men are excluded, ignored, or expected to be complacent about the pop porn perspective. Indeed, any consumer can become so immersed in its products that she or he becomes blind to its bias. And although more male bodies are on public display now than ever before, men cannot be objectified in the same way as women routinely have been, because a man does not count on his looks for social and economic survival in the way many women must.

Women are familiar with being in the awkward position of watching other women as objects of seduction, while also seeing their own mirror image. A woman learns to compare herself to, to *desire,* and to *desire to be* that idealized woman all at the same time. Yet, women rarely see women who resemble themselves on the screen. Only thin, able-bodied, beautiful, and young women fit the standardized pop porn image of what is sexy. This image is remarkably consistent across mainstream African American, Spanish-language, white, and Asian American media. The model female has an idealized body shape that is far from the norm for any group of women, and she is all-too-atypically white and blonde. Men from all ethnic and racial groups and every nationality learn to consume her image, and their female counterparts cannot escape being compared to it. Through the export of magazines, newspapers, books, radio, broadcast television, movies, videos, T-shirts, and the Internet, U.S. media's pop porn images affect how several billion people around the globe, especially young people, think about (and learn to equate) women and sex. Pop porn sells much more than just movies, consumer products, and services. It also promotes a certain brand of male-oriented sex. The medium is women's half-naked bodies. The message: This Is Sex.

What's Wrong with This Picture?

Hollywood films rarely portray women's stories, much less women's experiences of sex. Most popular films feature stories *about* men *for* men. They portray men's struggles, men's concerns, and men's adventures. Overall, men outnumber women in the movies three to one. Male characters dominate in most top-grossing films, including dramas, action films, and even children's movies and cartoons. Women rarely star, and even when they do, they are usually engaged in a struggle to help, find, free, or bolster a man. They are the wives or girlfriends of the male star, there to facilitate a film's action or provide sex for the male hero without being the beneficiary of either. As if the coin of a completely masculine realm, women are tokens of power and bargaining chips, one of many means—along with money, physical violence, cars—by which men compete among themselves to gain status and power. The fact that the best-selling combination for the cover of a video box is a sexy woman and a gun clearly indicates that the intended film audience is male.

U.S. films are geared to the tastes of young, heterosexual, white men who, from childhood, are molded by stories about themselves. Young men do not, in turn, go to movies whose protagonists are women. From *Tom Sawyer* to *Toy Story,* there is a vast choice in books, movies, and entertainment centered on the lives of boys. Stories about girls that do appear, such as *Pocahontas* or *Cinderella,* are both rare and boyfriend-centered. Boys' themes win out at the box office and toy stores because girls will accept stories about boys while a film with a female lead becomes a "woman's movie," a label that turns men and boys away. There is no such thing as a "man's movie"—there are simply "movies."

Girls learn the male-centered vision of the world at a young age. In toddlerhood, they watch "Sesame Street" with its predominantly male animal-character cast (more female animals, such as Zoe and Rosita, have been added recently). The humans the animals interact with are of both sexes and racially diverse. From Barney to Big Bird to Kermit, however, leading *animals* in children's entertainment are male. Yet few parents notice this. They tend to see these animal characters as "gender neutral."

The most popular entertainment products for children often involve stories that are brazenly masculine. Successful children's movies such as *The Lion King* and *Aladdin and the King of Thieves,* for example, are cartoons about patriarchal succession. Female characters fill roles as mothers, wives, or girlfriends who, although often intelligent, inventive, and strong, are clearly subordinate to males. If not altogether overpowered by male stars, female characters are far outnumbered by them. In the Muppet movies, even Miss Piggy, a character who frequently commits acts of daring and strength, is still a tagalong to a pack of animals who are all male.

In video games, women are often frail, helpless victims of evil that the child-combatant helps the hero rescue. Women can be quite powerful figures in some comic books, where they take their most bizarre form as leotard-clad counterparts to the male action-figure hero (Wonder Woman) or villain (Cat Woman). These characters send an especially peculiar message to children because, with Barbie-doll bodies outfitted with masks, whips, and boots, they share less resemblance to their male counterparts than they do to a miniature dominatrix. What strength they are attributed is diminished by being sexualized. Although they fight along with male action figures, women are only tokens among armies of good guys and bad guys. Like the female TV and film characters they see on screen, girls learn to accept a man's world of heroic exploits amidst car crashes, fiery explosions, gun violence, and dispersed blood and guts.

He's Gotta Have It

All adult viewers of mass entertainment must become accustomed to T & A (tits and ass) portrayals of women. Some young men relish the ready access to T & A that is available both on cable television and even prime-time network dramas, situation comedies, and advertisements. Breasts, thighs, and buttocks flash across the screen so regularly that a teen viewer could easily confuse the pop porn version of a woman's body with sex itself.

Sex is typically symbolized by a beautiful, young woman's body and a man's unruly desire. Movies play it safe and ensure box-office success by using only this tried-and-true formula and the standard conventions about gender. A man who acts without control of his passions is "sexy." A woman is "sexy" when she first resists and then succumbs to him. This seducer/seduced formula produces, at best, a fairy-tale kind of sex in which a prince sweeps a young woman off her feet. At worst, it produces sexualized violence.

A man's uncontrollable desire for a woman is something that some women consider thrilling. Although women know that Michael Douglas's furtive act of kitchen-counter penetration in *Fatal Attraction* is unlikely to bring Glenn Close to orgasm, some women like the risk, the danger, and even the violence of such scenes. They confirm existing gender roles in sex by presenting an irresistible woman (desirability is the only sexual trait a pop-porn culture encourages women to cultivate) and a driven man who will stop at nothing to "have" her.

Often women do nothing more than decorate the screen. In the futuristic movie *Soylent Green,* women came with the rental of an apartment and were even called "furniture." On TV's "Baywatch," women in bikinis appear in nearly every scene. A woman's beautiful body is like an expensive car that enhances the hero's image and acts as a medium through which he and other men negotiate status among themselves. Although clearly visible to the viewer, the men on the screen talk to one another past the decorative women, but never to them. Much of the time, women do not speak, act, or otherwise distract the audience from the actions of men. They are like product placement— there to be noticed just enough to sell a product.

Still-Life Pop Porn

Pop porn for the male consumer comes in a variety of forms and can be found at any pharmacy newsstand. A man has many choices: He can peruse the soft porn of the *Sports Illustrated* swimsuit issue, or reach behind the discreet plywood barriers to examine more hardcore photos in *Playboy, Penthouse,* or *Hustler.* He can buy or subscribe to these and other magazines to "read" in the privacy of his home. If such direct access makes him uncomfortable, he can turn to his wife's *Victoria's Secret* catalogue that arrives in the mail, or check the back-page ads of many magazines, newspapers, and even the phone book (under "escort services," "entertainment," and the like) for pictures and drawings of women frozen in seductive, often uncomfortable-looking poses, wearing G-string bikinis. Without any effort, a man has access to countless images of ideal female bodies.

Before mass marketing made pop porn more explicit and pornography more accessible to a wide market in the 1960s, the workhorses of generations of teenaged boys' sexual self-initiation were the still-life women of *National Geographic.* In their book *Reading National Geographic,* Catherine A. Lutz and Jane L. Collins report that the magazines and photo displays that accompanied descriptive articles often featured the naked chests of women. These pictures were selective: Only young, attractive females were depicted, even for societies where all women's dress regularly exposes their breasts. Ostensibly intended to depict the way of life of other peoples, the photographs were tailored to fit a U.S. sexual aesthetic, and they played a prominent role in young American men's sexual fantasies. Needless to say, men's sexual organs were never shown, even if they were in fact exposed in the culture being featured. The bodies of exoticized women and men were remade to fit into our society's pop-porn norms about sex and beauty. Those norms protected men from exposure and focused almost exclusively on young women.

Censoring all but attractive females from public view is typical of today's pop porn, whose images are derived from the bodies of real women picked for their proximity to a feminine ideal, then airbrushed to flawless perfection. This ideal woman calls out to the viewer. She exists for a man to consume and, in some ads, the product she sells consumes her. It is standard to see a women encased in the label of a bottle of liquor or molded into the shape of a sports car. When we see a picture of a naked man in ads, his nude body is subordinated to his brain. He is often a young, white man who poses as an Old World sage. He is a Greek god or Rodin's *Thinker*. One recent ad showed a naked man in a diver's tuck ready to plug his pronged head into a socket and go on-line with the World Wide Web. In contrast to men's thinking heads, women are frequently shown headless— their faces draped by opaque fabric, decapitated like department store mannequins, facing away from the camera, or chopped off at the neck. Faceless, a woman has no personhood. Headless, she does not think, nor can she speak. As a still life, she does not move, breathe, sweat, or smell. She is converted into a thing. She ceases being a person with desires of her own that could derail or interfere with the male viewer's (and potential buyer's) own sexual fantasy.

Pop porn turns a real woman into a soulless product. Unlike real partner sex between two people, pop-porn sex is a primarily visual exchange between man and object. A man can stare at a woman, even hold her in his hands, without having to interact with her. She has no name (even the identity of the highest-paid models usually goes unmentioned in fashion photography). The lack of any emotional demands or intimacy between the male viewer and this woman/image/lover/stranger/object, can actually enhance a still life's erotic value for some men. Having sex with an image carries no obligations or consequences. The woman remains separated from the man in time and space, yet she is all his. Her direct gaze and welcoming pose act as a mirror, inviting a man to indulge in his own immediate sexual gratification without concern for a real woman's desire.

Irreversibility

In the media and on the street, women are the observed, men the observers. These positions are not reversible. A popular television ad for Diet Coke offers an exception that proves the rule. The ad shows a group of women who gather at their office window to leer at a construction-site hunk as he removes his shirt on his break and enjoys a soft drink. While our sexual culture is losing its tolerance for men in groups who openly ogle women, the ad's reversal amounts to little more than a carnivalesque joke. Although believable—the man's torso ripples agreeably and the women are so engrossed they hold their breath—the ad is funny because it turns the usual gender relations upside down. This reversal only confirms for viewers that even the gaze of several women lacks the same power and authority of just one man's gaze.

Pop porn trades in women's but not men's bodies. There is no female-oriented counterpart to pop porn. Women do not have, nor do they seek, pictures of the bodies of men. An attempt has been made to market a playgirl image for women, with its accompanying centerfold and nude photographs of men (including exposed, often flaccid, penises). A magazine like *Playgirl* survives in part because of its popularity among gay men.

Desiring Woman as Evil

In pop porn, even depictions of female sexual pleasure become a measure of the man's masculinity, rather than a portrayal of the woman's own experience. If the pop porn camera shows a woman having an orgasm, the purpose is to excite the heterosexual male viewer and to demonstrate the sexual prowess of her on-screen lover. The camera shows a man kissing or caressing a woman's nipples, for example, so that the collective eye can observe her breasts, not so that women can identify with her arousal. In a scene from *9 1/2 Weeks,* a controversial film about a sadomasochistic relationship, Micky Rourke's fingers tease Kim Basinger's mouth with bits of juicy strawberry. Viewers are not meant to taste the fruit, but, instead, to imagine her rounded, red lips around, say, the head of a penis.

A woman rarely exhibits a true sexual appetite of her own. Even when a woman is shown "on top" during intercourse, she is put there to display her body, not her pleasure. A woman who is downright aggressive in sex is invariably a bad woman, one who also robs, or, like the character played by Linda Fiorentino in *The Last Seduction,* even kills.

Bad or good, a woman cannot escape her sexuality, which ultimately defines her fate. Typically, a woman ends up "losing" in one or more of three ways.

1. She loses her autonomy. In *Pretty Woman,* Julia Roberts as the prostitute with a heart of gold is saved from being the property of all men by becoming the property of Richard Gere alone.

2. She is raped. In Spike Lee's 1986 film, *She's Gotta Have It,* a sexually independent woman ends up being raped by the "nicest" of her three boyfriends as he forces her to choose among them.

3. She loses her life. In *Fatal Attraction,* Glenn Close's mistress-out-of-control is killed by the good wife who comes to the rescue of her victimized husband.

Lesbians in Pop-porn Limbo

Because women are supposed to be under the control of men, sexually autonomous women are usually portrayed as villains.

The only other reason a woman in the movies might be without a man is that she is a lesbian. Sometimes she is both lesbian *and* a villain, or, as in *Basic Instinct,* bisexual and bad.

Lesbian characters and performers now appear more frequently in mainstream media, yet their sexuality is filtered through a heterosexual lens. In an episode of the highly popular television series "Friends," when the ex-wife of a main character marries her lesbian partner, the show focuses on the heterosexuals' attitudes at the wedding. Two straight men express their frustration at being in a room full of women who are unattracted to them, one of them complaining that "I feel like Superman without my powers, you know. I have the cape and yet I cannot fly."

The "Friends" episode shows the lesbian couple hugging, but most pop porn completely averts its eyes from lesbian intimacy, not to mention sex. In the film *Fried Green Tomatoes,* the sexual relationship of the lesbian couple was limited to one kiss on the cheek. The film version of Alice Walker's novel *The Color Purple* portrays the awakening of Celie's lesbian desires, but it is so downplayed that it passes right by many viewers. Even when lesbian characters and couples are "out," as in *Boys on the Side* and the made-for-television movie "The Women of Brewster Place," they rarely so much as kiss, much less have sex. On TV, two women kissing on one episode of "Roseanne" created an uproar. Ellen de Generes has so far avoided the topic of sex, but by drawing out her coming out, she pokes fun at the lesbophobia of the sexual culture.

In contrast to being marginalized in pop porn, the so-called lesbian sex scene is a staple of pornography, where it is shown for the pleasure of heterosexual men. For those viewers, two naked women together just doubles the fun. It is not really sex between two women, however, because the women are there not for one another's pleasure, and certainly not for the lesbian and bisexual females in the audience, but for the heterosexual male viewer.

There have been important efforts to change the way lesbians are portrayed in film. A new genre of independent lesbian films such as *Desert Hearts,* and, more recently, *Go Fish, Bar Girls,* and *The Incredibly True Story of Two Girls in Love* are about women's lives, including their sexuality. When these films include sex, it is not meant as an object for straight men's titillation, but is for and about lesbians. The Oscar-winning film *Antonia's Line,* written and directed by a woman, portrays lesbians as part of a family and as human beings who also have sex. One segment of *Antonia's Line* cuts between several couples, including Antonia's daughter and her female lover, having sex in various rooms of their extended household.

In its typical renditions for heterosexual male viewers, lesbian sex seems to be more acceptable than sex between gay men. Nonetheless, lesbian sex disturbs the sexual culture because it is oblivious to men. In the universe of pop porn, women having sex that is neither *with* men nor *for* them does not draw an audience. After all, the true star of pop porn, the penis, is not even a member of the cast.

The Penis As Star

The greatest star of Hollywood never actually appears on camera. In even the most torrid sex scene, the man's penis remains hidden from view, especially when erect. Some American-made films excise even brief glimpses of a penis from all but its European and video versions. Mainstream films never subject male stars to the pressures that male porn stars face to produce "wood" on demand. They protect the actor's penis from scrutiny, not only for his sake, but for the sake of the heterosexual male viewer, who does not want to see another man's penis, especially one that is larger and longer than his own. The typical straight, male viewer fears being aroused by seeing another man's naked body. Hollywood does not think twice about imposing this experience on women because they so rarely have the female half of the audience in mind much anyway. To ask a man to expose his genitals for public scrutiny is to make him into a sex object, and part of the privilege of being a straight man is never having to be anybody's sex toy.

The View from Down There

Although camera-shy, the penis upstages everything else on the screen. During sex, its power is reflected in the facial expressions of the man's sexual partner. Although coupled, the woman's vagina, like the woman herself, is the penis's echo or shadow. Even more elusive is the clitoris. Although often likened to a penis, a viewer from Mars would never know the clitoris existed if she/he/it tried to learn about sex on Earth from movies. Since the clitoris does nothing to stimulate a man's penis, it remains invisible. And, in contrast to the camera-shy penis, the clitoris's absence does not anoint it with power, but rather reduces its importance to zero.

Clitoral invisibility is ensured by movie sex that consists mostly of intercourse in the missionary position. If we see anything different at all, it is the oral sex a woman gives to a man. Fellatio accompanied the arrival of VCRs in middle-class living rooms in the 1970s with the film *Deep Throat*. Star Linda Lovelace portrayed a woman who enthusiastically gave countless men "head" because her clitoris was in her throat. Her anatomical reengineering might seem to give attention to a woman's pleasure center, but the movie is about men's pleasure. Only in men's fantasies—and in pornographic movies like this one—does a woman get orgasms from fellatio. Although many women enjoy it, real-life deep-throat fellatio is rarely orgasmic, and it can be uncomfortable or even painful. Yet seeing this porn image on screen is believed to have pressured many women to perform this "trick" at home.

The fellatio that viewers see in pornography occurs offscreen in pop porn, and it is something the "bad" woman gives, not the wife or the steady girlfriend. It is the weapon of the conniving woman who gives fellatio to gain power over a weak man or to get men to do things for her. In *To Die For,* Nicole Kidman is a TV reporter who performs fellatio on a high school tough (Joaquin Phoenix) while she talks him into killing her husband. If a married man gets fellatio from a woman, he can rationalize that he has not committed adultery. Receiving fellatio can exalt a man's reputation, but it usually sullies the woman's. The woman who "gives head" is seen as degraded or evil. The man who gives cunnilingus, in contrast, is a great lover. The only good lover in *Waiting to Exhale* is the one who disappears below Whitney Houston's smile and off the lower border of the screen.

Films never actually show cunnilingus, but when they suggest it, women viewers sigh a quiet but collective "ooh." Giving cunnilingus is treated as a big sacrifice for a man, and viewers are expected to be impressed by his fortitude and selflessness. In *Annie Hall,* the audience laughs in sympathy with Woody Allen when he complains that cunnilingus makes his jaw sore. The joke also plays on the common wisdom that women take "forever" to come. In an episode of the television series "Seinfeld," Julia Louis-Dreyfuss finally convinces her new boyfriend, a jazz musician, to give her oral sex. His valiant efforts at cunnilingus ruin a subsequent audition when he is unable to hit a single note on the sax with his fatigued lips and tongue. Women are never shown joking about their sore jaws on TV or in movies because any woman who admits to "giving head" is morally unworthy of appearing on prime-time or the big screen.

Stranger than Fiction

Movies tend to favor quickie intercourse and not just in the interests of saving time. The choice reflects the way most heterosexual sex actually occurs. In both fiction and reality, sex goes according to a man's timing and pattern of arousal. Sex begins with a man's desire, quickly proceeds to intercourse, and ends with his orgasm and ejaculation. There may be some foreplay, but not to the point of the woman's orgasm. Intercourse can be so brief and perfunctory that, despite the woman's ecstatic poses and moans, it is inconceivable that she might actually have come. In fact, whether or not she has had an orgasm is unclear or irrelevant. Not only is the woman's pleasure overlooked, but birth control and safer sex are bypassed in most hurried cinematic encounters. Both in bed and on the screen, latex, lubrication, and other paraphenalia of safer sex are too often forgotten because they interfere with the pace of the man's arousal. They also contradict our sexual culture's fantasy that the hottest sex is spontaneous.

Movies and other media cannot take all the blame for sex that is either bad or unsafe. Besides, many women and men manage to have substantially more fun in sex than is typically depicted in pop porn. Sex often takes more than three minutes. Both the woman and man laugh. They listen to music. They engage in verbal play. They talk about contraception and condoms and about what they enjoy. They use their whole bodies—hands, tongues, as well as genitals—and invest their whole selves into sex. The man may concentrate a tongue or finger on the woman's clitoris and stroke her G spot until she comes. They may do it again and again. They take breaks for a sip of wine or water or tea and for trips to the toilet. They pause to put on a condom or spread more lubrication. They wrestle with clothes and sheets. They move from one position to another in ungainly and inelegant ways.

Some people eat in bed or involve food in their sexual play. They sweat. They make noise. And they come.

Perhaps it is unrealistic to expect screen sex to be so messy or so human. After all, a movie is an idealized visual rendition of life. There is no reason the typical sex scene in a dramatic film should carry any more influence or weight than a scene of a family meal. What people eat and how they behave at the table inform the audience about the characters' social status and their relationships to one another. The audience does not view the scene as a model for meal etiquette. Yet sex scenes can have this effect because, although people eat in public, they do not perform sex openly or even speak of it in realistic or detailed ways. In this vacuum, the influence of media portrayals of sex expands to ridiculous proportions. This is unfortunate because what is considered "normal" is actually a flat and one-sided view. Most of the sex in films is comparable to watching a meal where only men eat while the women cook the food, set the table, serve the meal, and clean up the dishes. Unfortunately, in cooking as in sex, on the screen and off, many women still do the bulk of the preparatory work but often end up with only the leftovers.

Waiting for the Man

It is little wonder that, given the orgasm imbalance in movie sex, women cling to romantic scenes that build up to and follow sex. Women seem to prefer tantalizing verbal foreplay rather than the often disappointing realities of genital sex. Accordingly, "women's movies" contain more allusions *to* than actual depictions *of* sex. This gap between desire and consummation, filled with sensual delights and erotic tension, often constitutes the whole focus of a woman's film. The woman is like a match searching for the surface friction that will make her burst into flames. Her sexuality ignites only upon the master stroke of a man who, as a roamer, a philandering lover, or an errant husband, happens or chooses to pass by.

Typically, a woman yearning for love waits years for pleasure to come, and when it finally arrives, it is fleeting. In *The Bridges of Madison County,* the meaningful and sensual relationship Francesca longs for lasts only four days and is romantic but not particularly orgasmic. In *Like Water for Chocolate,* sex and the sensuality of cooking are combined into such a potent brew that, after years of longing, when Tita finally has sex with her lover, they perish in the heat of their passion. Her lover dies with his orgasm. She burns up along with him, going with him in death if not coming with him in sex. In *Don Juan de Marco,* Johnny Depp portrays a young charmer who respects and revels in the sensuality of women, an attitude that consigns him to a mental institution. Women applaud when his "madness" ultimately wins out, and even his psychiatrist joins him in what is certainly worlds away from our own sexual culture.

Waiting to Exhale is a novelty in popular movies because it exposes a lot of women's frustrations with men, including sexual frustrations. The film features four women who yearn for male partners, but mostly find disappointment. They have sex with men, most of it bad. Eventually, each woman in her own way figures out that the answers do not lie with men at all, but in themselves and in their friendships with each other. This resolution works as far as it goes, but it does not resolve the problem of women who would like to have good sex with a man *and* retain their self-respect.

Even in the late 1990s, movies still feature female characters whose lives hang on a wire suspended by one or more men. If a woman has no male figure in her life, the film focuses on her search for that connection. Few recent domestic films have a female protagonist unless it is about women tangled up in a sexual web of men's creation. While this might be expected of a film that, like *Sense and Sensibility,* is set in the nineteenth century, it is also the case in contemporary dramas and comedies. Films that star women such as *Clueless, Waiting to Exhale, Up Close and Personal,* and *To Die For* all focus on women's relation to men or show how those ties influence a woman's life.

Movies men like to see are not about relationships with women. They are about male camaraderie and masculine autonomy from women. Highly successful movies such as *Forrest Gump, Pulp Fiction, Apollo 13,* and *Braveheart* all have male leads whose violent, heroic, or idiosyncratic actions are thoroughly independent of their female caregivers and lovers. The glass-shattering whirlwind of virility on the screen may intimidate some gentler souls, but most straight men at least share with the screen hero a desire to bond with other males and to gain a comprehensive kind of power, including power over women.

Movies confirm for male viewers that they have the right to consume women, both through the products of pop porn and in real life. This right is inherent to masculinity itself. There is no need to possess the face of a Denzel Washington, the biceps of a Keanu Reeves, or Bruce Willis's knack for wearing a pair of jeans. After all, in the movies, even Woody Allen gets the girl.

The Woman's Film

Women appreciate the few movies that depict female pleasure on its own terms, especially *Bull Durham, Thelma and Louise,* and *The Piano.* These films have reached nearly cult status among some female viewers, because they portray sexual women and sexy men. In *Thelma and Louise,* there is an extremely brief shot of Brad Pitt's muscular torso during sex with Thelma (Geena Davis), and we share her giddy joy when Thelma tells Louise that, after years of marriage, she has experienced her first orgasm with this young stranger.

Many women also loved *The Piano.* Although it dealt with a woman who was sold into marriage, maimed by her husband, and forced to gamble with another man for sex, it also showed the woman's remarkable resiliency and the eventual triumph of both her musical passion and her sexual desire. In one scene, the camera actually pans up the body of the man with whom she eventually shares both passions. The man's body is that of an average-sized, middle-aged man. Harvey Keitel's common good looks and character wrinkles stand in stark contrast to the young, thin, uncreased ideal woman we have come to expect as the standard object of desire in movie sex. We never see an average-looking, average-sized middle-aged woman portrayed as an object (much less the consumer) of erotic delight. In fact, except as mothers, we rarely see women in a major role of any kind.

The Disappearing Woman

In roles large and small, the only women we see are the ones that can meet a male-defined standard of physical desirability. The sex-love interest of the male star of any age is always young. Accordingly, there are few romantic roles available to female actors over forty. Molly Haskell notes in *From Reverence to Rape: The Treatment of Women in the Movies* that movies of the 1960s treated a woman of forty as an older woman. When Anne Bancroft played the evil mother-in-law-to-be who seduced Dustin Hoffman in *The Graduate,* she was an "older woman" of thirty-six. Today women can be sexy for a few years longer. But after forty—or whenever a woman can pass for forty—she is either asexual or a repulsive sexual predator. She is certainly not sexy. In contrast, a male actor at forty has several more decades of screen quickies ahead of him.

The few middle-aged female actors whom we still consider sexy simply do not look their age, or their age is obscured by good camera work and soft lighting. As these actors approach forty, they begin a battle against the signs of aging. While some performers speak out and challenge the stereotype as they start to feel its impact on their careers, a greater number rush to the plastic surgeon. Those who are sixty-plus take refuge on a theater stage where the audience sits at a distance. There, a mature woman like Julie Andrews or Carol Channing can still practice her craft without undergoing the scrutiny of the close-up camera shot.

A sex symbol, especially, has a screen life span that is brutally short. An actor in her forties like Kathleen Turner is sexy and sexual, yet on the screen, she has gone in just thirteen years from a sultry villain in *Body Heat* to a crafty detective in *V. I. Warshawski* to a demented *Serial Mom*. Yet audiences do not give a second thought to leading men over fifty playing romantic roles opposite twentysomething ingenues. Sean Connery was voted the sexiest man in the movies when he was already over sixty. In his late fifties, Robert Redford romanced women twenty years his junior in *Indecent Proposal* and *Up Close and Personal*. Clint Eastwood and Paul Newman still star opposite women who could be their granddaughters. Their deep wrinkles and gray hair make them look "distinguished," while a woman of similar age and appearance is rarely contemplated by the camera at all, much less considered a sexual being.

Females past their fourth decade are either sturdy mothers or pitiful spinsters whose sexuality is either out of bounds or nonexistent. A mature woman's romantic roles are limited to playing a charmingly eccentric Maude opposite her young lover, Harold, (with whom she is never shown having sex), or Faye Dunaway's cuddly wife to an older, heftier, and surgically unimproved Marlon Brando in *Don Juan de Marco*. Film critic Roger Ebert remarked how rarely one sees even a woman as large as Willeke van Ammelrooy, the lead in *Antonia's Line,* who is robust but average-sized. In Hollywood films, women must be not only young but slim and attractive to play roles involving sex.

A teddy-bear kind of sensuality is sometimes allowed older women as long as it occurs offscreen and involves women who are settled into a comfortable marriage. Often, they are the protagonist's parents, and they are usually "ethnic," especially Jewish, Greek, or Italian, or working class, like Holly Hunter's jovial parents in *Home for the Holidays,* who still dance, laugh, and even indulge in such old-country traditions as sex. These older women exchange winks and squeezes with their husbands, suggesting that some old gray mares still enjoy an occasional roll in the hay. It is a roll audiences are unlikely to ever witness.

Spectator Sex

Like Nikki, many women find that an evening of movie sex can quash a sensual mood. The plot of the film soon fades from memory, but visions of perfect female "10s" may continue to dance in a woman's head for months or even years afterward. Meanwhile, images *for* women or *of* a woman's own pleasure are missing. Over the years, the cumulative impact of movie sex on a woman is a state of alienation, both from the sexual culture and from her own body. As she lists in her head the many ways her body fails to measure up to the pop-porn ideal, she becomes a spectator rather than a partner in bed. Instead of participating wholeheartedly, she steps out of her body and sits on the sidelines of sex to watch.

Movies that make a woman want to crawl out of her skin rather than into bed are those that link sex with violence. Violence is rarely gender neutral. In action films such as *Rambo,*

True Lies, and *Total Recall,* the perpetrator is almost always male, as are the bodies that pile up in the aftermath of explosions, machine-gun fire, and vehicle collisions. But when women are among the beaten, maimed, and dead, the violence is typically sexualized. The extremes of sexual violence are reached in slasher and horror films. In *My Bloody Valentine,* the male murderer plunges a pickax into women's heaving breasts and in *Reanimator,* a woman is orally raped by a disembodied male head. These films make the sex in many pornographic films seem sweet by comparison.

Mainstream films include scenes of flesh-ripping assaults on and psychological torture of women, such as in *Silence of the Lambs, Leaving Las Vegas,* and *Rob Roy.* The erotic feelings that a woman might have at the beginning of an evening at the movies can easily drown in a sea of pop-porn images of blood and body parts. Their impact is increased by the knowledge that, although vampires may be creatures of the imagination, sexualized violence aimed at women is not.

To a woman who objects to sexualized violence, her companions may say, "It's only a movie. Just relax and enjoy it!" A movie is meant to be entertaining. But why does it entertain in precisely this way? Why are women the exclusive objects of this violence? Pop porn reflects the sexual values of the culture that creates it.

Single Exposure

Pop-porn images of women invade every woman's life because, whether she likes it or not, these images establish a standard by which each woman's body is judged and categorized. On the street, complete strangers feel entitled to tell a woman that she is skinny or fat, or to call her "honey" or "whore." Women and men alike silently rate every women on a scale from ugly to beautiful. Acquaintances, friends, relatives, husbands, or lovers feel free to remark on a woman's clothes, hair, makeup, or body shape. Some women's boyfriends and husbands leer at and discuss the sex appeal of other women in their presence. Women are at a loss about how to counter such comments and comparisons.

An atmosphere of belittling commentary can lead a woman to labor under the weight of a negative body image. Even when a woman receives compliments on her appearance, these daily evaluations are like individual bars of a cage that snap into place, eventually encircling the woman completely. No matter how much a woman accomplishes in her profession or her life, she can ultimately be put back inside that cage by a sexual culture that judges women by their sexualized bodies.

All of her life and every day, a woman's body is subjected to a kind of surveillance and evaluation that few men ever experience. Deborah Tannen points out that everything about a woman's body—her clothes, her shape, her shoes, her hair, and whether or not she uses makeup or perfume—says something about her. Every day, a woman makes a statement with her looks—indeed, with every part of her body—whether she likes it or not. Even though "Some days you just want to get dressed and go about your business," Tannen writes, a woman is never that free. Women are the "marked" category, Tannen suggests, the ones whose bodies are decorated and accented, while men are "unmarked." A man may choose to make a fashion statement if he wants (by sporting a beard or a hat, for example), but as long as he conforms minimally to standards of dress and grooming, his looks do not define him.

As teenagers, girls often wear the same type of clothes as their male peers, but the look is not unisex—it is male. Girls' clothes are never taken up by boys as the look of youth culture. When girls dress up and, eventually, when they grow up, they wear clothes that are marked as feminine. Women's clothes typically expose a lot of skin and accent the shape of the body. Even professional women go to work in skirted suits that expose their calves. Hillary Rodham Clinton's legs are exposed at every public appearance, but Bill Clinton's legs emerge in public only when he jogs in summer. Although the former President's legs were the brunt of jokes, as a man he revealed them exclusively in sporting contexts, not at a podium or while descending from Air Force One. A portrait of the Supreme Court shows seven men and two women. When they pose for a photo with their fellow robed colleagues, only Justices O'Connor and Ginsburg expose their legs from the knee down, while the men show only their heads and hands.

Men's bodies go on public display in one very important arena, the big business of professional sports. Heterosexual women can readily enjoy views of the basketball player's sweaty shoulders, the football player's tight pants, a wrestler's compact strength or the tailored suit and neat haircut of the coach at the sidelines. But professional sports for men have very little to do with women, who are a minority of the audience compared to the mass of male fans. In television coverage of men's sports, viewers rarely see close-ups of the tight end's rear end or of the male swimmer's Speedo. Instead, camera shots fill pauses in the competitive action with a cheerleader's bouncy skirt and breasts or the athlete's girlfriend in the stands.

Even women far removed from the age or circumstances in which they would be considered sex objects show the influences of the pop porn standard on their bodies and on the way they dress. No matter what her position, a woman engages in a constant back and forth between her mirror image and the pop-porn image on the magazine page or movie screen. This comparison is intensified in the darkened movie theater, where actors' bodies are blown up to the size of giants. This magnification makes the male romantic lead grow larger. It does not matter if he has a double chin, wrinkles, or a bald head, for he is judged by his charisma and character, not his looks. The female object of his desire, however, exposes herself to the detailed scrutiny of a magnifying mirror. She must display impeccable muscle tone in a backless dress, perfectly shaped thighs in a bikini, and a flawless and hairless complexion in a romantic close-up. The rules are the same for TV. As the "Baywatch" camera sweeps across breasts and chests alike, both women and men judge the erotically charged female body more harshly.

Whether on- or offscreen, a woman's entire body demands vigilance in grooming habits, diet, exercise, and fashion. Like a plastic Barbie, a woman must remain perpetually on her high-heeled toes. The sexual culture teaches even a young girl to be ever dissatisfied with the way she looks. As she grows, a girl may fail to explore her body's intrinsic pleasures because she is focused on meeting an outside standard. Rather than focusing on her body's potential for pleasure, a woman often sees only the ways she falls short of or deviates from the beauty norm.

Pop porn's beauty standard was made explicit in the 1980 movie 10, in which lovely, young Bo Derek earns that title from a pursuing admirer played by comedian Dudley Moore (he is not assigned a number). What constitutes a rating of "10" varies somewhat over the decades but this ideal always affects how women feel about themselves and about sex. Sometimes a woman may feel that sexual pleasure will have to wait until she has reached her beauty goals. But if good sex depends upon being a cinematic "10," then it will remain permanently out of reach to most women. Only a few women ever get included in this winning category, and, even when they do, they find that, no matter how hard they peddle, they eventually lose the beauty race to age.

For His Eyes Only

Large sectors of the economy revolve around the never-ending process of women pleasing men. Women not only spend a large amount of their time, they also spend a lot of their money on beauty. Cosmetics alone is a six-billion-dollar industry, and women's fashion, elective plastic surgery, diet and exercise products and programs, and hairdressing make fixing the body women's biggest living expense after housing. Men, in turn, spend billions on pornography. These two mammoth industries are grotesquely linked in our sexual culture's drive to satisfy men's socially induced sexual hunger.

In terms of volume, pop porn is what provides men with a daily diet of erotic stimulus. Both women's and men's magazines are sources of pop porn, but each sends a strikingly different messages to readers. Men's magazines exude confidence and a sense of economic and sexual entitlement. Women's magazines play on insecurity and encourage a culture of perpetual self-improvement. From the time a girl is identified as such at birth, rigorous but often subtle training begins in the art of attracting others. As she strives to fit that externally defined ideal, a woman often turns to magazines for beauty tips. Alongside articles on how to "Flatten Your Stomach in Two Weeks," magazines also offer sexual advice. Topics include not just "How to Give a Man What He Wants in Bed" but even "Eight Secrets to Orgasm for Women." Despite a veneer of post-feminist enlightenment, the articles never question how women's dissatisfaction with their bodies might be related to the products their publication sells. Nor do they explore how the norms of a sexual culture that views women as sexual consumer products for men might be related to the reasons why orgasm still eludes so many women.

It is often proclaimed that heterosexual men are easily aroused by the sight of a sexy woman because they are naturally more visually oriented than women, whereas seeing a sexy man presumably does nothing for most women. Women are not visually *or* libidinally impaired by nature, however. They simply are not socialized to find images of the opposite sex a turn-on in the way men are. Boys grow up masturbating to pop-porn images. Most girls put sexual feelings together with an object of desire only in the context of a relationship with a specific person. This sexual socialization leads few women to pay to see naked strangers. Strip joints and viewing booths for straight women have no audience. Some women consume moderate amounts of beefcake chosen from a small menu made up of fan magazines, *Playgirl,* the local gym, and male dancers. But when they go out to see the Chippendales, it is as a novelty on a celebratory girls' night out, not the way of life that it is for some men. The traffic in bodies goes one way only. It is a traffic in women.

If women are less visually inclined than men it is because their eye has not been trained. Women can now and then find images in pop porn that inadvertently appeal to their sensual tastes. For example, straight women have been known to rewind videos to a passing shot of Brad Pitt's torso in *Legends of the Fall,* and some lesbians enjoy watching the sexual liaisons between women (such as that between Susan Sarandon and Catherine Deneuve in *The Hunger*) that were created with a male viewer in mind. But the soft porn available at the local video store is aimed at heterosexual men, not women, because marketers know that even in mixed company, men are the ones who decide what to see. Some videos do have attractive men as well as women in female-friendly sexual interaction. That some women manage to make sexual sense out of pop porn's images attests to the resiliency and creativity of women's erotic potential. There is no telling how they would respond to media that portrayed women of every age and body type as sexual beings, not objects, and actually demonstrated an understanding of what women themselves find beautiful, provocative, or sexy.

The Sexual Woman in a Pop-Porn World

What people choose for sexual arousal is thought to split along gender lines. Stereotypically, women choose written erotica over the pop porn and pornographic pictures that men favor. This difference says less about the inborn sexual appetites of women or men than it does about a sexual culture that only recently has begun to cultivate women's erotic appetites.

Many heterosexual women get a rush from looking at an appealing man or even at isolated male body parts. What they go for varies—hands, a hairline, a chiseled face, veins in his forearm, a flat abdomen, a ballet-dancer's muscular behind. Although nice biceps are a nearly universal draw, heterosexual women tend to be idiosyncratic in their tastes. With fewer images of men as objects of arousal, women have been less conditioned than men to respond to a single model of male attractiveness. Also, women tend to perfer a nice person to go with the nice biceps.

How might the visual media more adequately portray women and their sexuality? The work of actors such as Susan Sarandon and Helen Mirren provide one model of mature sexuality. These actors look and act sexual and they tend to play women (in *Dead Man Walking* and *Prime Suspect,* for example) for whom sex is either on their own terms or irrelevant to what they do and who they are. Their predecessors, women like the late Greek actress Melina Mercouri *(Never on Sunday)* and, of course, Mae West, played roles more closely linked to sexuality. But they radiated a unique sexual confidence made possible because they coated everything with spunk and humor. On television, "Designing Women" and "The Golden Girls" feature real women who have real-life appetites and even grow old.

Madonna may be the most sexual of high-profile performers today. She uses her sexuality to sell, but she also uses it to subvert. She mocks the objectification of women by taking it to the extreme, using fashion (spiked breasts), images (with the photos in her book *Sex,* in which she dressed, undressed, posed, and pouted with a variety of partners in a variety of positions), and music (both rhythm and lyrics). Performers as different as Queen Latifah, Alanis Morissette, Tori Amos, and Courtney Love all explore new artistic routes for women and either ignore, indulge in, or thumb their noses at the sexual culture. Some female artists seem to do so consciously, but every woman makes a sexual statement of some sort whether she intends to or not. In contrast, male performers are "unmarked" and can be oblivious to the sexuality they project if they so choose. Although the macho lyrics of hardcore rock and rap still drown out the bedroom-smart lyrics of Bikini Kill and Salt-N-Pepa, the balance of the sexual culture is beginning to change, and women's words are being heard by the pop-culture audience.

Artists and performers who put forward feminist perspectives are drawing out the unexamined body of pop porn from its dark projection booth and applying to it the same scrutiny women's bodies have long endured. Comedy is one of the most important tools in this effort. Humor uncovers taken-for-granted absurdities while it offers fresh (both new *and* irreverent) alternatives. The feminist comedians' stage is one of the few places where the word *clitoris* is uttered in public. Female comedians are still in the minority. However, the classic comedy series "Saturday Night Live," has changed from mostly male in number and spirit to a more evenly gendered cast and, under writer Tina Fey, more feminist content. Other women in comedy such as Margaret Cho, Roseanne, and Ellen DeGeneres make their presence felt. Female audiences and critics have influenced some of the more traditional male comedians to ditch the sexist humor that has for too long been a quick and dirty source of laughs.

Of all popular culture, the television daytime talk show genre is perhaps the most thoroughly female setting. Whether these shows do women more harm than good is still up for debate.

What is undeniable is that long-running shows such as "Oprah" have given women and their concerns a public forum. These programs and their many imitators deal with women's concerns about everything from health and beauty to domestic violence and sex. The focus tends to be problems rather than pleasures, and on individual rather than social solutions. But at least women are talking about private issues that are rarely addressed in public.

Radio and television call-in programs and newspaper advice columns also provide a forum for people to discuss with experts and share with strangers the sexual concerns that they may not disclose even to their best friends. Some of these, such as "Real Personal," a call-in program about sex that ran on cable TV from 1992 to 1995, went beyond a discussion of problems to explore ways to actually enhance sex for women and men. The syndicated radio show "Love Line" is a youth forum whose focus is primarily sex. Yet for every useful and frank public discussion about sex and intimate relationships, there is a wall of sound coming from the Howard Stern wanna-bes who serve up hackneyed hunk-and-babe innuendos that boost ratings but do little either to change stereotypes or to enhance sexual awareness. Critics of pop porn may sometimes feel that the only solution is to retreat from mainstream culture. A more productive response is to confront pop porn with a critical eye and counter it with art and entertainment made by women that better reflect women's experience of sex.

Women's Erotica

The only erotica for women that even comes close to men's vast universe of pop porn and pornography is the low-profile but highly popular world of romance fiction. Millions of women enjoy romance novels. Despite being a multimillion-dollar busi-

ness, these novels are not included on major best-seller lists because, like pornography, romance fiction is considered lowbrow
literary fare. These inexpensive paperbacks are available nationwide at pharmacies and supermarkets. The bright red, pink,
or lavender covers with their titles in raised gilded script entice
readers with drawings of voluptuous women embracing brawny,
shirtless young men.

Romance novels create their erotic tension by exaggerating
the contrast between heroine and hero. Readers revel in descriptions of a hero whose tremendous chest strains against
chain mail armor, his gilded sword dangling on his thigh. They
identify with the robust but highly feminine heroine who always
wears a faint blush on her cheeks, her long hair and full skirt
flowing beyond the confining dimensions of the printed page.
When the two meet, the heroine sometimes simply "submits"
to the hero, who tears at her bodice, lifts her skirt, and, with one
or two thrusts, "takes" her. But romance-novel sex is not always
so quick or simple. Often the heroine receives clittage and cunnilingus. She comes before the man and she comes more than
once. The heroine and her lover often have sex that is creative,
exciting, and fun.

The goal of many a heroine is everlasting love, making sex a
mere stopover on a path toward marriage and children. This type
of heroine lusts after men, but keeps her eye set on one in particular. She convulses and cries out at the orgasm her lover inspires with his lips and hands but endeavors to save her "virginity" for her wedding night.

Despite the stereotype of women being interested *only* in romance, there is variety within the genre, and some of these books
drip sex and sensuality from every page. If the heroine is not actually engaging in passionate sex, she indulges in memories of
past encounters or anticipates the next one. Her thoughts and
utterances swell with double entendres and innuendo, and her
surroundings seem to come to life as inanimate objects sweat,

throb, and tremble around her. Every movement of the body is an invitation to sex. Eyes graze body parts, lips moisten, breasts heave, and muscles harden. The thickly sexual atmosphere is further enhanced by being set in distant times and places such as medieval and early Renaissance Europe, where the heroine lives amidst lusty foods, yards of velvet, crotchless drawers, drawbridges, towers, and rocking galleons.

Far more than any other popular medium for women, the sex in romance novels depicts a hearty female appetite. Yet romance novels are ultimately true to their name, because sex invested with romance usually prevails, and it usually occurs within the context of at least a potential relationship. Although the heroine gets "wet," reaches a crest, and crashes in orgasm, by far the most abundant bodily fluid to be shed in these books is tears.

While romance novels build up and sustain both erotic tension and a romantic mood in the reader, some women prefer sex books of fiction and fantasy that are less baroque. They select Nancy Friday's classic collections of sexual fantasies, *Secret Garden* and *Women on Top,* or they reach for the wide variety of erotic women's fiction now available, such as the annual collections of erotica edited by Susie Bright and Marcy Scheiner's *Herotica* series. Women can explore a variety of views and experiences of sex. Some accounts put off physical sex with suspense and tales of seduction, but lots of stories go straight to genital sex. Most combine the two.

Erotic videos made by and for women are adding to the array of sex entertainment for women. Candida Royale's videos, such as *A Taste of Ambrosia* and *Urban Heat,* offer heterosexual erotica that focus on women's orgasms. Fanne Fatale makes lesbian erotic videos such as *Suburban Dykes* and *Safe Is Desire.* Many films for women are instructional, such as Fatale's *How to Female Ejaculate.* In *Selfloving,* Betty Dodson shows women how to masturbate with a wand vibrator. Annie Sprinkle's *Sluts and Goddesses* combines instruction with humor in a film that spoofs the deification of a "temple prostitute" by Tantric sex advocates and the pop-porn image of woman as slut. The film is both funny and fun, especially when it climaxes with Sprinkle's own four-minute orgasm. After viewing this video, a friend exclaimed, "I want to be a slut-goddess!"

Erotica for women can come in any medium (including the visual ones) and it can be as genitally explicit as pornography. What distinguishes female-friendly erotica from pop porn and pornography is that it shows a woman's pleasure, complete with authentic orgasms. Erotica for heterosexual women does not objectify men or make their orgasms irrelevant; turning the tables on pop porn is not the point. Instead, the goal is to create sexual images in which both partners' pleasure is treated equally without subsuming one person's pleasure under that of another.

Babes On-Line

As women's erotica expands its reach, it can begin to act as a counterforce to pop porn by infiltrating and changing it. At the same time, however, pop porn has exploded into cyberspace. No one knows yet how, or whether, this new context will influence pop porn's content. What is already clear is that, despite the claims made by fans of the Internet, cyberspace is not user-friendly to all. On-line sex, for example, unfolds on the same terms as off-line sex. A woman who enters a sex forum is greeted with the same pickup lines from half a dozen strange men that she might hear in a singles' bar. There are, however, several advantages of computer sex for women. As long as a woman stays in front of her monitor, it is by far the physically safest form of sex. And, unless a woman has a video phone, it also allows her to engage in sex without worrying about her own or her virtual partner's looks, and a relationship can develop based purely on mutual interests. Yet people can easily wear disguises in cyber-space. They tease and play but they can also lie, exaggerate, in-sult, and even threaten. Fortunately, cybersex is easy-in, easy-out. A woman can quickly depart with a push and click of the mouse when things get uncomfortable. Its growing popularity, however, is mostly due to what it provides men. For men, sex on-line is the greatest thing since home videos because it allows ease of ac-cess, privacy, and anonymity. The man who owns a computer and a modem need no longer sneak furtively into the out-of-the-way theater or drive long distances to the strip-mall bookstore for pornographic materials.

Cyberspace offers users access to both pop-porn images and an immense new pornographic territory. Viewers can now be "interactive" with rounded, responsive female images. But whether indulging in sex with an image or venturing into cy-berspace for verbal intercourse, the standards regarding women and sex remain unchanged. A friend recently witnessed a com-puter student use a pop bottle to simulate the rape of an on-screen woman. According to pro-sex high-tech writer Lisa Palac, "A naked babe on a computer screen is just the same old babe, unless we add change. Technology does not magically trans-form—or even replace—erotic traditions. People do." A firm believer, she says, in the maxim to do it yourself if you want something done right, Palac produced the virtual-reality pro-gram called *Cyborgasm.*

Beyond Pop Porn: Multidimensional Sex

As pop porn expands to new contexts and technologies, it is up to consumers to demand that its content not only expand but change. People are not powerless against pop porn's grip on their minds and bodies. Through criticism and consumer choices, they can force the sexual culture to move beyond reruns of the visual and verbal cliché of sex as a woman's exposed body and a man's orgasm. Consumers have the power to challenge advertisers, filmmakers, television producers, and others to portray sex from the perspective of all sorts of human beings, not just that of straight men. They can support alternative media forms as well as artists and entertainers who explore new sexual frontiers. They can challenge those who control the media to retire sexist images and to break the link between sex and violence. By becoming a larger percentage of both the consumers and creators of sexual images, women can make the quality—and sexual equality—of popular culture grow. By supporting women-friendly media and boycotting magazines, programs, and films that perpetuate retrograde images of women and bad sex alike, people who want to bring about change can do so without bringing in the law or stifling creativity.

When women—typical, *sexual* women—raise their own profile, they will begin to counter the dominant pop-porn image of the stereotypical *sexy* woman. Instead of the narrow, two-dimensional view of sex, women and men can portray sex in ways that are multidimensional and a lot more fun. A new sexual culture would make room for vibrant, tangibly sexual women on the screen, including women who are older, disabled, large, or just average-looking. It would also include a view of the bodies of men in situations where they appear no more nor less vulnerable, attractive, dynamic or brave than women. Lesbian and gay sex would ensue on-screen in the same contexts as it does for heterosexuals. In short, the media would represent sex from the perspective of all kinds of people.

Daily acts of media criticism and of discriminating consumption will lead to the demise of pop porn so that a more diverse art and entertainment universe can rise in its place. Faced with the sheer vastness of the current sexual culture, it may seem a more manageable task to work at making sex good for women behind closed doors than to fend off or divert the tidal wave of pop porn in public. But these tasks are linked. When sex is good for more women, women will be able to make art and entertainment that portrays good sex from their perspective. And as women and their friends make inroads into the culture-producing industries, their influence will reverberate throughout the society and even be felt in the private erotic encounters of women and men.

Nobody knows what the fate of pop porn will be once art and entertainment regularly include women's experience, too. What is certain, however, is that women like Nikki deserve something better than the rancid taste of old, stale pop porn. When a woman's view of sex occupies its fair share of cultural space, Nikki and every other woman will enjoy a fresh, new kind of popular media that, instead of being a turnoff, both engages their erotic imagination and makes their PC muscle clench in recognition.

Sexual Self

Nikki lies in bed waiting for Joe. Tonight, they stayed home and made dinner together. Afterward, Joe cleaned the kitchen while Nikki took a bath. Now, as she rests between the soft, cool sheets, she smiles to herself and shivers slightly at the prospect of the pleasure to come.

Nikki smiles at Joe as he heads into the bathroom. But when she hears him turn on the shower, the sound of the pounding water reminds Nikki of a time when the prospect of sex filled her with dread. David, a man she lived with for almost four years when she was in her early twenties, always showered when he wanted sex. He didn't care whether Nikki was in the mood or not. He would expect fellatio and he insisted on coming in her mouth. He never seemed to notice how tentatively she stroked him with her tongue or how reluctantly she took his penis inside her mouth. When she suggested he return the favor, he refused. And David never gave Nikki clittage, because he thought she should come with intercourse alone.

Sometimes David wanted anal intercourse. Nikki tried to talk herself into liking it, but with David, Nikki always found it more painful than pleasurable. Nikki felt used. She felt that sex was out of her control. Yet she never said anything. Eventually, when David became verbally abusive, belittling her work as a third-grade teacher (he was an engineer) and criticizing her looks, Nikki finally left him.

Today, Nikki cannot believe that she put up with David's sexual and verbal abuse as long as she did. She remembers that she was extremely attracted to him initially, but she cannot understand now how she went on like that for years, having sex when she did not really want it, and performing sex acts she did not enjoy. Now Nikki cannot imagine having sex that is so one-sided again. And she knows she will never allow anyone to pressure her again into doing things in sex that go against her desire.

The shower stops, and Joe appears from the bathroom wrapped in a soft, thick towel. As the fragrant steam from his shower wafts over them, Joe and Nikki reach for one another.

Sex Against Desire

Nikki's experience with David was a turning point in her life. The relationship made her aware of the way power in sex is linked to other forms of control. After Nikki and David broke up, she remained uncoupled for almost a year. During that time, she set off to explore her sexuality without a partner. When, eventually, she began seeing Joe, she made sure to open up avenues of communication. Gradually, the two nurtured their relationship into one of mutual pleasure.

Today, Nikki enjoys sex with Joe in a way that she never imagined possible with David. Although David never used physical force, Nikki always felt sex was a service she was obliged to perform. She was expected to *give* pleasure, but could not ask for or expect to *receive* pleasure. She never complained or even brought up the subject of sex because she feared making him unhappy with her. So she acted as if everything was fine. She avoided having sex when she could, but she never turned David down. Only when his insults added to her growing aversion to sex did she determine to leave him. It was not until some time later that she looked back and realized that she had been having sex against desire.

Sex against desire (SAD) is what we call sex that both partners agree to, but only one partner enjoys. SAD is sex that denies—even negates—the desires and the right to pleasure of one of the partners, usually the woman. Because it is built into the way women and men typically have sex, sex against desire goes unrecognized in our sexual culture and is not seen as a pattern or problem. After all, a couple is simply performing sex as it is typically defined in the sexual culture, namely, intercourse to his orgasm. SAD is distinct from rape, (which includes date rape and marital rape) because it is consensual. But sex is SAD when a woman who *wants* pleasure is denied it.

Sex against desire has, as far as we know, never been specifically identified and named although virtually every woman has experienced it at some time in sex with a man. Some women have never known anything but SAD. Sex against desire occurs whenever the timing of sex, its frequency, or the sexual activities involved are on the man's terms. It is SAD, for example, when a wife has sex with her husband every night simply because he wants it. It is SAD when a woman gives her partner sex just to avoid confrontation or to keep him from straying. SAD also occurs when a woman feels obligated to have intercourse every time she has sex with her partner. Sex against desire is sex that is limited to slam-bam-thank-you-ma'am intercourse, with no attention to either a woman's readiness or her orgasm. It is sex like the kind Nikki had with David, giving fellatio without concern for her own preferences or desires. Many women can remember having sex in which they gave the man pleasure without concern for themselves. SAD occurs when the pleasure is one-sided.

Why do women do it? Some women have SAD because the alternative is to have no sex at all or to be without a man. A woman may agree to SAD to protect a man's sexual ego. She fakes orgasm (or simply lets him believe she has come) so he will not feel he has failed sexually. Meanwhile, neither partner addresses the absence of her pleasure. Some women learn to consider it normal that sex is, as one woman we know was told, "all for men," and to be content with whatever bit of pleasure inadvertently comes their way.

SAD is not something that most men consciously impose on women, however. In fact, many men want nothing better than their partner's pleasure. But the sexual culture leads a man to assume that whatever pleases him is good for her, too. Until one or the other partner is willing to stop and question the taken-for-granted in sex, SAD may occur even between two people who are otherwise loving and contented.

Sex against desire is sex and *not* rape in the strict sense of the term, that is, it is not an intentional use of force by an individual to obtain sex. A man does not have to force the woman because she has been taught to please him. Sex against desire is also not rape because the woman expects or hopes to get pleasure, yet she is continually disappointed. But sex is not truly mutual if one partner's pleasure is routinely ignored, excluded, or made secondary. In this sense, then, SAD *is* a kind of rape: *Sex against desire is a rape of women by the sexual culture.* It is a rape of a woman's mind, will, and sense of self when she has been socialized to say yes to sex that she does not enjoy.

Sex against desire requires no obvious coercion or force because the sexual culture recruits women into violating their own desires. Writer Sally Kempton once pointed out that it is hard to fight an enemy "who has outposts in your head." This is the kind of enemy women face in sex against desire. Nikki stayed with David as long as she did because, when disruptive or critical thoughts brewed in her head, she automatically muted them. She did not recognize that his behavior was out of bounds, or that her rights to be respected and to enjoy sexual pleasure were equal to his.

Nikki was not able to assert her sexual desires because she

had not yet developed a sexual self. Having a sexual self means that a woman asserts control of her own sexuality and ensures that she gets the pleasure she wants in sex. A woman with a sexual self has sex only when she wants to, engages only in sexual activities she desires—not because they are required—and makes sure that she gets the stimulation that gives her sensual pleasure or that leads to orgasm.

Few women either have the opportunity or take the time to create a sexual self. It is difficult to develop in a sexual culture that defines sex primarily as intercourse and the man's pleasure. It is difficult for a woman to cultivate her sexuality in a society that denies women autonomy and where sexual violence against women is an everyday occurrence. Although the sexual culture does not explicitly define all women as doormats, it routinely walks all over their sexual rights.

How SAD Puts Women at Risk

SAD encourages women to engage in sex that is degrading, without pleasure, and outright dangerous. Even women who are educated about the risk of HIV transmission may continue to engage in unsafe sex—the most selfless kind of SAD—because they have absorbed the sexual culture's instruction to put the satisfaction of others first. A woman therefore may succumb to even a casual partner's request for unprotected intercourse. *When a person cares more about any partner's sexual satisfaction than about her own life,* something is obviously and profoundly wrong with the sexual culture.

Even with a caring partner, a woman sometimes engages in sex carelessly and ignores contraception and safety. That a woman will neglect to protect herself reveals a profound self-lessness. Writer and feminist filmmaker Maggie Hadleigh-West offers at least twelve excuses she has used to justify to herself why, even though she knows better, she has agreed to sex without a condom:

> Sometimes I allow my unprotected vagina to be a nostalgic prize for a Good Man. Kind of like having my virginity back. Or distracting a man from my imperfect body. Other times, I'm embarrassed for the man's inability to stay hard, so I potentially sacrifice myself. Sometimes it's pure desire for pleasure. And the thrill of the risk. Or being incapable of asserting myself under pressure from a man for fear of being rejected. Or being forced to do something I don't want to do. And sometimes, I'm ashamed of how my body fluids are depleted by latex condoms. Or I hope some man will be there for me because my father wasn't. Or I mistake yearning for love. At times I think there will never be another man in my bed. A cacophony of reasons overpowers my fear of AIDS.

The doubts, excuses, and reasonable-sounding explanations play in a continuous loop like a tape recorder inside a woman's head. A woman justifies her selflessness in a variety of different ways, at different times, at different stages of life, with different men, and even over the course of a single sexual encounter. Even after making a safer sex resolution, a woman finds herself yet again in bed with a husband, boyfriend, or stranger having intercourse without a condom.

Sex against desire also contributes to the high rate of unwanted pregnancy. Teenage girls may have little power to resist SAD intercourse because their partners are older boys or men. Two-thirds of the babies born to girls under twenty are now fathered by adults. A man who is in his twenties or older typically has more social power than a teenage girl, and this inequality can affect how they have sex. She may look up to him, an older, more experienced man, and agree to intercourse to get his approval and attention. Some girls do have the self-confidence to insist on using a condom during intercourse. Other girls may fear incurring a boyfriend's anger or, knowing little about how else sex might be enjoyed, they give in when a man tells them, "But I don't feel anything this way."

It usually takes years of SAD before a woman realizes that she should engage only in sex that includes her desires, her orgasms, and her well-being. A girl may not want intercourse at all but her boyfriend subtly pressures her into it and, in order to "keep" him, she agrees. When a woman lacks a sexual self, she does not even think to ask herself, "Do I like this?" or "Do I want this?" much less, "What do I want?" These questions do not even form in many women's heads because the current sexual culture barely contemplates female desire. Nikki never questioned the way she and David had sex, because she presumed *she* was the problem rather than David, and the male-focused sexual culture that backed him up.

Eroticizing Male Power

Nikki avoided reflecting on what happened in sex because it meant confronting the power imbalance both in their relationship and in the sexual culture. Sex was just one of the ways David held power over Nikki. David was four years older, earned four times as much as Nikki did at the time, and he was taller and larger than she. This is not an unusual situation. Women typically have partners who are (or who would like to be) taller, richer, bigger, stronger, and in every other way greater than they are. Men are always busy pumping it up, while women work at toning it down, aiming for a profile that is petite and slim, with a voice, ego, and sexual demands to match.

Men generally prefer a woman of lesser status (except in appearance), while women seem to see sex appeal only in a man who has higher status in one or more ways. Henry Kissinger once said, "Power is the greatest aphrodisiac"—but this aphrodisiac works in one direction only. Women with power can have trouble just getting a date or keeping a husband, while powerful men are surrounded by female assistants and supporters smitten by their charisma.

Men seek out women of lower status, but women do not date or marry "down." Although a professional man seriously considers an attractive waitress as a potential date, it does not even occur to a professional woman to flirt seriously with a maître d', much less a busboy. Men can shop for a picture bride and hire a prostitute. May-December couples always involve an older man and a younger woman, hardly ever the reverse. Youth and beauty, not power, are the sexual cards a woman has to play, although occasionally a woman's wealth, personality, celebrity, or power can trump gender. It is a safe bet that Roseanne, for example, is not afraid to ask for what she wants in bed. But in and out of bed, women on top are still the exception. In Personal columns in papers, women seek older, "financially secure" men, while men want young, slim, "pretty" women. The woman is expected to trade her looks, youth, and sexuality for the man's status and money, not the other way around.

Women marry "up" in status and men marry "down." Even when couples meet as apparent peers in high school, college, or in the workplace and consider themselves one another's equals, a subtle status inequality based on age, job, or income almost always exists. The first-year college woman dates a man in graduate school, for example, and the female nurse dates the male doctor, not the reverse. Sometimes a man has direct power over the woman, as when the administrative assistant dates the male executive, or the pupil her teacher. The power difference may be more subtle when two partners share the same occupation, yet the man's specialty and his income are likely to be greater than the woman's in nearly every trade and profession: He is the surgeon, she the pediatrician. He is the principal, she the kindergarten teacher. He belongs to a union and has seniority, she is an apprentice.

Men tend to always come out "on top" in their work, in the economy, and in a relationship. When couples divorce in midlife, his standard of living typically goes up while hers goes down. In general, a man's value—based on wealth, power, and accomplishment—rises over his lifetime, while women typically lose the power of beauty as they age. The cliché of the middle-aged man who dumps a female contemporary for a newer model is one that many women, both rich and poor, live. Many older women find themselves, like a used Buick, parked on a vast car lot with other discontinued styles.

The Third Shift

How the status imbalance in marriage and partnerships affects sex becomes more obvious by looking at the full circumstances of women's lives. Most women still do the bulk of the housework. This seems justified because many couples still go into marriage with the unspoken expectation that the man will earn the family wage and, if she works, her job will supplement it. A wife's lower income and lesser work status ensures that she will feel obliged to be responsible for the "second shift"—child care and housework. Having children imposes upon a woman's career in a way it does not for men. It is simply assumed that a woman will be the primary caretaker of her children, work that is often invisible because it is taken for granted as a mother's duty. Meanwhile, a man who takes care of his children is praised as a "wonderful father" because he exceeds our expectations of men.

The woman generally takes responsibility for housework, and considers herself lucky if the man "helps" to cook, clean, shop, and do laundry. She typically does the bulk of the "emotional work" in the marital relationship and in the family, too, and is ready to feed hungry egos when needed. She must even do her husband's emotional "laundry." A woman may get little comfort in return, especially if she is in a relationship with a man who confuses the word intimacy with intercourse.

At the end of a day of doing it all, a woman crawls into bed with her partner, where she faces the "third shift." To a woman who is tired and who may be pissed off that her partner has not done his fair share of work, sex can seem like just one more chore. When she is not in the mood but feels it is her duty to comply, a woman may go through the motions of foreplay and intercourse, and then fake orgasm just to get some sleep. Or she says no to sex, one way women can wield power in a relationship. If sex is SAD, dispensing with it is a relief. Simply withholding sex or putting up with SAD sex is, ultimately, a dead end. A woman ends up cheating herself because she loses out on sexual pleasure and intimate play that could enhance and balance her life. For many women, however, good sex never even finds a place on their list of "things to do."

Princess or Seductress: Female Roles in Sex

A woman is trained from an early age to be the reactive rather than the proactive partner when it comes to sex. As a result of the feminist movement, women have begun to heed the warning about what Collette Dowling called the Cinderella Complex—the "If-I-only-had-a-man" solution to all problems. Women no longer expect a man to support them nor do they put off creating a life—building a home, even creating a family—until the perfect man appears. When it comes to sex, however, many still await Prince Charming, believing that the right prince will awaken them with a kiss from years of muted sex that has lulled them into a deep, sexual slumber.

Many women have taken to heart the fairy tales they learned as children. Women train from toddlerhood to be princesses who keep their eyes closed and lips puckered while they await that magic kiss. When a man she believes to be a prince eventually appears, a woman blindly yields to him and hands over all the responsibility for what happens in sex. She expects the prince to initiate sex and bring her to orgasm. Sex is something that *he makes happen,* while she learns that sex is something that *happens to her.*

The princess soon discovers, however, that true princes are rare (the T-shirt should read, "So many men, so few princes") because the sexual culture neglects to teach men much about women's sexuality. Despite this, women and men alike see the woman's orgasm not only as the man's responsibility, but also as a measure of his sexual prowess. Some men pride themselves on their sexual stamina and skill, measured by how long they can stay erect and keep intercourse going. These efforts are directed at an unappreciative audience, for a man's "performance" is not the source of a woman's pleasure.

Most women are careful not to criticize a man sexually or to be too demanding in sex. Yet, many men say they like a woman who is sexually assertive. The sexual culture encourages women in the role of seductress but only if she asserts her sexuality just enough to allure a man. This role is like that of a spider who lies in wait to trap prey in her sticky silk web. Unlike the spider, however, a woman does not poison her victim until rendered helpless and then suck its blood for her own nourishment. Instead, the woman-spider and her prey, once caught, suddenly switch places. The seductress takes on the role of the helpless and delectable meal, and the man she caught consumes *her.*

Women who seduce men may nevertheless expect them to initiate sex. A woman initiates sex only in indirect ways—dressing sexy, flirting, or even cooking a good meal. When a woman desires a certain man in sex, her first move is to get the man to make the first move. All women learn this reactive mode. One survey found that a common complaint that lesbians had about their sex lives is that their partners did not initiate sex enough. More than two-thirds said they wanted sex more often. Both women just wait for the other to act first.

Women and men fall almost effortlessly into their respective roles of seduced and seducer. Many women build their sexual fantasies around themes of surrender. They literally allow themselves to be "seduced," a word that means to be led away, even to be *mis*led, to be pulled away from their sexual selves and potentially into sex against desire. This dynamic allows one person—man, the seducer—to define how sex unfolds. His leadership in sex parallels the expectation that he will also dominate in other aspects of the relationship. The overall power inequality between partnered women and men is an important part of what fuels and perpetuates sex against desire.

Masculine Glamour

How much our society adores and indulges male power is nowhere more obvious than in the sexual culture's multibillion-dollar love affair with football, basketball, and other competitive team sports. The sexual culture so loves a winner that it throws millions of dollars and near-infinite social entitlement to the heroes who excel at throwing, catching, running, kicking, and slam-dunking a ball. Professional sports is a big business that is still largely male, and it plays an important role in keeping men on top of the economy and society. Former college basketball player Mariah Burton Nelson, in her book *The Stronger Women Get, the More Men Love Football,* details the ways men's competitive sports provide a model for aggressive, violent behavior both on and off the field. The physical and psychological pumping up of both male athletes and fans is often linked with violent social and sexual behavior against women. Nelson reports that at one series of baseball games, men passed around "plastic, life-sized, anatomically correct female blow-up dolls" that they fondled and simulated intercourse with while other men cheered.

The physical and social adrenaline that goes into both playing and watching men's competitive sports is also what is often behind some incidents of gang rape, the sexual assault of a woman by a group of men. Rapes have occurred in the aftermath of a game as players or fans "celebrate" a win or avenge their loss. There have been incidents of men using the date-rape drug Rohypnol to render a woman unconscious before sexually assaulting her. Men have raped women in institutions such as hospitals and prisons. Recently, a woman who lay in a coma for several years became pregnant. She was not dead, but one wonders just how passive men would like a woman to be.

In a sexual culture built around eroticizing male power over women, it is not surprising that the United States has one of the highest rates of rape in the world. Even though the sexual culture often confuses the two, rape is not sex. Sex is about consent and pleasure. Rape is violence, an act of power perpetrated on another person using sex as a weapon.

Precise rates of rape are impossible to discern, since only an estimated ten percent are reported. A *Ms.* survey of more than seven thousand college undergraduates found that one in four women has experienced rape or attempted rape. In a study cited by Catharine MacKinnon, Diana E. H. Russell found that forty-four percent of women interviewed in a random sample in one city said the same. For some, rape or attempted rape had occurred more than once. Russell also found that thirty-eight percent of young girls said they had been sexually molested or abused, usually by men who were friends, relatives, or acquaintances. One woman who was violated by a male family member as a child told us how the experience made her feel simultaneously help-less and responsible. It arrested her developing sexual self and made the prospect of ever enjoying sexual pleasure nearly evap-orate. For many girls unwanted sex affects every aspect of their subsequent development.

Along with rape itself, SAD is also part of what British re-searcher Susan Quilliam has identified as "a vast undercurrent of unwilling sex" in society. Some women, especially if they have experienced violence, feel perpetually under siege. All women, because they are women, are physically, socially, sexually, and psychologically circumscribed by sexual violence. Women live with a constant threat of rape that limits where they go, who they associate with, when they go out, and what they do. This fact shadows them when they have sex and during every other part of their day.

Sexual Self

It is difficult to plan a sex picnic when it is always raining vio-lence. It is hard to think about having fun in sex for those women whose experiences of violence make it impossible to put "fun" and "sex" in the same sentence. But each woman can work to sever the sexual culture's connection between sex and violence. Claiming control of, responsibility for, and a right to sexual pleasure can help to forge a stronger link between sex and plea-sure rather than violence. Making sex fun for women is not a friv-olous goal or a mere hedonistic diversion. It is an important part of the effort to reduce sexual violence and to make relations be-tween women and men more equal overall.

Individual women can fight violence by cultivating a sexual self. Gaining a sexual self takes effort and a willingness to scru-tinize one's sexuality and past and present relationships. Many women look back at their pleasureless "first time," or at the time they gave into a man's request to bypass condom use, or at all the times they "gave head" with little in return, and they regret the risks they took and the time they wasted. Nikki realized that she was having sex against desire with David only years after the fact.

As a woman begins to assert a sexual self, she asks herself why she seemed incapable of resisting a speedy bit of penetration on the deck with that sailor. *For what?* She shakes her head as she remembers spending hours giving oral sex to her high school boyfriend. *What did I get out of it?* In retrospect, she wonders why she was so selfless. Clearly, sex, even when it was SAD, met needs for acceptance and intimacy that she felt at the time (and still has on occasion). But why did those needs overcome her fear of disease, violence, or pregnancy? Why did it lead her to ignore—or never even develop—her own desires? Why did she repeatedly ignore her own right to pleasure? It was only after many disappointing, sometimes dangerous, sexual encounters before it occurred to her that she deserved sex on her own terms no less than any of those men.

Sex Escapes

Some women find that a sex escape can help them begin the process of developing a sexual self. They can benefit from getting away from the sex-negative messages in their heads, from a sexually restrictive environment or situation, and from getting out of whatever role they typically assume. A sex escape can involve changing roles, changing location, or changing partners.

Changing Roles: The Carnival Principle

Some women explore their sexuality by acting out their fantasies using sexual role-playing. Role-playing in sex can resemble the atmosphere of carnival, when people dress up as characters of their fantasy. Their looks and behavior flout the usual conventions, and roles are reversed—the servant is the ruler, the woman the man, the man the woman. Carnival traditionally allowed the powerless to "let off steam" by temporarily taking over the streets and poking fun at those who were really in power.

A carnivalesque escape can help a woman at least temporarily overcome the internalized message that "good girls don't enjoy sex." Playing the sexual culture's role of "bad girl"—whether as "top" or "bottom," domineering or submissive—allows them to break sexual taboos. Sexual role-playing allows a woman who learned that sex was dirty, or who was told that *she* was dirty, to send her mind on a vacation so that her body can play. For some women, transgressing sexual boundaries enhances erotic pleasure.

Changing Location: "Tourist Sex" for Women?

In the English play and 1989 movie *Shirley Valentine,* a working-class housewife has an affair with a local man while on a Greek holiday with a girlfriend. The experience is transforming for Shirley, and it hardly matters when she discovers the man declaring love to the next woman who steps onto the wharf. The brief romance renewed and strengthened Shirley's sexual self.

Most tourist sex is often no better than the sex at home; it can often be worse. But women nevertheless do have sex with people they meet when they travel. Sometimes they find pleasure, sometimes a lasting relationship. Sometimes if they are like Shirley, they gain fresh insight into their life or their sexuality.

Having sex far away from many of the usual restrictions of her own sexual culture often permits a woman to have sex without being in a serious relationship. It may be purely playful sex. The problem is that sex can become exploitative. The visitor from the rich and culturally dominant country, whether female or male, asserts her or his power over the citizen of an impoverished nation. The power differences between an unskilled hotel waiter living in an underdeveloped tropical seaport and a North American or European real estate broker on holiday cannot be dismissed. When the tourist is a woman, however, it is difficult to say who is the more vulnerable, the relatively impoverished male host or the female visitor who is not only on unfamiliar turf, but lacks the privileges of manhood. As long as a woman goes into sex prepared and protected, and as long as she treats others with honesty and respect, she and her partner may gain mutual benefit from their brief encounter.

A WOMAN'S WORLDWIDE GUIDE TO BOYS

Everyone knows what the Beatles and the Beach Boys thought of "girls"—Ukraine girls really knock them out, East Coast girls are hip and stylish, Midwest farmers' daughters make men feel all right, but California Girls, perhaps by virtue of being bikinied and blonde, knock them all out of the surf.

If women were to mark the map by the qualities of its men, would women rate, say, Southern men above Midwesterners? Or Asian men over Scandinavians? Would Adriatic Boys, perhaps, with their curly locks, coffee-colored eyes, and their alleged appreciation for and knowledge of women be voted the best lovers?

Such ratings make little sense for women, who know that looks do not indicate much about a man's romantic or sexual value. If men are rated at all, it is by themselves or other men, and it is based on alleged sexual prowess, an attribute that, as we have seen, has little to do with women's sexual pleasure. Women do appreciate romantic skills even though they are no guarantee of good sex.

Changing Partners: Affairs and Other Marital Escapes

In *The Erotic Silence of the American Wife,* Dalma Heyn suggests that women sometimes engage in adulterous affairs to fill an emptiness in their married lives. Heyn writes "It is *pleasure*— the independent pursuit of their wants and desires in their own lives—that is still denied many wives." Although an affair is not itself a sure way for a woman to get pleasure, it can be a catalyst for change. An affair can give a woman the strength or opportunity to get out of a bad relationship.

Sometimes a woman is not running *away* from a relationship, but *toward* a new kind of partner. A woman who has sexual de-

Women have sometimes rated men on a negative scale. As long ago as 1936, Helen Brown Norden revealed in *Esquire* magazine that "Latins Are Lousy Lovers." The illusion that sex is always better somewhere else is easily dashed: One woman told us about a sexual encounter with a man who romanced her on a moonlit Mediterranean beach, but as soon as he got her underwear off, he was inside her and it was over. Although the French are masters of seduction, the female half of the population finds orgasm to be no less elusive than American women. Northern European women are so frustrated with the men of their region that they travel in droves to southern Europe for romantic attention. Whether the sex is worth the effort is unknown.

Men in most of the world—on every continent and island— perform sex as a bit of foreplay and two minutes of intercourse. There is no place or type of man who provides superior sex. Such men appear only when women teach them what they have learned from first cultivating their own sexual selfhood.

sires for women but has had relationships only with men may gain not only a sexual self but a new sexual identity by exploring sex with a female partner. She can discover that she is lesbian or bisexual, and find sex that is not only pleasurable but expresses her true self.

What many women discover above all else is that gaining a sexual self is not only about who a woman's partner is. It is about who *she* is. What a woman needs in a partner is the support that allows her to express and develop her own sexual self. One woman in her fifties tells us that she never had an orgasm with her first husband, a man older than she. She had married young and when her husband died, she was on her own for the first time in her life. She looked at everything with fresh eyes, including sex. She purchased a vibrator—almost unheard of among her friends at the time—and learned how to have an orgasm. But she found that she could not translate her new knowledge into sex with men her own age or older, who all seemed to be set in their ways. They refused to give clittage and they believed that a woman's orgasm should come from intercourse alone. She finally met and married a younger man who, she says, was willing to be adventurous. The two of them explored oral and manual sex together and mutual orgasms became an integral part of their relationship. "My friends think I'm so lucky because I have a good sex life. But they could have one too if they would just explore for themselves."

A Sexual Self from the Start

Some women are lucky enough to have parents who help them cultivate their sexual selfhood. Writer Julia Hutton in *Good Sex: Real Stories from Real People* recounts the story of a sixty-five-year-old woman whose sense of sexual self was tested as a very young child.

The message from both my father and my mother was that women were as good as men, and it was important to get a good education as women, because we needed to be able to take care of ourselves, be independent and not be under the thumb of a man. My father would take me out on the milk route with him and talk politics. I argued with him, and he liked it. When I was four and a half, my neighbor's teenage son came into our garage, and he wanted to look at my sexual organs. He was really pushing me. I started to remove my pants and then it hit me that I didn't like him and didn't feel right about it. Suddenly I looked up at him and said, "No, I *won't!* And you'd better go away and leave me alone." I think I was able to be so forceful because of my parents' message that as a woman, you're empowered.

Although no woman or child can prevent sexual violence on her own, having a sexual self gives a woman the power to say no to unwanted advances, and to say yes to sex for her own pleasure, and to know the difference.

Making Sex Equal

When a woman and her partner both have a sexual self, sex can be playful, a game of give-and-take between two equally strong individuals. To put it in terms any man can understand: Sex needs to occur on a level playing field. And as sports fans know, the best games involve players who are equally skilled, knowledgeable, and ambitious.

A woman who begins to assert herself sexually may feel at first that she is being selfish. But a person with a sexual self does not impose her or his will on their partner. A person with a sexual self expresses her thoughts and desires and neither accepts nor imposes SAD.

Do-It-Yourself Orgasms

Most women have been trained to be selfless in sex. They never learn how to bring sex under their own control. Shere Hite found that women who regularly had orgasms with a partner had adopted a more "do-it-yourself" approach to sex. They made sure they got the stimulation they wanted whether they did it themselves or asked their partner. When women take responsibility for good sex, according to Hite, they keep and care for their own bodies rather than give them away.

Self-clittage in both solo and partner sex is a practical part of developing a sexual self. It not only allows a woman to learn how to have orgasms, she also learns that her orgasms are *hers,* not a gift a partner may or may not bestow upon her. Her sexuality is neither contingent upon having a partner nor dependent upon what her partner does or does not do. She takes control of her own orgasms by ensuring she gets the stimulation she enjoys.

Asserting a sexual self in partner sex involves changing the ingredients of sex. It means making clittage, not intercourse, the focus of partner sex for women. It means taking cunnilingus, clittage, and G spotting to orgasm, rather than abandoning them to "foreplay." It means a woman uses her PC muscle for her own pleasure as well as for the man's. It means she shifts the focus of sex away from a sole preoccupation with the man's erection, orgasm, and ejaculation and attends first to her own experience.

Proactive Penetration

A woman can make intercourse an act between two sexual selves by engaging in it only when she truly wants it. Intercourse is an optional part of sex, not its defining act. Intercourse should be like dessert: not necessary to have every time, but a great celebration and sensory delight when you do. It becomes dessert when both partners are equally hungry for it.

Making vaginal intercourse a pleasure means making sure a woman's cligeva is erect first. Erection allows a woman to be a proactive partner in sex because she can determine and control the timing, depth, and speed of penetration. (Proactive penetration is also important in anal intercourse.) Rather than being passive, the woman actively grasps or enfolds the man's penis with her vagina. Using clittage, the woman can intensify her erection and excitement. She can use her PC muscle to squeeze and press against his penis. She can angle her cligeva so that his penis stimulates her G spot or fits inside the cul-de-sac.

Partners who have developed their sexual selves have learned to talk about sex, to use safer sex methods, to respect each other's body rights, and to ask for what they want but accept no as an answer. They do not play games or do power trips on their partner. They do not expect the other partner to take care of their own needs, but they take responsibility for their own pleasure and give to the other person. In a new sexual culture, oral and manual sex will be mainstays, sex will be for mutual pleasure, safer sex will be common practice, and girls and women will be able to have sex for pleasure without unwanted pregnancies. Women and men alike will forge a new sexual culture in which the sexual selves of women and men will be developed and celebrated equally.

Making sex equal often means a woman has to help her partner learn. But she first needs to learn about herself. Knowing her own body in a way that is both conducive to pleasure and consistent with having a sexual self is the foremost task of redefining sex for women. By first reflecting on her own body and her own life, a woman can begin to cultivate the "power of the erotic" that the late poet and writer Audre Lorde describes as "the yes within ourselves":

When we live outside ourselves . . . rather than from our internal knowledge and needs, when we live away from those erotic guides from within ourselves, then our lives are limited by external and alien forms, and we conform to the needs of a structure that is not based on human need, let alone an individual's. But when we begin to live from within outward, in touch with the power of the erotic within ourselves, and allowing that power to inform and illuminate our actions upon the world around us, then we begin to be responsible to ourselves in the deepest sense.

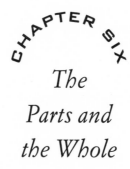

CHAPTER SIX

The Parts and the Whole

Joe has already fallen asleep, but Nikki rouses herself to go to the bathroom. As she sits on the toilet, she notices that her vulva still seems puffy and warm. Curious, Nikki washes her hands, then puts one leg up on the bathtub to take a closer look. Holding a hand mirror in one hand, she spreads her vulval lips with the other. Wow, it's so swollen! She presses a finger against her erect clitoris and moves its tip back and forth. She notices a small rise a little lower down and slides her finger over to stimulate it along with her clitoris—the good feelings at both points of pleasure merge. Spreading her labia wide, she notices that the skin at the vaginal opening is flushed and shiny. Nikki puts the mirror down, and with one hand still stroking her clitoris, she reaches inside with two fingers and applies pressure at her G spot. Nikki feels an orgasm building. But she wavers—Should I enjoy myself here, or wake up Joe . . . ?

The Mystery Spot

Through self-exploration, Nikki is getting to know her genitals and how they respond in sex. She is putting her new knowledge into practice in partner sex, too, and now enjoys the pleasure of orgasm every time she wants it. She has also become sensitive to her own genital arousal even when she is not having sex. Nikki's body awareness has grown since she embarked on a journey of sexual self-discovery. Like most women, Nikki had learned to ignore her genitals. Even during sex, they were the last thing on her mind. If she thought of them at all, her genitals only seemed to get in the way of enjoying sex. The body's prime pathway to pleasure is blocked for women by a sexual culture that tells them that their genitals are dirty and shameful. (The Latin word for women's genitals, *pudenda,* means "shame.") It is not surprising, then, that in contrast to men, who think of their penis as a friend and partner, many women treat their vulva and vagina like unwelcome guests at a party.

Women's shame about their genitals sometimes expresses itself as ignorance and a lack of curiosity. Girls learn not to look, touch, or think about what is "down there." Writer Sandra Cisneros describes how religious and cultural influences so filled her with shame about her "private parts" that it was not until she became an adult that she learned she even had a vagina. As a child she wondered where her menstrual blood would flow from: "I thought my period would arrive via the urethra or perhaps through the walls of my skin."

The lack of knowledge, and shame about their genitals, keeps girls from exploring them and discovering orgasm. For many girls growing up, they never hear about the clitoris, the G spot, and other pleasure-giving parts of their genitals. All they know is their vagina. Even women who know the pleasures of the clitoris may still believe the vagina is their primary sexual organ because it is where men put their penis. A highly informed woman thinks of her genitals as what sex educator Carol Queen describes as "a hole and a bud," a vagina and a clitoral tip. But many woman do not even think that far. Instead, their genitals are a gaping blind spot in their sexual self-knowledge.

The sex education girls get in school about their genitals is usually a brief lesson about reproduction intended to discourage teen sex and prevent pregnancy. A girl learns where her uterus,

> Really that little dealybob is too far away from the hole. It should be built right in.
>
> —COUNTRY SINGER LORETTA LYNN

ovaries, and fallopian tubes are, that "sex" will make her pregnant, and that menstruation may make her miserable. One woman said to us that when she was in school, "all they told you in sex education was that you will get your period and that you will get cramps. That was it." If a girl uses tampons, she may study the insert in the box to find out where the vaginal opening is. But the illustrations leave out the clitoris, G spot, and other pleasure-giving parts of the genitals. In the era of AIDS, girls are told that sex can be deadly and are advised of ways to negotiate condom use by their partners. But a young woman gains little knowledge of her sexual anatomy or of how her body can give her orgasms, the kind of information that can help her to build a sexual self, which ultimately may be the best protection against SAD and unsafe sex.

Many women walk around with a mystery spot occupying the place where their genitals should be. The mystery surrounding women's genitals contrasts with the early intimacy and easy familiarity a boy develops with his penis. Men's lifelong love affair with their penis is usually attributed to its obviously greater accessibility. There it is, in front of them, asking to be handled. Men grab hold of this appendage several times a day to urinate, so it is never far from their attention. And when it responds to stimulus and becomes erect, it seems to demand a man's attention. Women's lack of genital awareness is not simply due to the fact that their genitals are out of immediate sight. If the sexual culture encouraged women to explore, they would discover that their genitals are well within reach. They would also learn to recognize the taut and full feeling of their own erection.

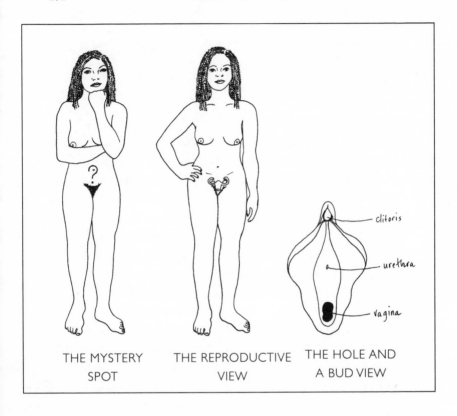

THE MYSTERY   THE REPRODUCTIVE   THE HOLE AND
SPOT   VIEW   A BUD VIEW

Sanitizing and Censoring the Genitals

> Sex is dirty, save it for somebody you love. I mean that was
> the message I was given. . . . Why would you want to save
> something dirty for somebody you love?
>
> —BEVERLY WHIPPLE

The sexual culture teaches women to ignore and to cover up
their genitals, implying (and sometimes stating outright) that
they are dirty. Much of the attention women's genitals receive is
meant to ensure their obscurity. Television commercials and
print ads remind women that their genitals can easily offend others or embarrass women themselves. Deodorizing douches sug-

gest that women's vaginas are forever in need of cleansing, and feminine hygiene sprays imply that women need to mask genital odor with cologne. Women must be especially careful to conceal any odors or spots during menstruation. Every woman knows the fear that a smell or stain will make it obvious that she is having her period. Women are grateful for the existence of tampons (literally, "plugs") not only because they are comfortable and effective, but because they are better than pads at hiding the odor of menstrual blood, diminishing the likelihood of leakage, and avoiding the lumps that indicate a pad is in place.

The sexual culture speaks only indirectly about menstruation. A normal process experienced by half the population is treated like a shameful secret. Ads for menstrual products are vague (they rarely if ever show the actual product) and they hide discreetly in the pages of women's magazines. In 1995, the Women's Tennis Association rejected a $10 million contract for global corporate sponsorship from the makers of Tampax because local tournament sponsors did not want to be linked with the distasteful fact of menstruation.

Women themselves adopt the sexual culture's genital-hating messages and obediently keep their hands and eyes averted. Some women decline to use tampons, or they use only the applicator type to avoid having to insert a finger in their vagina. As one woman told us: "I don't mind touching the outside, but I feel funny about touching inside. It's wet and icky in there!" A woman may choose an oral or injected form of birth control rather than a diaphragm or other device that requires that she reach inside her vagina. A colleague recently recounted to us the story of a woman whose honeymoon turned into a disaster when she could not find the diaphragm she had inserted into her terra incognita. Instead of spending her wedding night in pursuit of sexual ecstasy, she and her groom went in search of a doctor who could retrieve what neither of them was willing to find for themselves.

Information about a woman's genitals is so vague that a woman who actually explores on her own is likely to be in for a surprise. Betty Dodson, the "Mother of Masturbation," describes how she reacted upon first seeing her genitals as a child:

> Around the age of ten, I wanted to see what I looked like "down there." One afternoon when the house was empty, I got Mother's hand mirror and went into my bedroom. Sitting by the window with sunlight pouring in, I looked at my sweet little child's genitals and was instantly horrified. There hanging down were the same funny-looking things that dangled from a chicken's neck. Right on the spot, I swore off masturbation and made a deal with God. If He got rid of those things that hung down, I promised to stop playing with myself, keep my room clean, and love my little brothers.

Dodson grew up thinking that her genitals were "funny-looking," even "horrifying." She is unusual, however, because she actually looked at them. Many women never even peek at their vulva, much less place their genitals up close to a mirror to take a good long look. For some women, of course, looking only confirms their aversion. A woman who saw the drawings in this book commented to us, "It just shows you how disgusting women's genitals are."

What familiarity women do gain with their genitals can be easily thwarted by cultural messages that treat them as unworthy of attention and love. When this message comes from a partner, it can abruptly put an end to a woman's sexual enjoyment. A friend in her forties remembers that her first lover "enjoyed having me do oral sex on him, but he refused to do it on me. It made me feel unappealing and dirty. It's probably why I have never enjoyed receiving it since." Even when a woman's partner offers to give cunnilingus, a woman may decline, for reasons that Betty Dodson describes:

At the age of thirty-five, I still had an ugly mental image of my genitals. In the past, men had "gone down" on me, but I was always much too uncomfortable to reach an orgasm. The thought of someone tasting my genitals struck me as being unsanitary. Worse yet, he might see everything. I could only allow oral sex to continue for a few moments before I pulled my lover back up on top of me for "normal sex."

Women expect their partners to be turned off by the way their genitals smell, taste, or look. One woman tells us that she was shocked when her lover said he actually wanted to pull up a lamp so he could see her genitals in the light. His interest embarrassed her at first, but his appreciative attitude—and great cunnilingus—eventually helped her overcome her own negative feelings.

Dodson believes that she could have been spared a lot of pain and confusion growing up if women's genitals were not veiled in secrecy and shame. "What a difference it would have made in my self-image and sexual development," she writes, "if I could have seen pretty pictures of adult genitals in a sex book." Today, Dodson's *Sex for One* and other books on women's health and sexuality, such as *Our Bodies, Ourselves, A New View of a Woman's Body,* and Joani Blank's *Femalia* have photos and drawings of vulvas that show a remarkable variety of colors, shapes, and sizes. Dodson herself is dedicated to teaching women to love their vulvas and to exploring the empowering pleasures of masturbation. Yet Dodson and other sex educators have their work cut out for them. Although feminism has made big strides toward knowledge and empowerment, only a minority of women are any more familiar with the sexual possibilities of their genitals than were their mothers or even grandmothers.

Recently we invited some women friends, all college students and mostly in their twenties, to watch Dodson's video, *Selfloving*. The students expressed embarrassment about watching Dodson's "Bodysex" workshop participants examine and admire their vulvas. They were especially uncomfortable about seeing other women make the inner lips into different shapes. But they laughed when one woman said her hooded clitoris and draping inner labia looked like Meryl Streep in *The French Lieutenant's Woman*. And several women later told us that the video inspired them to go home and look at their own vulvas for the first time and embark on a sex journey.

Like most women, these students had internalized a disdain for the female genitals. This is not surprising in a sexual culture that puts women's vulvas on display only in the "beaver shots" of men's porno magazines, a format hardly designed for women's (or men's) sexual self-knowledge. The genital themes in the political art of feminist painters and performance artists such as Judy Chicago and Annie Sprinkle were provocative for simply dealing with the subject. Their work, along with the sensuously contoured petals of Georgia O'Keeffe's flower paintings (which O'Keeffe herself denied were vulva images) begin to provide some balance to the phallic skyscrapers, sports cars, neckties, missiles, cigars, and guns that penetrate every aspect of the sexual culture. But vulva symbols do not do justice to the richness of women's cligeva because they represent only the outside. A more appropriate and inclusive symbol is needed that expresses how the cligeva encompasses all the sexual parts of women's anatomy.

Some women-oriented health clinics help women get to know their genitals by looking at their cervixes and by teaching them to do a self-exam using a speculum, flashlight, and a hand mirror. One woman recalls learning how to examine her cervix in a small group at a women's health clinic during the 1970s. Seeing her own and other women's cervixes for the first time completely changed how she thought about her genitals. It also improved her sex life. Familiarity with the shape and location of her cervix enabled her to become more aware of what she was feeling during intercourse. She learned how to use her PC muscle to "lift" her cervix and open up the cul-de-sac. She showed

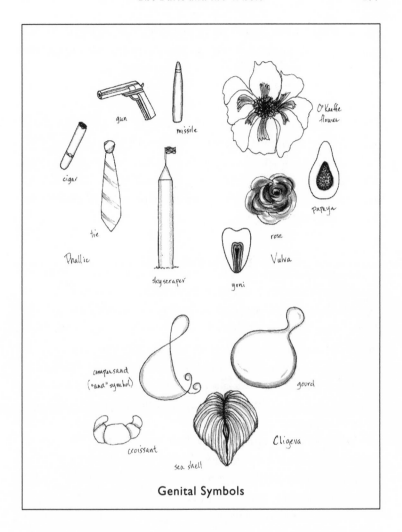

Genital Symbols

her cervix to the man who was her partner at the time, and he became much more aware of what his penis was touching. Years later, he told her that the lesson had fundamentally changed his view of women's genitals and of sex. Instead of treating the vagina as a dark, mysterious hole, he was able to avoid hitting the cervix on his way to the cul-de-sac during intercourse, a skill his current partner (and all women) appreciates. When women's genitals come out into the light, they cease seeming dirty and mysterious, and the quality of sex improves.

Women's access to the pleasure of their genitals is cut off by society, not by their anatomy. Indeed, if anatomy were destiny, all women would revel in the ability of their clitoris to give them orgasms every time they had sex. Instead, because women's clitoris is ignored by the sexual culture, most do not even have one orgasm during sex. Society largely determines how women and men experience their genitals, whether they feel pleasure, revulsion, or nothing at all.

The Deepest Cut

A woman's clitoris is quite literally cut out in cultures that practice clitoridectomies and other types of genital mutilation. Over 100 million women and girls living today, mostly in Africa and the Middle East, have had parts of their clitoris removed. Female genital mutilation is sometimes called female "circumcision," but it is far more radical than the foreskin removal of male circumcision (literally, a "cutting around"). True female circumcision would involve cutting away the clitoral hood. A clitoridectomy involves the removal, at minimum, of the tip and shaft of the clitoris and is comparable to cutting off the tip of the man's clitoris underneath the head of the penis. Some women also have their labia removed and undergo infibulation, in which the vaginal opening is sewn shut except for a small hole to allow the flow of menstrual blood.

Genital mutilation is a rite of passage for girls done at infancy, puberty, or later that prepares them and makes them eligible for marriage. Defenders of the practice say it needs to be understood in the cultural context in which it occurs. They point out that women themselves usually want the rite performed on their daughters, nieces, and granddaughters. They would feel negligent if their young relatives did not undergo this rite of passage because a girl is otherwise considered unfit for marriage. African women leading the fight against female genital mutilation and Western critics such as Alice Walker say that this practice is not culture but torture, a brutal and terrifying procedure performed on female children that effectively denies them of sexual autonomy and contributes to preparing women for a life under the control of a husband.

One young woman from Nigeria told us that it was only as an adult that she became aware that a clitoridectomy had been performed on her when she was eight months old. She discovered her mutilation after moving to the United States when she compared the diagram of a vulva in her college anatomy class textbook with her own body and realized that the tip and the shaft of her clitoris and outer labia were missing. No one, including her mother, had ever mentioned that she had undergone genital mutilation. She still can have orgasms by rubbing her vulva because the legs of her clitoris were overlooked and spared.

Even in Europe and the United States, where the procedures are against the law, female genital mutilation sometimes takes place among some immigrant groups. Similar procedures are not new to the West. In the 1860s, doctors sometimes performed clitoridectomies and female circumcision (removal of all or part of the clitoral hood) to control women's sexual appetite. They also removed the healthy ovaries and uteruses of thousands of American women to cure hysteria and other psychological ills. These procedures occurred in addition to gynecological surgeries that were medically sound and that would be considered indicated today.

Western women are still subject to questionable genital surgery today. Though becoming less frequent, women who ejaculate sometimes undergo surgery to correct "urinary incontinence." Other women have their ovaries (whose role in regulating hormones is not fully understood) or their uteruses removed (with little or no concern that the uterus contracts during orgasm and may contribute to pleasure), when less radical procedures might be more appropriate. Women beyond their childbearing years are especially vulnerable because if a woman is no longer having babies, she is not thought to need these organs. The authors of *A New View of a Woman's Body* write that, "physicians often connect the uterus with reproduction alone instead of acknowledging that it also plays an integral part in sexual response. So when a physician tells you that you won't really need your uterus, you can tell him [sic] that indeed you might."

Psychological Clitoridectomy

The rates of cesareans in the United States are among the highest in industrialized societies, revealing how commonly the surgical knife is poised to cut women below the belt. Although surgery to reduce sexual enjoyment is uncommon in the West, the sexual culture regularly performs "psychological clitoridectomies" on women through guilt and shame. One woman told us that she was orgasmic when she was four years old. But her mother told her that if she masturbated, she would be punished. When at six she had kidney problems, she thought the pelvic pain she suffered was her punishment, so she stopped masturbating. She did not have an orgasm again until she was in her thirties. Another woman remembers that as a child she was told that she was a "slut" if she even thought about, much less touched, her genitals. She learned to cut off her genitals from the rest of her body and to this day has never experienced an orgasm. If a woman who touches her genitals and enjoys sex is seen as a "bad girl," women have no model of what a sexually healthy woman looks like. In their efforts to be "good girls" who do not think about or enjoy sexual feelings, young women may give up their journey toward a sexual self.

Different Strokes

Women learn to deny their genitals and to forego pleasure, while boys receive constant but subtle signals that their penis is something to enjoy and be proud of. To most men, the penis is a symbol of strength, virility, and pride. Some men even name their penis and, once a sexual partner becomes sufficiently intimate, the two get introduced. One woman tells us that, as a teenager, she and her boyfriend called his penis "Eddie," after her pet parakeet. They regularly consulted Eddie (the penis, not the bird) about sexual matters, and they responded to his desires. Eddie knew what he wanted and when he wanted it. The young woman's genitals had no name, no identity, and, apparently, no desires of their own.

In comparison with the outgoing penis, women's genitals live the life of a recluse. They remain anonymous and, although they do receive visits, they are not expected to go out and initiate contact or to make any demands of their own. Women themselves are rarely on speaking terms with their most intimate parts. Like a cloistered nun, many women's genitals take a vow of silence.

Hands-on Knowledge

Women who want to develop their sexuality can do so by taking a hands-on approach to genital pleasure. As women become more aware of genital pleasure, they may find that their own experience of them is inconsistent with what the sexual culture has taught them. They discover sensitive areas such as the G spot but find little confirmation or information about it from sex experts, some of whom question women's experience of it. Magazines, sex manuals, and some gynecologists tell them that a normal woman has orgasms from intercourse or that ejaculate is just urine. They see anatomical drawings that show their clitoris to

WHAT'S IN A NAME?

John Thomas and Lady Jane (of D. H. Lawrence's *Lady Chatterley's Lover*) are perhaps the most famous genital protagonists in modern literature. Yet most names given to female and male genitals reflect the different esteem in which they are held. In Nicholson Baker's novel *Vox,* the male caller refers fondly to his "Werner Heisenberg" (after the physicist who noted the impact of the observer on the success of an experiment). Although he has numerous names for women's breasts, the only nickname for the clitoris is "candy corn," and the caller's female counterpart offers no endearing nicknames for her own genitals.

In common slang, women's genitals are often compared to fruit—the tip of the clitoris is a "cherry" and the vulva is a papaya—suggesting that they are sweet to the taste when fresh but decay quickly. Fruits are short-lived and vulnerable, quite the opposite of the long-lasting reign of the powerful penis suggested by condoms named Trojans, Sheiks, and Ramses. No such fantasies of power, glory, or immortality are attached to women's genitals. The single brand of a condom for women is called simply Reality.

be the size of a pea, rather than an organ that extends into the body and is much longer and larger than the visible tip. The parallel between a woman's clitoris and the erectile tissue of a man's penis is overlooked. The pleasure women feel at the cul-de-sac is ignored, unrecognized, and unexplained. The list of controversies, misconceptions, and gaps in knowledge goes on and on.

Every woman can contribute to a better, more healthful, and more pleasure-centered understanding of sexuality by looking at her genitals for herself and exploring the sensations they offer. A woman can become her own best authority on erotic pleasure.

As she explores, she can compare her experience with the existing model of her genitals as well as with alternative models like the one we suggest in this book. When women share their questions, answers, and ideas with one another, they spur the sexual culture as a whole to reformulate the way it imagines both women's anatomy and the nature of sex.

A new view of women's genitals requires a new vocabulary. The alternative concepts and terms we present below are intended to help women identify and understand the sensations they can discover, as well as the ones they have already felt but could not name. This new view also pictures the genitals not as a bunch of unconnected parts, but as a sexual whole—the cligeva. Our aim is to bring clarity, common sense, and simplicity to what has for too long been a muddled mystery.

The Not-So-Opposite Sexes

The sexual culture regularly refers to women and men as opposite sexes. They are more accurately described as unequal sexes, because men are considered the standard model to which women are compared and found lacking. Whatever men are or have, women are not or need. Thus, men are sexually aggressive, women are not; men have a penis, women do not. The penis is seen as the quintessential sex organ, and women apparently have nothing that compares to it in either size or importance.

What women do have of interest is a vagina, seen as the complement to man's penis. The vagina is viewed as a passive, empty space for the active, ample penis to fill. The woman's clitoris holds less interest, since it provides no direct genital pleasure to men. Mistakenly thought to be no more than a dot, the clitoris's apparently small size is taken as proof that women are the second and inferior sex.

Anatomy books typically present a woman's clitoris as an

PARTS LOST AND FOUND

Knowledge about women's sexual anatomy and functions known for centuries has been repeatedly "lost" and then "found" again. Freudian ideas about sexuality ignored the clitoris in order to focus on the psychosexual role of the vagina. It was not until the 1960s that people such as sex researchers Masters and Johnson and feminists such as Shere Hite and Mary Jane Sherfey rediscovered the clitoris.

The G spot, too, has been "discovered" and "lost" several times. The G spot's contribution to female pleasure was recognized in ancient Greek medicine, described again in seventeenth-century Europe by Regnier de Graaf, but then was largely ignored in the scientific literature until 1950 when Ernst Grafenberg described it anew. The work of de Graaf and Grafenberg was brought to the attention of sexologists in 1978 with the publication of an article on the female prostate and female ejaculation by Josephine Lowndes Sevely and J.W. Bennett. Sevely and Bennett's work inspired further research that culminated in the publication in 1982 of *The G Spot and Other Recent Discoveries About Human Sexuality* by Alice Kahn Ladas, Beverly Whipple, and John D. Perry, which named the G spot after Grafenberg and brought it and female ejaculation to public attention. Yet, fifteen years later, many sex experts continue to doubt that either exists, despite women's enthusiastic affirmations that they indeed do.

underdeveloped penis. In illustrations of genital development in the human fetus, the same erectile tissue that grows in the male fetus shrinks in the female. The clitoris is presented as a penis that shrivels on the vine. Yet more recent research indicates that female fetuses grow erectile tissue, too. Adult women and men have sexual organs of the same respective size. They are just placed differently in the body.

This view of the clitoris as small and unimportant compared to the penis is reinforced in medical training. Norma Wilcox, a nurse and sexologist who teaches medical students how to do pelvic exams, told us that medical students and physicians report to her that they learn about the anatomy of the penis but often run out of time before they get to the clitoris. They also say that they do not learn the anatomy or physiology of the periurethral glands (or G spot). Wilcox believes that these organs of women's sexual anatomy are "not valued, not taught, and therefore, not valued," and that medical students could benefit from human sexuality instruction from a sexologist.

In the new view of sexual anatomy that we present here, women and men are shown to be more alike than different. Both sexes develop the same sexual organs, and they are roughly the same size. Although the reproductive organs develop greater differentiation and serve different functions, the parts of

---

THE OPPOSITE AND UNEQUAL GENITALS OF WOMEN AND MEN CURRENT VIEW

FEMALE	MALE
vagina	penis
clitoral tip	penis

The sexual culture views the familiar parts of women's genitals in terms of men's penises. In reality, the vagina is many things besides a receptacle for penetration. It has sensitive parts that are not necessarily best stimulated by a penis. The clitoris-penis comparison is also false because it compares a part with a whole. A woman's clitoral tip, often described as a tiny version of a man's penis, is only the visible part of a much larger internal organ.

women's and men's genitals dedicated to pleasure are remarkably similar. The major difference is the way they are placed in the body. The woman's clitoris extends the same length into the woman's body as the penis extends out of the man's body. Its tip is exposed at the vulva, while in men the entire clitoris is enveloped in the penis. The differences in their external appearance and location in the body are exaggerated by the distinct names given to parts that serve similar functions in women and men. For example, what is essentially a clitoris is called the *corpora cavernosa* in men. Yet the similarity is rarely noted, even though the anatomical term for the woman's clitoris is *corpora cavernosa clitoridis*. The man's clitoris is usually ignored altogether in favor of a view of the penis as a whole. Similarly, women's prostate gland or G spot is neglected and only men are thought to have one. When partners recognize that both women and men have the same organs for pleasure, and understand that they are differently situated in the body and require different techniques to stimulate them, they can exchange and enjoy pleasure more equally.

Showing how women and men are alike subsumes neither sex under the other, but asserts instead a radically equal view of the genitals and of sexual pleasure. Men are as much like women as women are like men. Typically, women have been viewed in male terms, so Shere Hite suggests we begin viewing men in terms of women for a change. "Think of a penis as just the externalization of a woman's interior bulbs and clitoral network," she advises, challenging the sexual culture to see women as neither men's opposites nor their inferiors in sexual pleasure, but as essentially the same.

Josephine Lowndes Sevely advocates a view of genital similarity between women and men in her book *Eve's Secrets: A New Theory of Female Sexuality*. Her work has been extremely influential for some women who are rethinking sex because it lays the groundwork for a more egalitarian view of sexuality in which the only difference of consequence between women and men is, as Sevely puts it, "one of organization, not of substance."

The Parts

The Clitoris

At the center of a new view of women's sexual anatomy is the clitoris. The clitoris is made up of erectile tissue that becomes engorged with blood and is the most sexually sensitive organ of women's (and men's) sexual anatomy. Most women are aware of the capacity of their clitoris for pleasure and know that it is a major site of women's orgasms. Yet they may have only a vague notion of what the clitoris looks like.

The word *clitoris* is thought to derive from Greek words meaning "close" (because it is hidden from view by the labia) or "little hill." The little hill is, however, only the tip of a much larger organ. Most people think that the small tip and shaft is the whole clitoris and presume it is shaped like a small penis. But as *A New View of a Woman's Body, Eve's Secrets,* and other sources show, the woman's whole clitoris is over four inches long and Y-shaped like a wishbone. (Sevely compares it to a maple tree seed.) The legs of the wishbone extend into the body on either side of the vagina.

The clitoris is commonly considered to be a structure that is exclusively female. Sex manuals often laud the woman's clitoris as the only organ whose sole purpose is pleasure, an inaccuracy that only calls attention to the way that purpose is routinely overlooked. Few authors concede that men have what is essentially a clitoris of comparable size to women's that serves the same purpose—pleasure. In both women and men, the clitoris becomes engorged with blood when aroused and becomes stiffer, larger, straighter, and more sensitive to touch and pressure. (It is because the woman's clitoris straightens that the tip appears to retract under the hood.) In a man, clitoral engorgement causes the penis to enlarge and stand up. In a woman, clitoral engorgement makes the cligeva expand and tent up. Because a man's erection is external and visible, men's sexual organs seem much larger than those of women, whose erection occurs inside the body. In fact, the clitoris in women and men is of the same size relative to the body. (It is roughly four inches long in a woman, five inches in a man.) The proportions of the Y varies: The female clitoris has a short body and long legs that embrace the vagina; the male clitoris has a long body that runs the length of the penis and short legs.

The two organs also differ in the way they are placed in the body. In women, the sensitive clitoral tip is outside of the body, while the man's clitoral tip is encased in the penis. (Ironically, this inverts the usual perception that women's genitals are internal and men's external.) Because it is exposed, the tip of the woman's clitoris is accessible to touch, while the tip of the man's clitoris is under the head of the penis and cannot be touched directly. When the penis is stroked, the entire clitoris as well as the urethra that runs alongside it receive stimulation. The urethra in women and men alike is wrapped in sensitive spongy tissue, or spongiosum. In the woman, the legs of the clitoris are adjacent to the sensitive tissue of the urethra, while in men, the body of the clitoris and the urethra run parallel to one another inside the length of the penis.

Understanding the different orientations of the clitoris in women and men helps clarify the reason why intercourse makes men come but not women. In intercourse, the tip and length of the man's penis is stimulated by pressing against the vaginal walls. When the woman contracts her PC muscle, her vaginal walls apply pressure against the body of the man's clitoris and

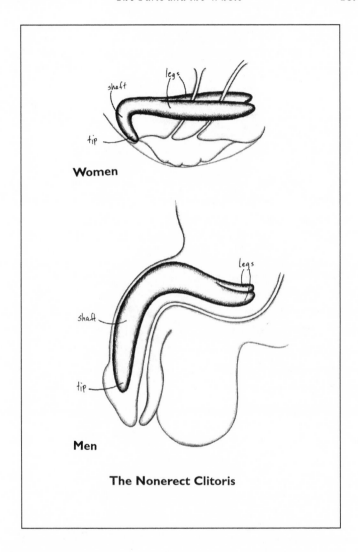

The Nonerect Clitoris

his urethra with its surrounding spongiosum. All the sensitive parts of his penis receive stimulation. But during penetration, the penis bypasses the woman's clitoral tip and passes in between the legs of her clitoris. It also bypasses the sensitive tis-

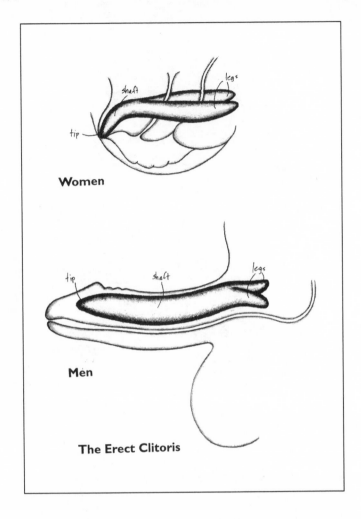

sues of the woman's urethra. His penis can stimulate the legs of her clitoris and her urethal tissues, but *only if the woman's genitals are erect.* The man's body or his penis may press pleasantly against the woman's clitoral tip or her U spot, or urethral opening. But the stimulation is neither as direct nor as continuous as the clitoral stimulation the man gets during intercourse. Women need the same clitoral stimulation that men receive to have an orgasm. This is best provided by manual sex, not intercourse.

The Orgasmic Crescent

The "orgasmic crescent" is the name we give to an area of women's sexual anatomy where several sensitive parts come together. The key to the orgasmic crescent is the clitoris, which lies at the outer end of the crescent. The clitoris is the first stop on the quarter-moon-shaped arc that extends from the tip of the clitoris outside to the G spot inside. From the clitoris, a finger passing along the crescent crosses over the U spot and the frenulum (see below) and then enters the vagina to the G spot. We call this the *orgasmic* crescent because it combines the pleasure powers of the clitoris, the U spot, and the G spot.

The clitoris leads the orgasmic crescent into an erect state. When stimulated, the clitoris heats up, making the whole area puff up like a mouth-watering croissant. Like a croissant, the orgasmic crescent is both firm and fluffy, and to a woman and her partner alike, it is delicious. Stimulating the whole orgasmic crescent produces intense orgasms and, for some women, ejaculation.

The Frenulum. After the sensitive clitoral tip, the next stop along the orgasmic crescent is the frenulum, where the inner labia join. It is so close to the tip of the clitoris (sometimes joining above, sometimes below) that the frenulum may be easily confused with it. (The man's frenulum is the small fold of skin attached to the underside of the head of the penis.) In both women and men, the frenulum has lots of nerve endings that respond to touch.

The U Spot. One of the least-known and most important sites for a woman's sexual pleasure is the U spot, the third stop on the orgasmic crescent. Josephine Lowndes Sevely describes the sexually sensitive area around the opening of the urethra as sim-

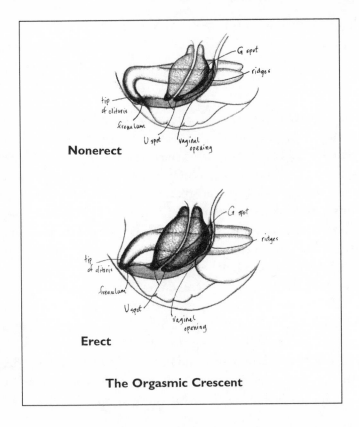

Nonerect

Erect

The Orgasmic Crescent

ilar to the head of the man's penis (she calls it the woman's glans). Barbara Keesling is one of the few popular writers who recognizes this area and treats it as a sexual part. Keesling calls it the U spot, because it lies at the external opening of the urethra. Women may notice sensitivity at their U spot but never hear the area talked about in relation to sex. One friend told us that she was worried when she first noticed a "thing sticking out" below her clitoris; she thought she was deformed or that she had two clitorises. Her gynecologists had never said anything about it. After reading this chapter, she realized that it was her U spot.

The U spot lies about three-quarters of an inch below the tip of the clitoris. Women may experience erotic sensations from the

U spot, but because it is so close to the clitoris, they may not distinguish between the two. When doing clittage or applying the large round head of a vibrator to the clitoral tip, a woman is likely to also hit the U spot. The U spot is very mobile. During penetration, a woman's U spot is pulled back and forth as her partner's penis, his fingers, or a dildo slides in and out of the vagina. Stimulating the U spot affects the whole urethra, including the G spot, which may be why some women ejaculate from what seems like clitoral stimulation alone.

A woman can locate the U spot by spreading her inner lips and pulling up on the clitoris. Using a mirror, she can see that the U spot is outlined by a deep recess and its lower edge forms

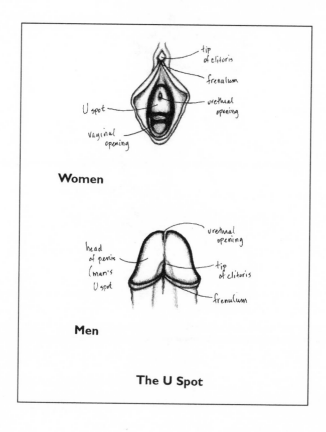

The U Spot

the top edge of the vaginal opening. It is often difficult to see and may not stick out, but when erect, the U spot puffs out into an acorn shape above the vaginal opening. It may be irritating to touch when not erect (use lubricant), but becomes sexually sensitive when erect.

The head of the man's penis is typically considered the equivalent to the tip of the woman's clitoris, but it has more in common with the woman's U spot. Both the U spot and the head of the penis are perforated by the urethra. Both are acorn-shaped

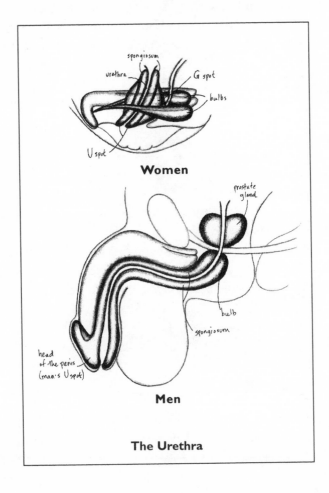

The Urethra

(usually only apparent when the U spot is erect) and both are sensitive to direct stimulation. The U spot and the clitoral tip are about three-quarters of an inch apart in women; the tips of the urethra and the clitoris are set one on top of the other in men. For both women and men, the clitoris *and* all the parts of the urethra (U spot, spongiosum, and the prostate or G spot) in combination are the primary sources of sexual pleasure.

The Urethra. The woman's urethra is not usually seen as a sexual organ. Most people realize that the man's urethra automatically gets involved in sex because it runs through the center of the penis and because it is a passageway for semen during ejaculation. A woman's urethra runs through her orgasmic crescent and is associated with female sexual pleasure and ejaculation.

Josephine Lowndes Sevely has been one of only a few writers on sex to describe the woman's urethra as a sexual organ. The urethra is surrounded by the sexually sensitive tissue of the spongiosum (erectile tissue that encases the length of the urethra), and it lies near the bulbs (erectile tissue that extends along the legs of the clitoris on either side of the vagina) and the G spot.

The Spongiosum and Bulbs. In both women and men, the sensitive tissue surrounding the urethra is called the *spongiosum.* The spongiosum is erectile tissue that is connected to the U spot. During sexual arousal, the spongiosum fills with blood, becomes erect, and responds to pressure. Although it cannot be touched directly, the spongiosum is stimulated by pressure from G spotting and U spot stimulation.

The *bulbs* are made up of the same erectile tissue as the spongiosum. The bulbs are split in two in the woman, while the man has one bulb. The two bulbs in the woman lie on either side of the vagina, along the clitoral legs. The woman's bulbs are stimulated whenever the clitoris, U spot, spongiosum, or G spot is stimulated. The swelling of the woman's bulbs is visible in erection. This swelling causes the labia to puff out and the outer third

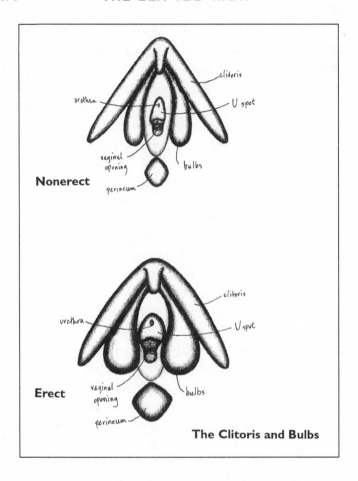

Nonerect

clitoris
urethra
U spot
vaginal opening
bulbs
perineum

Erect

clitoris
urethra
U spot
vaginal opening
bulbs
perineum

The Clitoris and Bulbs

of the vaginal opening to tighten. The puffed bulbs also increase the sensation of friction and pressure against the vaginal walls during intercourse.

The G Spot. The fourth and last stop on the orgasmic crescent is the G spot, the second most important site of women's sexual pleasure after the clitoris. The G spot is often associated with women's vagina because it is reached by penetrating the vagina. But the G spot or female prostate gland surrounds the urethra and has ducts that open into it (as does the prostate

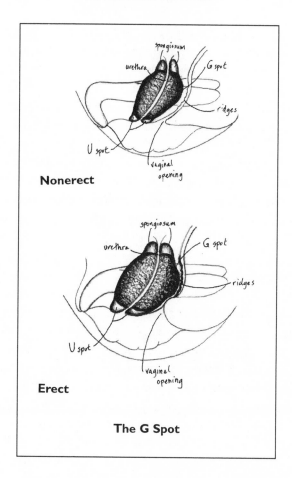

Nonerect

Erect

The G Spot

gland in men). The G spot is best stimulated by G spotting, stroking or pressing with the fingers. It can also be stimulated by a G spotter (a curved vibrator attachment), penis, or a dildo.

Stimulation of the woman's G spot creates sexual pleasure that can lead to orgasm and ejaculation. Female ejaculate is fluid that resembles male prostatic fluid without the sperm. In women and men alike, ejaculate is expelled from the urethra.

The G spot is a sexual part in the making. There are disputes about whether it exists, whether all women have one, and what it should be called. Beverly Whipple and John Perry named the area the G spot after Ernst Grafenberg, the man who brought it to the renewed attention of anatomists in 1950. Sevely calls it the female prostate gland because it is equivalent to the male prostate gland. The authors of *A New View of a Woman's Body* call it the urethral sponge because it holds and expels fluid. Others call it the periurethral glands because it is made up of glands that surround the urethra. Tantric sex practitioners Carolyn and Charles Muir call it the "S spot" for Sacred Spot. The G spot is the term we use because it is the most familiar, although some critics dislike the implication that by pressing on a magic "spot," orgasm will result. We believe that calling it a spot is helpful because it emphasizes how stimulating a specific area provides pleasure.

The G Spot and Female Ejaculation. When women learn how to stimulate the orgasmic crescent—including their G spot, U spot, and clitoris—they may experience the erotic sensations of ejaculation. Largely unmentioned in sex education, female ejaculation inspires great controversy among the people who study sex. Some refuse to believe it occurs and suggest that women who appear to be ejaculating are urinating. Beverly Whipple, who has researched the phenomenon extensively, asserts that what is known is that "some women expel fluid from the urethra . . . [and] the fluid expelled is different from urine. . . ." According to Whipple, the fluid comes at least in part from the female prostate or G spot. She and other researchers speculate that other glands may also supply some of its contents.

Women's ejaculate typically looks like watered-down skim milk. It smells slightly sweet or is odorless. It is of a thinner consistency and usually more abundant than men's ejaculate. The amount of ejaculate varies in quantity but can be enough to soak a towel. It is possible that some women produce just a small amount of ejaculate and are not aware they are ejaculating.

The sexual culture has difficulty accommodating female ejaculation into a view of sex in which women and men are opposites. The ancient Greeks believed that women ejaculated a fluid that contributed to conception. But female ejaculate does not come from the vagina and, aside from the relief from pain in childbirth as the baby's head passes under the pubic bone during labor, the G Spot has no known practical purpose beyond providing sexual pleasure.

The Vagina

Many people reduce women's genitals to the vagina. They think of the vagina in its role in intercourse and childbirth. It is also a major orifice of the body, of course, not only for the pleasure of the penis but for the flow of menstrual blood and vaginal fluids. In a sexual culture that defines sex in male terms and sees women in relation to men, the vagina seems only an empty "hole" waiting to be filled by the penis.

By thinking of the woman's genitals as the cligeva (an integrated whole and not just a "hole"), the vagina can be seen as much more. Wonderful sexual parts lie behind its walls. The vagina acts as a passageway that provides access to the internal pleasure parts of a woman's cligeva. Viewing the vagina as "full of things" rather than as an empty hole, and as an area that can be activated by the PC muscle allows a woman to become a *pro*active—rather than a *re*active—partner in sex.

PC Muscle

The PC or pubococcygeus muscle is actually a group of muscles that forms the floor of the pelvis and supports the genitals. It begins as two bands at the pubic bone, rings the vagina an inch from the opening, and comes together at the base of the spine.

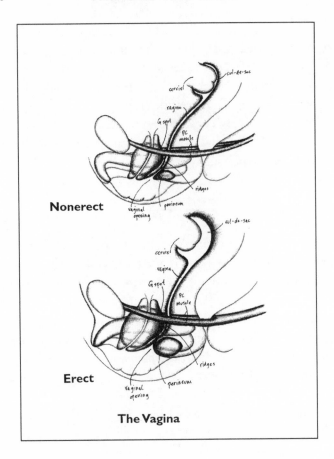

Nonerect

Erect

The Vagina

In erection, the PC muscle contracts, tightening like a lasso around the vagina, urethra, and rectum. The muscle can be consciously used to enhance sexual pleasure. A woman can contract her PC muscle to enhance her erection and can push out or bear down during ejaculation. A man can use his to lift his erect penis and to control ejaculation.

Many women learn to use their PC muscle to give men pleasure during penetration, but do not know how it can also in-

THE VAGINA: PASSIVE OR ACTIVE? EMPTY OR FULL?

How girls and women think of the vagina depends on what they learn from their culture. U.S. culture generally sees the vagina as empty and passive. Researchers who explored the vagina using a Q-tip–like probe concluded that the vagina lacked sensitivity. They did not take into account that the vagina becomes sensitive only when the cligeva is erect. It is not surprising that researchers overlooked this, since the sexual culture lacks the concept of female erection.

Not all societies consider the vagina to be passive or empty. Sevely notes that on the Pacific atoll of Truk, people consider the vagina, not the penis, as the primary symbol of sexuality. A woman's vagina is thought to be "full of things." For the Trukese, these "things" include the clitoris, inner lips, and a "small projection below the clitoris," what we call the U spot. In our view, the vagina is even fuller: It includes the PC muscle, cul-de-sac, and perineum and provides access to the G spot. It is also "full" in the sense that its walls engorge during erection.

crease their own pleasure. By tightening and releasing her PC muscle, a woman draws blood into her genitals and makes them erect. Squeezing the PC muscle also increases friction during intercourse. By pushing out or bearing down, the G spot bulges out and allows a woman to increase its stimulation during G spotting and intercourse.

During orgasm, a woman's (and a man's) PC muscle involuntarily contracts for a few wonderful seconds. One woman tells us that she uses her "stomach muscles," which include her PC muscle, to bear down to have an orgasm. Others contract the muscle and lift up. Some women push out with the PC muscle when they ejaculate. Strong PC muscles assist for both or-

GOING FOR THE TURN-ON

A strong PC muscle can enhance women's ability to reach orgasm and to ejaculate. Women can strengthen the PC muscle by doing "kegels," named after the physician who pointed out their value.

To exercise the PC muscle, a person first must know where it is and how to consciously contract it. The easiest way is to try and stop the flow of urine when the bladder is nearly empty. The PC muscle can be strengthened as most other muscles can be— by squeezing and relaxing the muscle at short intervals, gradually increasing repetitions, by holding the contraction for several minutes, and by tightening and releasing slowly. A woman can even do some vaginal weight lifting by inserting fingers, a dildo, or a "kegelcisor" (a small dumbbell made expressly for this exercise) while contracting. Women can do kegels discreetly anywhere—while driving, waiting at a bus stop, or reading this book. Of course, the most fun way to exercise the PC muscle is in sex.

gasm and ejaculation. Women and men alike can strengthen their PC muscles during sex and by doing "kegels."

Cul-de-Sac

Some women are familiar with a sensitive area at the cervix that opens up during erection, especially after orgasm. This sexual part has been largely ignored or, if a person does feel or experience it, she may be unaware of what it is. Barbara Keesling is the only writer we are aware of who gives it a name: the *cul-de-sac*, a French term meaning "bottom or end of the sack." The cul-de-sac is an area created at the cervix during erection. The vagina straightens out and the muscles supporting the uterus lift up, creating a "tent" or archlike area. One woman told us that when her cul-de-sac is erect, it feels like a door opens up, allowing the head of her partner's penis to snuggle in. To a man, it feels like a crown or a ring is placed on the head of his penis. It is not clear why pressure in this space is pleasurable for women. Sevely suggests that "the arch is very close to the sacral nerves and . . . any stimulation of the area could induce stimulation of these nerves." Whatever the reason, both partners can enjoy the gentle pressure (not thrusting) of the head of the penis against this tented or vaulted spot. More delicious than a French kiss, cul-de-sac stimulation allows lovers to meld their genitals into one.

Perineum. Some women are aware of pleasurable sensations at the perineum, a sensitive, muscular body that is attached to the lower opening of the vagina. When the perineum is erect, it can be seen puffing out between the vagina and the anus. (In men, it is between the testicles and the anus.) One woman told us of a lover who liked doing cunnilingus for a long time and called the perineum a "chin rest." Along with the bulbs and G spot, the perineum helps tighten the vaginal opening upon erection and increases friction, pressure, and pleasure. This tightening allows women to experience the most intense sensation in the first third of the vagina.

Anus

The perineum lies next to the most taboo area of the body, the anus. Many women and men enjoy anal stimulation during sex, whether from touching sensitive nerve endings at the opening of the anus or from penetration. Many people engage in finger penetration as an enhancement to other stimulation during sex. Those who enjoy anal intercourse like the sense of fullness it provides. And inside the rectum, a penis, dildo, or finger can stimulate the perineum and G spot in women and the prostate gland, clitoral legs, and bulb in men.

As with vaginal intercourse, penetration using latex-covered and lubricated fingers, dildo, or penis is crucial to safer sex. Also crucial is that the receiving partner be erect. The receiving partner's erection and orgasm helps relax the sphincter muscle that closes the anus. Therefore, "ladies first" orgasm *before* and clittage *during* anal sex are a must for making it a pleasure.

The Sexual Whole

More Than the Sum of Its Parts: The Cligeva

It is difficult to get our minds around all the sexual parts of women's genitals. By becoming aware of sexual areas that have gone unnoticed or unnamed, such as the U spot, or learning names for sexually sensitive places they may already enjoy, such as the cul-de-sac, women can begin the process of transforming sex. Naming and recognizing the special features of the clitoris, G spot, urethra, and vagina separately is a crucial first step. The next step is to enjoy their pleasures through "caressing the (orgasmic) crescent." The final step is to involve the entire cligeva and to tap its full capacity for pleasure.

Our term for the whole of women's sexual parts, *cligeva,* suggests the order in which most women like their genitals to be stimulated—first, the clitoris, then the G spot, then vaginal penetration. When the clitoris is stimulated, its erection sends sexual sparks to the rest of the cligeva. When the G spot is stimulated, it can lead to orgasm and possibly ejaculation. When the sexual parts of the vagina are erect, the walls become sensitive to pressure and friction and the cul-de-sac opens up. Using her PC muscle, a woman can bring all the parts of her cligeva together in erection. The concept of cligeva brings the genital whole (and not just the clitoris or the G spot as isolated parts) together conceptually. The word *cligeva* allows women to talk about their sexual anatomy in terms that can contribute to pleasure. With *cligeva,* women can put a name and a practical concept where a mystery spot has been.

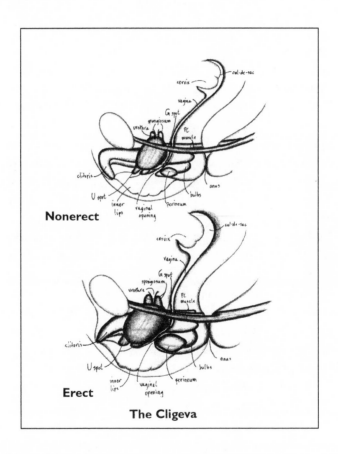

The Cligeva

Orgasm
or Bust

Nikki and Joe rest against pillows, their legs and arms entwined. They talk, kiss, and gently touch each other. Nikki pours lubrication into Joe's gloved hands. He warms the thick liquid between his fingers and gently strokes her clitoris. Nikki feels her cligeva come alive in erection. She moves Joe's other hand toward her vagina and he slides two fingers along her orgasmic crescent and inside to her G spot. The combined effect transports Nikki's whole body to orgasm.

Now Nikki wants Joe's penis inside her. She applies a condom and lubricant to his warm, hard penis. Nikki climbs on top of Joe, and slips his penis into her vagina. She contracts her PC muscle and presses his penis against her G spot. Joe massages her clitoris with his fingers. Nikki leans over and Joe plays with her nipples with his lips and tongue. Nikki comes again. Joe has an orgasm, too, but slows down and squeezes his PC muscle to keep from ejaculating; he wants to wait until Nikki is fully satisfied.

They change to rear entry, and as Nikki performs clittage, Joe strokes her engorged G spot with his penis. Orgasm rushes through Nikki's body. She turns over on her back, and with her hips resting on pillows, Joe gets on his knees and focuses again on the orgasmic crescent, simultaneously massaging her clitoris with one hand while pressing two fingers on her G spot with the other. She reaches orgasm and before it subsides she brings Joe to her and he penetrates deeply. The combined clitoral stimulation and pressure

*on her cul-de-sac sends Nikki toward an orgasm. Seeing her plea-
sure inspires Joe to come with her.*

*Sweating and hearts beating fast, Nikki and Joe slowly descend
from their high to complete stillness. Radiating erotic heat, they
hold each other and fall into contented slumber.*

Thinking about women's genitals in a new way is more than
a mental exercise. It changes how a woman feels about and
enjoys her body. Nikki has learned that when sex incorporates
her clitoris and G spot, she reaches orgasms every time she has
sex. She knows that when intercourse follows orgasm, her pleasure is exceptionally intense. The orgasmic facility Nikki has
developed eludes many other women largely because the information available to them about sex is vague and disembodied.
Women are told how to decorate for sex instead of being told
about how their genitals work. "Light candles and wear something lacy" is not useful sexual instruction.

The sexual culture makes orgasms unnecessarily complicated
for women by teaching them to either ignore or underrate them.
When women learn to visualize their genitals as a whole—as a
cligeva rather than just a passive vagina and a miniscule clitoral
tip, having an orgasm becomes a straightforward and readily at-
tainable experience.

When Sex Is Just a Bowl of Warm Oatmeal

When a woman is lukewarm about sex, it is often because she
never has, or only rarely has, an orgasm. The reason a woman
does not reach orgasm is usually that sex with a man centers on
intercourse. One respondent to Shere Hite's study described her
experience of orgasm:

I believe that this is true for countless millions of wives, in spite of all the claims to orgasm, that they really don't know what orgasm is. Almost no one is willing to admit to not having orgasms—what, me frigid? I used to say, during my marriage of thirty years, and quite sincerely, believe it or not, that yes, I had orgasm almost every time. But then, taken by surprise in a lesbian relationship, I experienced real, buffola total eclipse orgasm for the first time. Wow. I'd never felt anything like *that* before. Suddenly I understood all kinds of strange masculine behavior. The rather pleasant, generalized sensation I was accustomed to feeling with men—vaginal stimulation—were in a class of sensuously warm oatmeal. No wonder women have never made a big thing out of sex—it's nice, really, but one can do without it.

Many women are indeed indifferent about sex. Ann Landers once asked her (presumed to be heterosexual) readers about which they preferred—to cuddle with their partner or to have sexual intercourse? Answers divided neatly along the gender lines: Over 70 percent of men preferred intercourse, while 70 percent of women wanted to cuddle. This difference happens to mirror the orgasm gap: Over 70 percent of men regularly have orgasms and 70 percent of women regularly go without. Women's attitudes about sex change when they have orgasms that are both readily available and satisfying. Once a woman has a powerful, full-bodied orgasm, she says, "Wow, *now* I get what all the to-do is about!"

Sex without orgasm is not without value, of course, but perhaps it should be called something else. Sex without orgasm is more like sensual play, which can be lots of fun. The problem is that sensual play and sex are gender-specific activities: The man has sex while the woman gets sensual play. When women reinvent sex, there is no reason why women and men cannot enjoy both of these pleasures equally.

Women can make having an orgasm a choice rather than a

challenge. Few men ever choose to have sex without orgasm, while women accept this fate by default. When women say they do not care about orgasm, writes Shere Hite, "Most women are not speaking from a position of strength. . . . We are not always *having* orgasms (or able to orgasm) during sex, and *then* saying they are not important." A woman can say no only to something that is actually available to her. Sometimes sex resembles the uneven situation of a couple sitting at a restaurant table together but with separate menus. The man can choose from an array of delectable dishes and a long list of fine wines. Her menu offers only one dish: warm, cozy oatmeal. We think women deserve something better.

From Hot and Bothered to Just Plain Bothered

Many women have had the experience of sex that stops just short of orgasm. They know the physical frustration of *almost* getting there. But the unreleased blood and muscle tension in the woman's genitals is nothing compared to what having "blue cligeva" does to a woman's morale and to her sexual self-esteem. A woman may fake orgasm so that she does not have to confront her own lack of fulfillment or her partner's disappointment. When orgasm does not occur, she considers that *she* is responsible and that *she* has failed.

Once "sex" is over, a woman may react in a number of ways. While her partner sleeps, a woman may get up and go to the bathroom to quietly masturbate. She may go to another room to read a magazine or down to the kitchen to finish off the pint of ice cream. Usually she just lies awake, waiting for her erection to subside and trying to convince herself that orgasms are not really what sex is about anyway. *It's OK, really.*

Many women put up with orgasmless intercourse in order to get some cuddling. But for a lot of women sex is just not worth all the effort they have to put into it. In a Nicole Hollander "Sylvia" cartoon, one woman asks another, "Do you think cake is better than sex?" The other woman hesitates. "What kind of cake?" When sex is without orgasm, it is no wonder that some heterosexual women develop a closer relationship with sweet, edible things than with either the man in their bed or with themselves. For sex that is, in editor Roz Warren's words, "unquestionably better than cake," we think a woman needs a healthy serving of orgasms with her sex.

Many women say that orgasms are not important to them. Susan Quilliam reports that over half of the women in her English survey say having orgasms is not what matters in sex. The large-scale 1994 U.S. sex survey found that women reported being almost as physically and emotionally satisfied with their sex lives as men despite women's much lower rates of orgasm. This may be a case of women accepting the inevitable. They forego a pleasure they would not think of denying their partner.

Sex cannot be truly mutual when one partner has a four-star meal while the other spoons in the gruel. Women rarely complain, however, because gruel is what they believe they deserve. They do not feel they should expect anything more, and many buy the explanation that if sex is not orgasmic, it is their own fault. The sexual culture diagnoses a woman who does not have an orgasm—who is labeled *preorgasmic, anorgasmic,* or even the old-fashioned but lingering term, *frigid*—as suffering from a personal or psychological problem. Individual or couple therapy is advised. Men have acknowledged sexual problems, too, of course. Premature ejaculation and erection problems can be at least as distressing and embarrassing for the men who experience them. But men are offered medical explanations and cures for their sexual afflictions. Their problems are often treated as matters of plumbing that special clinics stand ready to fix, while a woman's sexual problem tends to call for a long series of visits to the therapist's office. The problem is not in her genitals; it is all in her head.

The sexual culture generally shrugs its shoulders at women's sexual problems. Although some women do seek help to improve their sex lives, others do nothing because they think women are naturally cool to sex. They believed they are inherently less sexual than men. In fact, the notion that women are erotically numb is a recent invention of the sexual culture. Through most of Western history, women were considered so extremely libidinous that only marriage or the convent could tame them. Their hot sexual nature necessitated imposing strict codes of conduct reinforced by a culture of shame and even, as we mentioned, by recourse to genital surgery. A woman who actually expressed her sexual desire was (and still is) considered ill, a nymphomaniac (literally, "crazy vulva lips").

In our society, women's sexual desire hardly gets expressed. Why should it be when all women have experienced is sex without orgasm? Not all women are happy with this state of affairs, of course. As one woman told writer Harry Maurer:

> It might be a revelation to the world to find out how unsatisfied women are. The men act like they're the ones who always want sex, and the woman always has a headache. Well, she has a headache because it's a headache to bother getting all excited, and the guy leaves you high and dry. It's easier to just say, Forget the whole thing, I won't bother having sex.

Men leave women high and dry in sex not because they are all gluttonous boors or unfeeling heathens. Many men care a great deal about their partner's pleasure and would love to make sex better. But they do not know how, and their partner is equally in the dark. So both go into sex on automatic pilot. They blindly follow the sexual culture's script in which men are always eager for sex while women need to be coaxed or romanced into sex with candlelit dinners. Women and their partners may take it for granted that it was nature's plan for the female of the species to forego sex in favor of a cuddle, a kiss, or, if not warm oatmeal, perhaps a satisfying bowl of soft ice cream.

What Women Are Missing: Defining the Orgasm

Orgasms are notoriously difficult to describe, and even the best erotica cannot communicate what it is like to have one. The subjective experience is hard to put into words. Most people probably prefer to simply enjoy them. A person who has never had an orgasm and wonders what to expect is usually told, "You'll know it when it happens." Orgasms are such a unique experience, that if a woman only "thinks" she has had one, she probably has not. The best way for a woman to know what an orgasm is and whether she has them is to have one that is so powerful that it is completely unambiguous.

Although there are many ways to feel good in sex, orgasm is a very distinct type of good feeling. Sex researchers held an international congress in India in 1991 that dealt solely with the phenomenon, yet even these experts have been unwilling or unable to define orgasm in any hard-and-fast way. They do, however, offer a baseline set of physical events that regularly occur with orgasm. Researchers have found that in both sexes orgasm is indicated by raised heart rate and blood pressure, dilated pupils, and increased blood flow to the genitals. The PC muscles of both women and men contract at regular intervals that researchers have measured at exactly 0.8 seconds (which more mystical observers see as resonating with the vibrations of the universe). An orgasm can include just a few or up to fifteen contractions. When the PC muscle contracts, the blood that has concentrated in the genitals during erection rushes away from the area, creating a pleasurable sensation of release. Orgasms also may occur without PC contractions, however. In a woman, her uterus often contracts during orgasm, producing a deep pleasure sensation.

In both women and men, the sexual high is linked to the feel-good hormone known as oxytocin. With orgasm, oxytocin levels quintuple in men, and women's bodies are flooded at even higher levels. Women's bodies tend to hold on to that good sexual feeling longer than men's, so that even after an orgasm, a woman may desire more stimulus and continued sexual activity.

What part of the body a person perceives to be involved in orgasm varies. Some orgasms seem localized in the genitals while others rush through the whole body in a wave. Others affect a number of areas: Some orgasms cause a tingling in the soles of the feet, nipples, or on the palms of the hands. Orgasm can make the tongue and palate respond to the contractions of the genitals. The toes curl, legs tense, mouths go slack, and breathing is suspended. (Tantric sex practitioners advise breathing deeply through the orgasm.)

An orgasm begins with what feels like a gradual climb to the top of a high peak. At the top, there is a moment of suspension, then a feeling of pulsating pleasure, followed by a sense of release. Once the orgasm starts, there is no stopping it. It lasts a few seconds and is immediately followed by an afterglow, a sense of satisfaction and well-being that can last for hours or even days.

Dueling Orgasms

Orgasms vary depending on the who, what, when, why, and how of their creation. They can be all-encompassing and explosive, or a more low-key thrill. A woman who has orgasms can explore them in all their diversity as she gets to know her own body's potential for types of orgasmic experiences.

WELL, IT'S HARD TO DESCRIBE . . .

Orgasm merges body and mind so completely that it reduces most people's vocabulary to "ohs" and "ahs." When people try to describe how orgasm feels when they are not in the middle of one, they use words as diverse as "explosive" and "restful." Many people feel released from the hold of their body during orgasm. They "float" beyond its physical constraints. This is an important benefit of orgasm for women who feel shame about sex or have negative feelings about their body. One woman told Susan Quilliam that orgasm made her feel "slim." Orgasm can make a woman feel beautiful or it can take her so thoroughly inside her own experience that she will not care whether she is or not.

Some people feel overtaken, engulfed, or swept away by orgasm, as if seized by an external force. The power of nature is a common metaphor for the experience. Orgasm is a tidal wave, a rumbling volcano, electricity, a bolt of lightning, or a seismic tremor. As with earthquakes and other devastating acts of nature, an orgasm demands surrender and submission. It cannot be controlled. How this loss of control affects the body varies widely: To some orgasm is like a sneeze or a sigh, while others feel like they black out, stop breathing, or even, for a moment, cease living. In French, orgasm is "a little death," yet, undeniably, it also reaffirms life. After orgasm, people describe feeling a deep sense of well-being. They feel refreshed, renewed, and at peace with themselves and the world. If they are with a partner, they feel a tighter connection to that person.

Most women do not talk about their orgasms and what they feel like, but women need to hear about other women's experiences so that having them becomes less of a puzzle and more of a pleasure.

The only really significant category for orgasm, in our view, is being able to have them if and when a person wants. Yet the sexual culture is intent upon categorizing, labeling, and ranking them. Orgasms have become commodities of the sexual culture as if they were an item of market exchange. Counting and categorizing orgasms goes against the advice of sex educators who fear that making one kind of orgasm better than another, pressuring women to have multiple orgasms—even mandating orgasm at all—just moves them further out of many women's reach.

Clitoral versus Vaginal

The Freudian idea that a "vaginal orgasm" is superior to a clitoral one has cost (and still costs) millions of women their sexual pleasure. Despite research by Masters and Johnson in the 1960s, by Shere Hite in the 1970s, and by others who concurred that orgasm is usually due to some form of clitoral stimulation, the clitoral versus vaginal orgasm debate continues today. Women still confess that they "only" have clitoral orgasms. They feel deficient because they believe vaginal ones not only exist but are superior. Some sex books reinforce the idea that vaginal orgasms, especially through intercourse in the missionary position, are superior. They teach women techniques such as the "bridge maneuver," for example, a way of transferring what a woman feels in her clitoris to her vagina. The technique involves combining clittage with intercourse but gradually using your fingers less and less until the same orgasmic feelings occur with intercourse alone. Other books advise using the coital alignment technique, a man-on-top intercourse position that allows the clitoris to be rubbed by the man's penis during penetration. Some women come with intercourse because the layout of their genitals or their fit with their partner is conducive to it. But other women "grow" their cligeva through lots of sexual activity that

helps increase and heighten their genital sensitivity and awareness. They have learned to bring all the parts of their cligeva together into an orgasmic whole. Their orgasm is not vaginal, however, but cligeval, and it involves the clitoris.

Not all women consider vaginal orgasms superior to clitoral
ones, but they still accept them as distinct types of orgasm. One
woman told Susan Quilliam, for example, that her clitoral orgasms were "usually shorter but more intense" than orgasm
from vaginal intercourse, which were "not so intense but softer
and longer." A woman may develop her own system for categorizing orgasms. But categories are problematic when they set unrealistic goals or when they limit women's orgasmic potential.
Externally defined categories and goals can lead a woman to go
after a prescribed type of orgasm rather than exploring the possibilities that grow from her own body and from her own body
of experience.

The G Spot's Mistaken Identity

When the G spot became a hot topic in the early 1980s, many
feminists dismissed it as sounding dangerously like a return to
the Freudian vaginal orgasm that has haunted women for most
of this century. Although it has become identified with the
vagina, an orgasm from G spot stimulation usually comes from
manual sex rather than vaginal intercourse. To see the G spot as
the site of the "vaginal" orgasm is to hand the vagina back to
Freud instead of encouraging women to define its pleasures for
themselves.

Solo versus Partner Orgasms

No matter what their source, all orgasms provide pleasure, yet
the sexual culture treats orgasms with and from a partner as superior to the kind a woman gives herself. Orgasms with a part-

ner are considered more meaningful than self-made ones. Although there is no denying the pleasure of being skin-to-skin with a lover, or the enhanced meaning orgasm takes on when it occurs with a partner, a woman with a sexual self is her own best lover first.

Masturbation is an activity that can help a woman to develop a sexual self. The idea that solo orgasms are inferior keeps many women from fully appreciating the pleasures of masturbation, and they choose to go without any sex at all rather than to have sex alone. They wait to find a partner who will give them orgasms, rather than taking responsibility for themselves in sex. A woman is kept from becoming sexually independent and from growing sexually because she believes, "I have a partner. I don't need to masturbate." Masturbation allows a woman to have a sex life and orgasms whether or not she has a partner.

The Orgasm Race

Men are thought to be sexual sprinters; women are long-distance runners. The immediacy and urgency of men's sexual style matches a U.S. temperament that values speed and aggression. Women's greater endurance in sex is rarely praised. Instead, it is seen as a problem. Women's slow and steady sexual style is taken as evidence that they are less sexual than men. Women always lose when sex is measured in categories designed for men.

The reason men are faster to come is that sex is organized in their favor. Men's orgasm is the primary goal of sex. Women are encouraged to stay apace of men's arousal but this is difficult given the context: Women and men are partnered in sex as a two-person relay race. The woman is the starter who warms up and sets things in motion. When she is at her own top speed, the man takes the baton into his own hands. Her energy and excitement give him momentum and inspire him to race across the sexual finish line to orgasm. The woman never gets to break the final ribbon when she is solely concerned with passing that baton to her partner. Her mind cannot concentrate on her own pleasure. All she can think about is, "I'd better hurry and get this baton (pleasure) to him." But if she is so distracted that she cannot give her own best performance, both partners lose the race.

Men are sometimes told to slow down in sex, but because they worry that they will lose their erection, some men rush to orgasm and ejaculation. With equal amounts of practice, both women and men can learn to go as fast or slow as they like. The pleasure of orgasms can be enhanced by maintaining a high level of arousal over a longer period of time. When women and men attempt to make sexual timing complementary (with women enjoying orgasms in quickies and men able to play for hours and have multiple orgasms), both discover that getting there is far more than half the fun.

The Timing of Sex

As we have seen, sex that goes according to a male clock deprives women of pleasure. But it also robs men of multiple and more intense orgasms. A man may not be aware that ejaculation and orgasm can take place independently of one another. A man may be cheating himself out of more intense or multiple orgasms because he is heeding the pressure to ejaculate, the event the sexual culture treats as the high point of sex.

Heterosexuals spend an average of only fifteen minutes for sex, which is not enough time to build up a high level of arousal. Expanding sex to an hour or more would give both partners greater opportunity for fun. Taking more time for sex can mean it happens less often, but the actual frequency of sex is less important than its quality. In fact, having sex only once a week— or even less often—can allow for great excitement as the anticipation of pleasure intensifies sexual enjoyment. For many people, one luxurious sex session once a week is more satisfying (and more manageable) than a nightly routine of rushed intercourse. When women's orgasms are included, sex can alternate between mutually orgasmic quickies and longer, more relaxed sexual encounters.

People vary in their opinion of which time of day is best for sex. Most people have sex at night because that is when they are in bed, but it is also when they are most tired. Setting aside a morning or afternoon when they are more energetic can make sex a special treat. What time of the week or month partners choose often depends on life's other demands. It also depends on body rhythms. For example, any time there is increased blood flow to the genitals a woman may be more in the mood for sex. Many women's desire rises just before or during menstruation and often during pregnancy. After childbirth, a woman may be thinking about her new baby and her sore body, but her flushed genitals want sexual release. Levels of desire are also influenced by environmental and social factors. Women and men feel like sex when they are happy and respond with an increased sense of verve after winning the lottery, getting a promotion at work, or getting off the plane in Bermuda. Good times foster good sex, and good sex enhances good times.

Masturbation: Practice Makes Pleasure

Partner sex requires coordinating schedules with an intimate other; sex for one is far more convenient and can be highly satisfying. Masturbation is treated as the poor relation of partner sex, even though it offers many benefits to women. Masturbation reminds a woman that orgasms come from their own efforts. They are not something a woman seeks from a partner, nor are they a gift bestowed or withheld by him or her. When a woman realizes that she is responsible for her own orgasms, it takes great pressure off the relationship and her partner. Masturbation becomes a sex act to be enjoyed in its own right.

The key to orgasm is practice. Masturbation provides the opportunity for a woman to learn to orgasm without worrying about having to please another person at the same time. From the age of puberty men diligently masturbate. That is one reason why men have orgasms more easily than women. Men are not inherently more orgasmic, but they do get a lot more practice. Think of learning to play the piano or ride a bike. It does not happen overnight because it takes time to train the body and mind. But with practice comes results, whether in music, biking, or sex. The 1994 U.S. sex survey researchers suggest that, "The more often people masturbate, the more likely they are to report experiencing orgasm when masturbating." Women can also practice learning to ejaculate without worry about what her partner will think or how wet she gets the bed.

As we have seen, men reach orgasm more quickly than women because their clitoris and the urethra are stimulated at the same time when their penis is embraced by the vagina during intercourse. Women can also come quickly and easily when their orgasmic crescent is caressed. This can be easily accomplished once women and their partners become aware of her genital map. What is more, with time and practice—including practice at masturbation—women's bodies may actually begin to grow nerves and capillaries between the separate parts, increasing blood flow and nerve impulses and making orgasm easier.

The difference in how much stimulation women and men usually receive may also explain why women and men seem to experience a different aftermath to orgasm. When a woman has a less intense orgasm, she often wants to keep going and feels energized. The man's orgasm combined with ejaculation makes him want to sleep. One woman told us, "My experience always is, you have sex, he comes, and if you're lucky, you come too. And then he goes to sleep and you're waiting, thinking, 'Come on, let's keep going.' I just got my interest going around about the time he starts to snore." The man may feel depleted because he ejaculates. Some women describe feeling similarly satisfied and relaxed, and even fall asleep, after receiving the kind of intense stimulation that leads to a powerful orgasm.

Women who masturbate regularly reach orgasm easily. Clearly, the orgasm gap they may encounter in partner sex is not a problem intrinsic to a woman or her partner but a problem in the way heterosexual sex is defined and carried out.

With the knowledge a woman gains from masturbation, women can begin to change sex. Once a woman learns how her body responds through masturbation, she can better explain to her partner what she wants and likes. Partner sex is more fun and playful when she knows she is not dependent on her lover for orgasms. Because they make her more sexually independent, solo orgasms also give a woman the strength and self-confidence to force open a dialog with a partner who has yet to learn that sex is learned.

Many Roads to Orgasm

Women and men share a similar physical capacity for orgasmic sex: Both have a clitoris, a prostate gland, and erectile tissue around the urethra. Both are sensitive at the perineum and anus. Both experience erection and may lubricate, women vaginally and men with pre-ejaculate. Both are capable of orgasm, but because the sexual culture does not make women's roads to orgasm obvious, nor is it built into the standard way heterosexuals have sex, women get trapped in the orgasm gap. By reinventing sex,

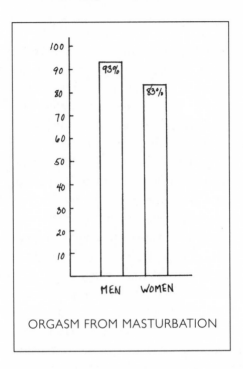

ORGASM FROM MASTURBATION

women can reveal to themselves and others that there are many paths to female pleasure.

Orgasms from Clittage

Women easily reach orgasm with masturbation because it involves clittage. Both women and men need continuous and rhythmic clitoral stimulation to have an orgasm, but each requires a slightly different kind of touch. Most men enjoy pressure against their penis, while women tend to prefer a massaging of their clitoral tip. In both solo and partner sex, clittage can be performed with either lubricated fingers or a vibrator. Most women like a gentle and slow start, but once erect, they often

ONE OR TWO ROADS TO ORGASM?

TRADITIONAL VIEW

Woman	*Man*
Wetness	Erection
Intercourse	
Orgasm?	Orgasm!

NEW VIEW

Both

Lube

Manual, oral, and genital-to-genital stimulation

Erection

Orgasm!

want more pressure and a faster pace. As a woman nears orgasm, rhythm and continuity become crucial.

U Spot Clittage

Because of its location near the clitoris, the U spot may benefit indirectly from clittage. When the external part of a woman's orgasmic crescent is touched by the fingers, a tongue, or a vibrator, both her U spot and the tip of her clitoris receive massage. In both women and men, stimulating the urethral opening (the U spot or head of the penis), arouses the erectile tissue along the length of the urethra. Some women ejaculate from clittage that includes U spot stimulation, because the G spot, which is adjacent to the urethra, becomes aroused.

Vibrating Clittage

The main sexual use of a vibrator is to stimulate the clitoris, but many people believe that vibrators are stand-ins for the penis and meant for vaginal penetration. As more women buy them and learn to use them properly, the word is getting out that a vibrator's first sexual use is to provide clittage. (The vagina is not best stimulated by vibration but by pressure.)

Vibrators come in many sizes, shapes, and types. There are heavy-duty plug-in types for long sessions and portable battery-operated purse-size junior vibrators for travel and spur-of-the-moment pick-me-ups. Battery-operated dildo-shaped vibrators are usually sold as novelty items. The best for clittage are plug-in types because they provide strong, continuous vibration. For women who like simultaneous penetration, there are novelty two-armed vibrators that work simultaneously inside and out. One arm penetrates while the other is a suspended "tickler" (often in the shape of a friendly animal) for the clitoris.

Dildos are for penetration. They come in a wide variety of shapes, sizes, and colors. Vibrators and dildos can be ordered by mail or purchased at a woman-friendly sex-toy shop. Although vibrators can be off-putting to a newcomer, most women quickly warm to their power. Once a woman has discovered the handy pleasures of her vibrator, she won't want to leave home without it. One woman told us she ran out to buy a new vibrator on a recent business trip when she realized she had left hers behind.

Many women like to combine vibrator clittage with penetration. While stimulating the clitoris with the vibrator, they use a dildo or a specially curved attachment to press against the G spot. Some women also combine vibrator clittage with anal penetration. Anal penetration should be done only with a dildo with a flared end so that it will not get lost. The combination of any kind of penetration and a vibrator gives the whole cligeva a thorough workout.

Vibrators are not only for solo sex. Vibrator clittage can make intercourse go quickly from ho-hum to hummingly. Vibrators also add electricity to all kinds of partner sex. One woman whose partner was slow to get interested in sex, told us that rather than wait for him, she uses a vibrator to turn herself on first, and her excitement helps get her partner in the mood.

Some men fear that vibrators make them redundant. One woman reported that she used a vibrator during intercourse and had one of the best orgasms she had ever experienced. But her partner was not pleased and did not want her to use it again. He felt threatened that the vibrator offered her a more powerful orgasm than he could. One male student voiced the same concern to us. "How can I compete with a vibrator?" he asked. Many men think of the vibrator as an oversized penis that can go forever. Women explain to their male partners that the vibrator is not a substitute for them or their penis. By making it clear that women use the vibrator to stimulate their clitoris, not for penetration, a man takes a step toward unlearning the myth that only the penis can make a woman come. Instead, a man learns that clittage, whether with an ever-ready hand or a vibrator, is the key to a woman's enjoyment. His frisky fingers, with their infinite variety of speeds and motions, can keep up with and easily surpass a vibrator when a man learns how to use them. He also has the backup of another set of fingers (as well as the woman's own) and his tongue.

Clittage Intercourse

Partners can make intercourse orgasmic for both of them by adding clittage. Clittage intercourse combines clitoral stimulation with deep internal stimulation of the cligeva. This brings a woman to orgasm with the pleasurable feeling of connection that comes from intercourse. Clittage intercourse allows the woman to maintain her erection through intercourse. With fingers on the clitoris, she can control the level of her arousal and, when she wants to, take herself over the edge to orgasm. Clittage intercourse brings the external and internal parts of the cligeva together into orgasm. Clittage intercourse can transform the traditional one-way quickie into a mutually orgasmic adventure.

Cunnilingus: The New Gourmet Sex

Long the secret of success in lesbian sex, cunnilingus has become the darling of some young heterosexuals. The 1994 sex-survey researchers note that cunnilingus came into fashion because it could bring women to orgasm. They note, however, that, althought it has grown in popularity, oral sex in general "does not occupy the essential and defining role that vaginal intercourse does in the sexual event for heterosexuals." In other words, oral sex is still optional, and when cunnilingus is performed, it may not always take a woman all the way to orgasm. Instead, it is treated as foreplay, an appetizer to the main dish of intercourse. Many women say they want more foreplay, by which they usually mean more cunnilingus and other direct clitoral stimulation. Making cunnilingus to orgasm a staple of sex rather than a rare treat would expand and enhance the choices on women's sexual menu.

Going for the G Spot

After clittage or cunnilingus makes the cligeva erect, a woman's G spot becomes fully sensitive to the stroke of fingers, a curved dildo, or the head of a penis. Because the G spot is felt along the front vaginal wall, fingers are most effective for reaching it. (Most penises are not curved enough to reach the G spot, and if a man goes in too far or at the wrong angle, he will bypass it entirely.) To engage in G spotting, a woman's partner uses latex-covered and lubricated fingers and begins with clittage, and then follows the orgasmic crescent inside the vagina, around the curve of the pubic bone, then in, up, and forward to the G spot.

Once a woman knows where it is and what it feels like, she and a male partner can try G spotting with the penis. The woman's cligeva should first be erect. She may lie on her back with her hips raised by pillows and either pull her legs up against her chest or straddle his neck or waist. This helps her to angle the head of the penis toward the front wall of her vagina. Rear entry intercourse with the penis angled down can also hit the G spot. A woman may experience a powerful orgasm from G spotting, and also ejaculate.

Caressing the Orgasmic Crescent

A woman and her partner can combine clittage with G spotting and engage the whole orgasmic crescent. A partner may either use one hand to slide from the clitoris, past the U spot, and into the G spot and back, or use both hands simultaneously on the orgasmic crescent—one at the G spot, the other providing clittage. Caressing the crescent can also be done with a vibrator on the clitoris and and dildo or fingers on the G spot. The orgasmic power of caressing the crescent is demonstrated in a not-so-farfetched parody by Annie Sprinkle in her video, *Sluts and Goddesses.*

Camping at the Cul-de-Sac

Orgasm ensures erection, and erection brings the cligeva to life. When the cligeva swells with blood and its muscles become taut, the first third of the vagina tightens and becomes sensitive to friction and pressure. The PC muscle contracts and brings the midvaginal walls into contact or against any stimulus present in the vagina. In the upper or back third of the vagina, the cervix lifts up, creating a tentlike area known as the cul-de-sac.

After orgasm, most women find that there is nothing they want more than vaginal penetration. They want to feel a penis or dildo against their engorged vaginal walls. They want to contract their PC muscle around something firm. They may want the head of the penis to stroke their G spot. Orgasm makes the cligeva fully erect, and causes the cul-de-sac to tent up and become highly sensitive to the head of the man's penis, which fits snugly into place there. As they rock together, a woman and a man can enjoy what is perhaps the most intimate erotic embrace possible.

Orgasm and the Cligeva

> What we want is *everything* being stimulating effectively so we have our best orgasm. . . . Who would want to make a choice between either/or? I want it all!
>
> —BETTY DODSON

We have suggested the term *cligeva* as a word and concept to describe women's genital whole. By seeing the female genitals as a whole, a woman can make and enhance the connections that bring on orgasm. By emphasizing the three most sensitive areas of the genitals, the term *cligeva* reminds women of the interconnection of their genital parts. The cligeval whole is greater than the sum of its parts. Erection makes the G spot, vagina, anus, and other areas become more sensitive to stimulation. The more parts that are stimulated, the more intense the orgasm. When the whole cligeva is erect, it is primed for an orgasm that can transport a woman to a new dimension of pleasure. Her ecstasy can reach a spiritual level, to the point of feeling, as one women told us, "I don't just see God, I *am* God."

Orgasm or Bust?

It is controversial to suggest that women make orgasms a goal of sex. Sex educators fear that setting up such a goal will make women anxious and more likely to fail, actually diminishing the pleasure of sex in the process. Men endure anxiety about sexual performance, yet no one protects them from the consequences of failure.

In our view, it is patronizing to protect women from feeling bad about not having orgasms, especially since it is not their fault. As more women realize that sex can be orgasmic when it is oriented to their own pleasure, they can more appropriately place the blame where it belongs—with the sexual culture. Cathy Winks and Anne Semans write in *The Good Vibrations Guide to Sex,* "Orgasms are a simple pleasure which we'd all benefit from taking less seriously." But orgasms are not simple for many women. Rather than giving less attention to orgasm, women would fare better by boldly asserting their right to pleasure equality.

Orgasmic Mystery Solved!

Until recently, getting information about how to have an orgasm was like piecing together the clues of a great mystery. Sex educator and writer Carol Queen told us of her first efforts as a teenager to learn about sex:

I figured out from a women's magazine that there was such a thing as orgasm. I figured out from the context in which it was discussed that it was a desirable thing, that I might like to have one or more than one, but where to get them I had no idea because I didn't know what they were. . . . Orgasm is talked about as though we all understand what that means but if you haven't had that experience how are we going to know?

A woman we know in her forties tells us she had orgasms as a child but that when she looked up *orgasm* in the dictionary, it was defined as "convulsions." She did not connect that definition with what she experienced, but she remembers thinking she did not want to have orgasms if they were like having a seizure.

Young women are now more likely to get the message that orgasms are fun, but they are still unlikely to be told how to have one. A woman could easily become frustrated with the magazine articles, books, and sex classes that offer no guide to exactly where, what, and how the body needs to be touched to make orgasm happen. It is a credit to female perseverance that, against all odds, many women who make the effort eventually *do* learn to have orgasms. The only difference between women who learn and those who do not is that orgasmic women decide to take their sexuality into their own hands. A lot of practice (and a little lube) are the ingredients to "going all the way" to orgasm. A woman can develop the art of sex as she cultivates any other skill or craft: by gathering the needed equipment, learning the techniques, and getting lots of practice.

Three Keys to Orgasm

Making sex orgasmic for all women means breaking with the arbitrary prescriptions of the sexual culture and getting physical about sex in a new way. Making sex orgasmic for women means grounding sex in the body. Once a woman has an image of the whole cligeva, she can experiment with techniques that are most appropriate to female anatomy.

The three keys to orgasm are:

- lubrication
- manual sex
- erection

Lubrication

The road to orgasm, including intense and multiple orgasms, is paved smooth with lubrication. Once a woman and her partner use bottled lubricant they will wonder what they ever did without it. Affectionately called *lube,* this water-based commercial product is the biggest boon to women's orgasms since fingers. Water-based lube has a slippery consistency that allows two surfaces to slide smoothly against each other. Instead of irritating the sensitive clitoral tip or tugging on the labia during intercourse, a partner's hand or penis can glide smoothly along the orgasmic crescent or into the vagina.

Lube can be used regardless of whether or not a woman's vagina gets wet. It can be used on all parts of the orgasmic crescent and can be reapplied or refreshed with a spray of water. Lubricant makes longer sex sessions—and multiple orgasms—possible because sex can continue without irritation. It can make quickie sex—indeed, any kind of sex—more likely to lead to orgasm because it makes clittage go more smoothly. Lubricant is also essential for safer sex. It must be the water-based type that keeps latex barriers effective.

Manual Sex

If women replace the intercourse imperative with the manual sex imperative (for it *is* one of the few essentials of sex), they can easily bridge the orgasm gap. Manual sex is one of the finest and most convenient ways to provide effective clitoral stimulation. The fingers are magnificent sexual appendages. Experienced clittage with a lubricated, latex-gloved hand or cot-covered finger (a cot is a finger-sized condom) can quickly make a woman erect and arouse her to orgasm. Clittage can be done in combination with G spotting or penetration. It can be performed by either partner. With one hand on her clitoris, a woman can take control of her own orgasms.

Erection

Women's erection prepares her genitals for orgasm. Yet, it is difficult to grasp the idea of women's genital erection since the sexual culture defines erection by what happens to a man's penis. But if erection can be seen as something other than the mounting of a skyscraper and likened in women's case to a rich croissant filled with good things and hot from the oven, the concept can work for both sexes.

Know It and Grow It

Just as muscles grow stronger and bigger with use and the brain grows sharper with mental activity, the genitals grow more sensitive to pleasure and more able to reach orgasm when they are regularly stimulated. The genitals work better the more they are used. In a positive twist of the "use it or lose it" axiom, we say "know it and grow it." Exploring and engaging the whole cligeva not only improves muscle tone, but also encourages the growth of blood vessels in the area and trains a woman's nerves to send messages of pleasure more efficiently. The more a woman stimulates her cligeva, the greater its sensitivity and the more intense her orgasms.

A woman can also "grow" the feelings and awareness of other internal parts of the cligeva. Once she has experienced erection, a woman may become aware of a feeling at her cervix when erection causes it to tent or lift up, opening a new space for pleasure. The cul-de-sac also responds to the pressure of penetration, and this stimulation can produce orgasms that some women describe as deep, whole-body orgasms.

Multiple Orgasms

Sex is not a competition and no one needs to keep score. In sex that focuses on pleasure, what counts is not the number of orgasms but the feeling of satisfaction. But it is important for women to know that they are capable of having more than one orgasm in a sexual encounter. For many women, it takes more than one orgasm to feel satisfied. A woman may have enough after one big orgasm, several small ones, or any combination thereof. What matters is not the type, size, or number of orgasms, however, but the feeling of sexual satisfaction.

Satisfying sex is more likely for women when sex lasts more than the fifteen-minute average. Whereas coming to orgasm quickly can be an exciting experience, delaying orgasm and letting erotic tension build up can increase its quality and intensity.

Coming Together

When a man can control ejaculation and a woman controls her orgasm, heterosexual couples can meet halfway and enjoy their last orgasm together. Simultaneous orgasms can be a powerfully bonding sexual and emotional experience. Sex experts, however, warn against setting up simultaneous orgasm as a goal. Yet skilled lovers increase the likelihood that it can occur when they learn how to be in control of their own pleasure. In heterosexual sex, a man who knows how to delay his ejaculation can readily allow a "lady" to go "first." In our opening scene, Joe waited until Nikki was ready for her last orgasm, then came with her. Whether coming together is desired or not, increasing sexual skill and body awareness can enhance the mutuality of any two partners' pleasure.

Female Ejaculation

Female ejaculation is a sexual experience that some women stumble upon and others cultivate. Some women may want to learn to develop the ability to ejaculate. Others find the whole notion unappealing and find even the mention of female ejaculation distasteful. Yet the sexual culture fully accepts and acknowledges the same phenomenon in men, and for women who do ejaculate, it is the source of great sexual pleasure.

In ejaculation, a woman enjoys a sense of release that is distinct from orgasm. Ejaculation occurs from stimulating the sexual parts surrounding the urethra in sex. The G spot, U spot, and the spongiosum are all sexual parts that are linked to the urethra. One woman says she ejaculated for the first time with a vibrator on high speed. Although she applied it to her clitoris, the vibrator stimulated her whole cligeva, including her G spot via the U spot. Most women ejaculate by stimulating their G spot

MULTIPLE ORGASMS FOR MEN

People often fail to distinguish between orgasm and ejaculation in men. But in both women and men, orgasm and ejaculation are two separate events. Men who learn to control ejaculation can prolong sexual activity and experience multiple orgasms.

By slowly building up to and then pulling back from the brink of ejaculation several times, a man begins to identify the point of no return and learns to pull back and postpone it. By staying at a high level of arousal for a longer period of time, he also can intensify his orgasms. After one or more orgasms, a man can reach orgasm for the last time with ejaculation when his partner is ready for her final orgasm.

One technique for learning to be multiply orgasmic is the stop-start technique. Just before ejaculation seems inevitable, a man reduces or stops genital stimulation. He has an orgasm, but does not ejaculate. Another method is the "squeeze technique." A man can press his penis below the glans between his thumb and forefinger to prevent ejaculation. A man can also stop the flow of ejaculate by contracting his PC muscles tightly.

Many of the timing problems of traditional sex are eliminated when men slow down. When two people spend more time having sex by postponing intercourse and extending the time before the man's ejaculation, both partners have a better chance of coming in their own time and on their own terms.

with fingers or a dildo, usually combined with clitoral stimulation. At the point of ejaculation, most women use their PC muscle to push out and the ejaculate spurts from their urethra like a fountain.

Women who ejaculate typically have strong PC muscles. The more a woman stimulates her genitals, the stronger her muscles get and the more she "grows" the cligeva as a sexual organ. In

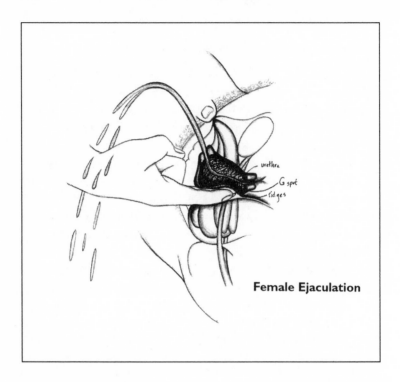

Female Ejaculation

their book *Ultimate Pleasure: The Secrets of Easily Orgasmic Women,* Marc and Judith Meshorer quote one woman who ejaculates frequently and forcefully. She describes the importance of being erect from orgasm first.

> I usually need clitoral contact for my first orgasm. . . . After the first, my vagina and my clitoris and everything's more sensitive, and it's easier to orgasm again. At least once every time we have intercourse, at some orgasm, my muscles all contract and contract and contract and this fluid pushes out like a man's ejaculation. . . . It always happens at least once, and sometimes more than once, at the beginning, middle, or end of a session. I've sprayed five feet and soaked my husband's feet.

Ejaculation usually occurs right before, during, or just after an orgasm. A woman may have several orgasms and then ejaculate, or have an ejaculatory orgasm (she ejaculates and has an orgasm at the same time). If her orgasm is especially intense, a woman may feel as spent as many men do after they come. But if ejaculation occurs by itself, a woman will want to continue to orgasm. Fanny Fatale's video, *How to Female Ejaculate,* describes the phenomenon and includes a demonstration by four women who masturbate to ejaculation and orgasm. One of the women explains that she taught herself to ejaculate, while others first experienced it inadvertently during G spot stimulation.

All women may have the capacity to ejaculate once they know how. The likely reason that only a small number of women do it is that women, unlike men, do not spend years practicing ejaculation through masturbation because the sexual culture does not tell them this is possible. Most women and girls do not even know that ejaculation can occur in women, which makes women who do experience it feel embarrassed or ashamed. They believe they are lubricating excessively or urinating. When women get to know their cligeva and "grow it" by stimulating it, they may develop their capacity for ejaculation. When the sexual culture acknowledges female ejaculation, more women will enjoy—without shame or concern—their fountains of pleasure.

Some women may be concerned that female ejaculation sounds like yet one more sexual hoop for women to jump through. Although ejaculation is not necessary for a woman's sexual satisfaction, it is one more pleasure she can cultivate once she has the information and an adequate framework for understanding her genitals. She also needs a sexual culture that is oriented to providing women and men alike with pleasure.

Both individually and as a group, women are moving into a new erotic frontier. Instead of dismissing any new pleasure she

THE ACCOUTREMENTS OF ORGASMIC SEX:
A BASIC BEDSIDE SEX KIT

An orgasmic sex environment can be created by a combination of comfort and equipment. Basic equipment includes: a vibrator, dildo, water-based lubrication, condoms, latex gloves or finger cots to protect both partners in manual sex, and latex barriers for cunnilingus, either dental dams (latex sheets like the ones dentists use, available in pharmacies) or plastic wrap. (Those who are allergic to latex should explore alternatives, such as vinyl gloves.) A small spray bottle for water can be kept beside the bed to revive lube when it gets tacky. Massage oil for nongenital skin can add to overall pleasure and provide tactile excitement, muscle relaxation, and an aromatic environment.

Having towels on hand is essential for a woman who ejaculates. The towel should be folded under her to avoid soaking the sheets. Pillows are needed to raise the woman's hips for better G spot stimulation during man-on-top intercourse.

Some people choose their bedroom furniture—even all their home decor—with good sex in mind. The bed needs to be fairly high for rear entry or man-on-top intercourse in which the man is standing and the woman lies or kneels on the bed. A couch or a rocking chair can be used for sitting position intercourse and for cunnilingus. For the more adventurous, a hammock or suspended chair allows a woman to float as she enjoys cunnilingus.

encounters, a woman can decide for herself which sexual paths to explore and feel free to follow her own curiosity. All a woman needs to get started is a fresh perspective on the body and a Basic Bedside Sex Kit. She has nothing to lose and everything to gain.

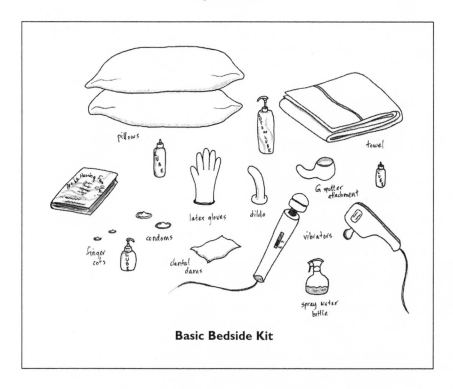

Basic Bedside Kit

Closing the Orgasm Gap

Pleasure is the primary reason to have sex, and one of the finest pleasures of sex is orgasm. Orgasm is like a carefree and refreshing week-long vacation concentrated into a moment of bliss (and with none of the time, expense, or inconvenience of actual travel!). Mae West believed in "an orgasm a day." Most of us believe we cannot give the same daily attention to sex as the Hollywood star once did, yet we spend time on other less enriching activities: Is sex less entertaining than watching a B-movie on video? Is it less important than spending three hours every two weeks at a hair salon?

Sex belongs in a balanced and healthy life. All it takes is for a woman to decide that she wants it. Rather than an orgasm a day, however, the motto should be, *an orgasm every time* a woman wants one, whether in masturbation or in partner sex.

Orgasm can be within every woman's reach when she develops her cligeva by knowing it and growing it into an erect whole. A woman can make sex better than cake or ice cream (not to mention warm oatmeal) when it includes her orgasm(s). Sex is sex only when two partners share its orgasmic pleasures.

CHAPTER EIGHT

A Lingo for Love

"Touch me here. Yeah, there. A little more to the left. Aah, yes. Gently . . . Now a bit faster . . . Ooh, that feels good. Can you put your fingers inside? Right there. Mmmm . . . Yes, yes, yes. A little harder. That's it. Don't stop!"

The Other Oral Sex

To communicate sexually, partners need to communicate verbally. Nikki and Joe now enjoy great sex because, both inside and beyond the bedroom, they have learned how to talk. They do not always talk during sex, but neither of them hesitates to say what they want, or to tell the other when "a little more to the left" could make sex feel so much better. They also tell the other when something feels especially nice. As a result, every time they have sex, it is as good or better than the time before.

Good lovers are made, not born. They are made through practice and through thinking and talking about sex. Being able to talk allows two lovers to grow sexually as they bond emotionally. Sex should get better and better as a relationship matures, but for many people it stagnates because they do not talk. Even the closest of partners cannot read one another's mind, yet many people act as if they expect their partner to magically sense what they want. Yet lovers who can ask for what they want during sex are not only more likely to receive—and to give—orgasmic pleasure, but more likely to enhance intimacy.

Sometimes chemistry makes sex good from the start of a relationship. But even a relationship that starts off with so-so sex can grow into something superb if both partners are willing to communicate. Good communication is also the key to making a sexual relationship endure. There is no need for sex to become tedious, even for two people who have been together for decades, as long as there is communication and interest in sexual growth.

Speaking openly and honestly is an essential ingredient of good sex. Sex talk is more than the *ooh, baby* or *give it to me* that people sometimes use to spice up sexual play. It is also that highly erotic form of verbal communication that tells a partner she or he is doing something right. The right words get us in the mood for sex. The cooler words of affection that follow sex enhance intimacy. Sex talk, words well chosen and gracefully timed, can lubricate the wheels of sexual passion.

Some women and men have sex in silence as if words would break the enchantment of the moment. While appropriate and desirable at times, silence about sex can cause a relationship to wither and may prevent partners from discovering new pleasures. Sexual silence *must* be broken if there is to be safer sex and sex that avoids unwanted pregnancy. Not talking about sex also permits pop porn and other negative influences of the sexual culture to define sex for women and their partners instead of letting an erotic language grow organically from two partners' own experiences.

. . .

Breaking the Silence

Instead of mouthing love lyrics like a karaoke singer, women can get into the practice of speaking from their own minds and hearts about sex and desire. If a woman does not express her desires to her partner, she becomes an audience for the man's sexual performance rather than fully participating as one of two lovers in an erotic conversation. Getting the sex conversation started can be awkward and difficult for women, because the words that describe female pleasure do not yet exist. In order for women to break the sexual silence, they first need to create a new language for sex. A more equal language for sex can give voice to women's pleasure and encourage the kind of communication that enhances both lovers' enjoyment. That language will emerge as women explore sex on their own terms.

Talking about sex is an important part of enabling women and men to close the orgasm gap. Women and men would also benefit if there were similar conversations about sex going on in the wider sexual culture. Women need to see sex represented in a way that reflects their lives, their bodies, and their experience. They need to feel that it is alright to talk to both lovers and friends about sex. They need an environment that encourages them to develop a sexual self, and to encourage men to think about and talk more openly about sex.

For most women, however, sex is not now a topic of conversation with either partners or friends. Women talk about sex even less than they think about it, which survey researchers report is not very often—on average less than once a week. Few women ever talk to friends, perhaps not even to sex partners, about more than the generalities of sex. They are unlikely to exchange ideas, experiences, or information about the details of oral sex, for example, or about how they like to have orgasm, or about what protection they use for safer sex. These issues are seen as either too intimate or too embarrassing to discuss. A person may fear that others will find out she does not have orgasms, even though this problem is a direct result of the silence around sex.

Sexual silence leaves a vacuum that fills with the negative vocabulary and narrow vision of pop-porn sex. That the words for sex are "bad" words reflects the culture's deep discomfort with sexuality. There is plenty of talk about sex in the culture, but most of it is not the kind of talk that enhances a woman's sexual self. Depriving young people of sex-positive, woman-friendly information only puts them in harm's way. And among adults (who need continuing sex education), there is very little frank talk about the best techniques for sex especially when compared to the attention given to other activities and hobbies such as cooking or car repair, even though many people have at least as much need—indeed, some have an urgent need—for helpful advice on the subject.

A new voice about sex is now being heard—that of women's health activists and AIDS prevention educators. Also offering fresh perspectives on sex are sex columnists in regional weekly papers and in some women's magazines. TV shows like *Seinfeld* and *Sex and the City* have made masturbation, oral sex, and women's pleasure the focus of entire episodes. This public discussion may help to spur private conversations about sex.

Silence in the Bedroom

Most lovers avoid sex talk altogether, especially when they are in the bedroom. They avoid the subject because they feel that words will spoil romance and eroticism. They are also simply not in the habit of speaking explicitly about sex. During sex may be the worst time to discuss a sexual problem, but it is the best time to communicate desire. It can be a time to learn, too. Men who are taught to feel they should be born lovers may be reluctant to ask questions or take instruction from their partner. Women may refrain from offering suggestions to a man because they fear offending him. This combination is the perfect recipe for bad sex.

In the view of many social conservatives, the less people know and the less they talk about sex, the better. They seem to think the silence about sex means that people are not having it. Yet the less people talk about sex in the culture and with their partner, the more risky sex becomes for all, but especially for women. Unwanted pregnancy is seen by some as just punishment for sin but it is only teenage girls and their children (but not their babies' fathers) who pay its wages. A shaming and punitive attitude about sex has a devastatingly powerful impact on public policy, affecting people's access to birth control and to safer sex education. Research conclusively shows that teenage girls have lower rates of unwanted pregnancy when they have access to education. Safer sex education has been crucial to slowing the spread of HIV. That campaign has had an impressive impact despite the efforts of sexual reactionaries and other forces to limit funding for AIDS research and prevention.

Conservative, antisex groups are just part of a much larger problem of the sexual culture. They are to the sexual culture as pornography is to pop porn—not necessarily the greatest danger to safer and better-quality sex, just the most obvious one. Indeed, pornography and "dirty" sex are the flip side of prudery And just as pop porn may ultimately have a more pernicious effect overall than pornography, the most extreme anti-sex groups are only one voice (albeit a vociferous and well-financed one) in a generally prudish mainstream U.S. culture that pushes all frank discussion of sex underground. They are powerful because they fill a vacuum that the majority of Americans leave empty when they remain silent about sex.

Sanitizing Sex and "Talking Dirty"

> In America sex is an obsession, in other parts of the world it
> is a fact.
>
> —MARLENE DIETRICH

Many people avoid broaching the subject of sex directly. Instead
they use euphemisms in polite company and "talk dirty" for humorous or erotic effect. Euphemism and talking dirty are two
sides of the same repressive coin. People resort to using either
euphemism ("making love") or slang ("fucking") because the
sexual culture provides no adequate way to talk seriously (but
not drearily) and accurately (but without using clinical language)
about sexual fun. Both extremes fail to get at the heart of sex
for most people. Euphemism is inappropriate mostly because it
is inaccurate. Is it "making love" if, for example, a woman has
sex with someone with whom she is only "in like?" Have you
"slept" with someone when neither of you closed your eyes at
all?

A related type of sanitized sex talk is the clinical language of
the medical profession and sexologists. Medical terms, usually
in Latin, have an air of authority and seem to provide a neutral,
descriptive language for sex. Yet many of these terms are actually words that disparage women's bodies or silently perpetuate
the view that sex is as natural as breathing. Medical language also
emphasizes pathology, not sexual health, and usually has little
to say about pleasure. Women can hardly rely on doctors as a
source of a language for sex. Most doctors locate the problem
of being "frigid" or "anorgasmic" within the individual woman's
body (or, more often, her psyche) rather than in society and the
sexual culture. Some women prefer to attend women-staffed and
women-oriented alternative health clinics because they feel that

in traditional health care settings, even a female doctor cannot always escape the reach of a medical training whose model and concepts are oriented to the male body.

Many people use sexual euphemisms and clinical language because they are uncomfortable with the other, more explicit language available to them: talking dirty. Most talk about sex uses slang, a language that seems casual but is also typically violent. For example, take the popular word *fuck*. Slang for sexual intercourse, *fuck* also means to be taken advantage of (get fucked), to be cheated (fucked over, also "screwed over"), to bother or harass (fuck with), to become drunk or high on drugs (fucked up), or to make a mistake (fuck up). You can even *be* a fuckup. "Fucking," especially if you are the one being "fucked" (that is, in the feminine role) does not sound like a position that gets a lot of respect or is a lot of fun. Yet women and men alike use the word both to describe something that is messed up and to talk about intercourse.

Yet, used properly, the word *fuck* can be fun, strong, and sexy. This one-syllable and percussive word is a verbal powerhouse that many women find exciting when used in the right context. The word carries a lot of power because to utter it is so taboo, especially for women. Talking dirty in a sexual context is a way some women free themselves from feelings of shame and guilt. Some women get an erotic charge from using words that are typically forbidden to "ladies." Such words give them a feeling of control in sex and a (false) sense of equality with men.

It is hard to reconcile the sexy uses of fuck from the violent ones. Although a woman may like the sound of dirty words when used in a playful way, it is hard to disregard the way they are linked with sexual violence and with disrespect for women. The same word a woman's partner may say to her during sex can be used in public by a man who wants to assert power over a woman.

The existing language for sex adds to men's social power because any man, no matter his age or status, can use dirty words to assault, bother, threaten, and intimidate women. A young woman was recently reminded of the power of both words and men when, as she bent over to pick up her toddler's picture book on a busy street corner, a panhandler commented that she had a "hot pussy." Weeks before the same words had been uttered to her by an obscene phone caller. A woman does not have the power to wield words against men in the same way. A woman who calls a man a "prick" delivers only a mild and humorous insult, not a threat (calling him a "hot dick" would sound like a compliment), and we cannot imagine a man being harassed by a woman on the telephone just because his voice is male.

A woman who is the target of dirty words often feels their effect long after they have been spoken. They may even infiltrate her experience of sex. Any woman who has "pussy" hurled at her by a stranger probably does not want to hear "pussy" whispered in her ear that evening by her lover. A woman who hears she is "frigid" cannot then easily peel off the label when she is in bed with her partner hoping to have some fun. Sexually belittling and controlling words are not a turn-on.

Women now may be more willing than ever to talk about sex, but when they finally open their mouths, they cannot find the words. They are silenced because there is no language for sex that seems to fit their own experience. In *Good Sex: Real Stories from Real People,* Amanda, a twenty-nine-year-old woman, tells author Julia Hutton:

> The language we use to describe sex is so hard-edged. It's either used in a derogatory way—"jerk someone off"—or it's so soft, "making love." Neither really describes what you're doing. The language bugs me. Nothing describes loving sexual acts without being clinical or vulgar. There's something to be said for reclaiming the vulgar language, but that doesn't really work, because the mainstream negative undertone is so pervasive.

Women and their friends need a new, more woman-friendly vocabulary. Many men are also uncomfortable with the language available to them for sex. Perhaps women and men together can come up with better ways of expressing their desires, not only by talking but also through the practice of sex.

Private Language

Just as families develop a vernacular of their own over a lifetime of experiences together, two lovers may develop their own language for sex. Part of getting to know a new lover is learning his or her sexual language, and gradually building an intimate vocabulary with that person. Having a personal name for the genitals or a favorite slang term for sex can be an affectionate way of bonding with a partner. Like nicknames, this vocabulary helps establish and reaffirm intimacy. However, private languages sometimes reflect the social imbalance in the sexual culture. That the names for men's genitals are more often those of a person, for example, while women's genitals are typically named after a fruit or a pet reflects how people expect male, but not female genitals, to be assertive personalities. As partners and friends begin to talk more openly, they can examine the inequality embedded in the current language for sex and begin to fashion their own alternatives.

A New Public Language for Sex

A new public language for sex cannot be handed down from on high, but emerges through active use. New words for sex will develop as changes take place among women and men in all their relations. When friends and lovers actually begin to talk to one another about sex, they will have to invent new words because no adequate vocabulary currently exists. When more people engage in sex talk, there is a greater chance that words will emerge that are neither derogatory nor so dry that they lose all sense of fun or sexual play. As more women gain a greater ease about talking to themselves, to each other, and to their partners about sex, a new lingo for love can develop organically from that conversation.

THE POWER OF CUNT: TWO PERSPECTIVES

The word *cunt* is perhaps the most hotly contested sexual term for women. Until a few centuries ago, the related word *cunnus* was the standard term for "vulva." Today the word has a meaning that vulva does not. The following excerpts demonstrate the power of this word and how women can put it to their own use.

Andrea Dworkin writes in her novel *Mercy:*

If I was famous and my name was published all over the world, in Italy and in Israel and in Africa and in India, on continents and subcontinents, in deserts, in ancient cities, it would still be cunt to every fucking asshole drunk on every street in the world; and to them that's not drunk too, the sober ones who say it to you like they're calling a dog: fetch, cunt. If I won the Nobel Prize and walked to the corner for milk it would still be cunt. And when you got someone inside you who is loving you it's still cunt . . . and your heartbeat and his heartbeat can be the same heartbeat and it's still cunt. . . .

My mother named me Andrea. It means manhood or courage. It means not-cunt. She specifically said: not-cunt. This one ain't cunt, she declared . . . [but] it failed . . . because before I was even ten some man had wrote "this one's cunt," he took his fingers and he wrote it down on me and inside me, his fingers carved it in me with a pain that stayed half buried and there wasn't words I had for what he did, he wrote I was

It's a Man's Word

Words we currently use to describe sexual behavior are gender-specific and unequal. For example, a woman who has many partners is a slut, while a man who sleeps around is a stud. A woman who eagerly seeks sex is a nymphomaniac; a man who has sex often has a healthy appetite. A promiscuous man is sometimes condemned publicly but privately admired by other

cunt, this sweet little one who was what's called child but a female one which changes it all. . . .

Pseudonymous writer Jane Air likes the word *cunt*. She describes an incident that occurred when she was a go-go dancer at a biker bar in Bridgeport, in her article "A Vindication of the Rights of Cunt."

I love CUNT. . . . Cunt has all the power of a magic word . . . in order to remain sane, it was very important that I act like a cunt, because that's really the only thing the guys in the bar would respect. . . . It meant holding my own and not playing the nice girl.

So I'm on stage and one of these guys says, as a little conversational gambit, "You really have an attitude, don't you?" He doesn't say it very nicely. Then he says, "You know what you are? You're a little cunt!" and he lunges at me. At which point the other dancer on the stage very coolly grabs a beer bottle and hits him over the head with it, thus taming his impulse (don't try this one at home). Luckily he came to his senses (losing consciousness can do that to guys) and things settled down.

When I asked my savior why she did what she did, she simply stated, "He called you a cunt," and went back to doing the splits for singles. The point here is that cunt is such a powerful word, with so many associations, that if it's used incorrectly it can set you off in all your feminine avenging fury. Now, don't you want a word like that, carefully and correctly used, at your fingertips?

men. The woman with multiple partners may be desirable to some men, but is admired by no one.

Some pro-sex feminists and other women hope to remake the language for sex by taking negative words like *cunt* and *fuck* and giving them new, positive meanings for women. Simply employing these words can have great political impact, because women typically do not use them. When women call themselves "bitch," for example, a word normally used as an insult, the sexual culture sits up and pays attention. If nothing else, this attempt at rehabilitation makes it obvious that until now, the language has not belonged to women.

To some women, words like *cunt* and *pussy* are beyond rehabilitation. They prefer coining new words that are free of emotional baggage. Other women and men think everyone has become oversensitive about language. They suggest that women should stop complaining and grow up. But expecting women to accept the verbal status quo begs the question of why women face verbal sexual abuse to begin with. Why is it that only a woman can be reduced to her genitals? Why is it that specifically *sexual* words are used to berate, control, or frighten her? It is difficult for women to freely use the language for sex when that language is so often used against them.

Women lack appropriate words for their experiences of sex and for their genitals. The absence of an adequate word for women's genitals as a whole contrasts with the list of proud terms for men's sexual appendage. Synonyms for a man's penis are words almost uniformly pointed, even cocky. Slang terms such as *cock* and *dick,* while vulgar, express confidence and pride of ownership. *Cock* (from British English for a "watercock" or faucet) evokes a rigid projection that spurts fluid, and *dick* (also slang for "detective") transforms the penis into a sexual agent that tracks down "pussies" for its own pleasure.

There is a sense that men's visible penis and testicles present a clear and complete genital whole in a way women's genitals do not. Of course, "penis" fails to take into account the prostate gland, PC muscle, and anus. Still, there is far less ambiguity and vagueness about where men can be touched for pleasure. Indecisiveness surrounds women's genitals, in contrast, and there is less attention paid to the clitoris than to the vagina in its role as the source of men's pleasure. Slang terms for the genitals of women and men alike reflect the male view and experience.

Some researchers who want to redefine women's genitals recognize the need for an all-inclusive term. For example, Sevely redefines the *vagina* to include all the parts that are capable of pleasure. The women of the Federation of Feminist Women's Health Centers underscore the importance of the clitoris to pleasure by calling all of women's genitals the *clitoris*. Some women call the genital whole the *vulva* because it is external and can therefore be seen and touched. But this term excludes important sexual parts that are internal. *Female genitals* seems like a neutral and inclusive term but does not distinguish between sexual and reproductive parts. Other all-encompassing names for women's genitals include the sexual-spiritual mix of the term *yoni,* a Sanskrit word which means "womb," "origin," and "source." This South Asian term reflects cultural and religious traditions that view female genitals as sacred symbols of the goddess. This is certainly a more positive portrayal of women's genitals than that in Western culture, but *yoni* is sometimes used to mean a spiritual transcendence over the sexual or to emphasize its role as the "gateway of life."

A useful name for women's genitals is one that would help women climb down from the sexual pedestal and get more concrete, more practical, and more specific about pleasure. The name we propose—the *cligeva*—emphasizes this practical goal. It also suggests how the clitoris, G spot, and vagina come together in erection and orgasm to form a whole. The term highlights the dynamic and unified character of the body parts that give women pleasure but have too long remained in the dark.

We offer *cligeva* in order to get women talking, debating, and exploring new words for sex. Linguist Julia Penelope calls reinventing language by and for women a "sifting process," for it is only through discussion and use that women will formulate the right words and establish a woman-centered language for a new sexuality.

Growing the Language

New words like *cligeva* (for the genital whole) and *clittage* (for clitoral stimulation) are intended to be simple, practical, and fun. These new words develop out of existing words without reproducing the old framework for sex. Some people use terms like *outercourse* for sex that avoids vagina-penis penetration, but this derivative word only reaffirms the centrality of intercourse. It makes nonpenetrative sex seem like a consolation prize for the real thing. We prefer to give the activities within outercourse names of their own. By specifically naming manual sex, for example, the practice gains an integrity of its own, and (as anyone who engages in it knows) it stands second to no other kind of sex.

Erection and some of the other terms we suggest are words that have been traditionally used to describe men's experience of sex. These words have the advantage of familiarity, and they point to the experiences that women and men share in sex. When a man hears that a woman also has an erection, he will understand that she experiences a process of arousal similar to his own, and that she no less than he needs to be erect before penetration can occur, he will also understand its importance for her orgasm. Similarly, identifying the man's clitoris inside the penis helps people recognize the importance of the woman's clitoris for her pleasure.

A new language for sex will make women's sexuality a legitimate part of the sexual culture rather than seeming a mere by-product of the actions of men. Women could use such a language to share experiences and information with one another. Women do not need more talk about sex that simply reinforces sex against desire, male-oriented pleasure, and a heterosexual norm of inequality. Talk about sex will improve women's experience of sex by disrupting the existing pop-porn culture of sex and creating a whole new framework for thinking about, talking about, and enjoying sex.

Starting the Conversation About Sex

Talking to Oneself

Changing the language for sex means creating words that make sexual sense to women. Once women have access to a language they feel describes their experience and that they find comfortable, they can begin to broach the subject of sex in their own minds. Becoming aware of desires, fears, questions, and concerns and articulating them to oneself is a beneficial exercise that can start a process of sexual growth. Women can name the physical sensations they feel, giving their experience legitimacy and enhancing its pleasures.

Talking to Friends

Women typically share intimacies with one another about their emotional lives and about relationships, but carefully skirt the issue of sex. Women do not confess even to a best friend about finding it difficult to have an orgasm, for example. They do not exchange information about how to find the G spot. They may not reveal their concern that they have engaged in sex against desire. When they talk about what they enjoy in sex, they are likely to avoid giving details and speak only in anonymous generalities.

There are several reasons sexual topics are avoided, including lack of habit, embarrassment, and fear of disapproval. Most people also consider sex a private issue and are reluctant to betray intimate details about themselves or, especially, their partner. Women can protect their partner's privacy by speaking instead about the way sex is portrayed in pop-porn movies or on TV. The important thing is to speak: It is a shame to waste the tremendous resource women have in one another. A person may not be able to talk sex with every woman she knows, but she can gradually open up the topic of sex with one or two close friends. When women start to say to each other, "I don't always come from intercourse but I do when I masturbate," they begin to chip away at sexual myths that keep women from good sex.

Women can learn how to talk about sex by following the motto of "each one, teach one." Women can benefit from having access to people and to environments where they feel free to talk about sex. Women can also learn from other women who have a healthy sexual self. Each woman who begins her own sex journey becomes a role model for other women.

Talking in Public

Breaking the silence is a powerful way to loosen the grip of pop-porn definitions of women's sexuality. Sometimes public figures are able to get an unmentionable topic or problem on the table. When Dr. Joycelyn Elders suggested that masturbation be a part of sex education, a few powerful people disapproved, but many other Americans were glad to hear someone finally speak frankly and realistically about sex.

Women need not be public figures to speak up and speak out about sex. If they initiate honest discussions with others, they are likely to discover that they, their friends, and their partners share many of the same sexual concerns and passions.

> What is wrong with sex in North America is simply the inability to talk about sex. . . .particularly with people you are having it with.
>
> —JOANI BLANK

Talking to a Partner

One of the greatest problems women face is not being able to talk to their partner about sex. A couple may have engaged in sex hundreds of times, but never talked about it even once. They follow the "don't ask, don't tell" approach to sex. There are women who are afraid to confess that they do not come, and their partner is afraid to find out. Other women do not talk to men about sex and go on having sex against desire because they do not want to confront the problem.

When partners do talk, they may feel they are speaking different languages. Talking about sex with an opposite-sex partner can be difficult because of the different styles of language women and men learn to speak. As Deborah Tannen suggests in her book *You Just Don't Understand: Women and Men in Conversation,* women and men often misinterpret one another. They also have different conversational goals. In general, women talk in order to develop intimacy with others, while men engage in competition. A woman wants to share and compare experiences. She fields a question to a group of friends not to get a precise answer, but to open discussion and to gather a set of opinions. She sees conversation as a way to make ties and get closer to other people. A man, in contrast, sees conversation as a means of getting things done and of establishing rank. When a woman throws out a question, a man may think he is being asked to answer it or to solve a problem. Tannen suggests, when all she wants is simply to talk.

If women and men talk for different reasons in everyday conversation, they are likely to do the same when they talk about sex. For men, to merely bring up the subject with a partner gives the impression that there is a problem. A woman may see such a conversation as an opportunity to get closer, while the man may feel his sexual abilities are being challenged. If he expresses reluctance to talk or becomes angry, a woman may begin to edit what she says. She may avoid saying anything at all for fear of provoking him. She would rather fake orgasm than address a sexual problem with her partner. The man, meanwhile, may have his own concerns about sex, but he feels uncomfortable about bringing them up. So they go on in silence, and sex for both becomes a performance, not a pleasure.

Negotiating Sex

If women and their male partners do not talk about sex then, by default, all the pleasure falls into the man's lap. This imbalance drains the pleasure of sex for both partners and may end it altogether. But this imbalance can be redressed by consciously making pleasure mutual.

The Principle of Reciprocity

Many women are reticent to ask for what they want in sex. One woman told us, "I give him fellatio, hoping he will return the favor, but usually he doesn't. But I don't say anything. I just don't know how to ask him to go down on me." It is difficult to ask for something when sex takes place in silence. Through conversation, however, women and their partners can open the lines of communication that will allow them to articulate their desires. That conversation can also facilitate turn-taking in pleasure and lead to a stronger relationship overall. When partners keep a conversation going about sex, both can feel more comfortable about asking for what they want.

An ongoing sex conversation also helps reserve the right of either partner to say no to sex or to a particular sex act. Even when two people disagree—for example, when one partner wants to receive oral sex and the other does not want to give it— the topic is at least out on the mattress and not left lurking under the bed. When each person feels she or he can bring up a desire or fantasy for discussion, a happy resolution is a greater possibility. By dealing with the issue openly, both partners may be willing to work at a compromise.

Women and men need appropriate words and concepts to make sex more reciprocal. The vocabulary we have suggested may facilitate greater reciprocity because it emphasizes women's and men's equal capacity for pleasure. A woman can make a man understand that she needs the same type of stimulation that he does by telling her partner, "We both have a clitoris. Mine enjoys being stimulated to orgasm as much as yours. If you touch me there, I can enjoy an orgasm, too." Through both words and actions, using "show and tell," women can help men see sex through a female lens and share with them the new, bright prospects for pleasure that await.

Show and Tell in the Bedroom

Tell Him

Most men want to please their partner. They are just waiting to be told how. If a woman clearly tells her partner that she wants clittage or oral sex, she is likely to get an honest and possibly an enthusiastic response. A woman may need to give explicit genital directions—"a little to the left . . . aah, right there"—or words that help a partner provide the right intensity or speed of stimulation. The satisfied look on his partner's face is usually more than enough reward to convince a man of the value of following directions.

> What's the worst thing that can happen? If you ask, you might not get it. But if you don't ask, you certainly won't get it.
>
> —JOANI BLANK

Show Him

If words are not enough or seem inappropriate, a woman can show her partner what she likes. A woman who enjoys masturbation and does not mind an audience can show her lover exactly what kind of stimulation makes her come. Masturbation in front of a partner is not something that appeals to everyone, but it is an exercise that is widely used for couples in sex therapy. When the man sees how she gives herself clittage, he may improve his own manual technique. Some people use fantasy, role-playing, dressing up for sex, or otherwise adopting another persona to make show and tell easier. (For inspiration, see Carol Queen's book *Exhibitionism for the Shy*.) By assuming a different role, a woman or man may find it easier to physically play out personal desires.

Guide Him

A woman can instruct her partner in good sex technique without words. Nonverbal communication—body language—is the fundamental language of sex. By shifting her body or gently moving his hand to the right spot, a woman can make sure her partner's efforts are not wasted. A woman can let a man know when he is on target by making noise, squeezing his arm, or otherwise expressing pleasure with her body. A woman can perform what she wants on the man first, then letting him know that she wants the same. Nonverbal communication is easiest between long-term partners who know one another intimately and who are unafraid to speak out with their bodies.

Do It Yourself

A woman who does not want to wait for a partner to give her the stimulation she wants can give herself clittage whenever she desires it. Clittage can be crucial to making intercourse orgasmic and with do-it-yourself clittage, a woman never has to go without.

Don't Give Up

What is a woman to do when she lies awake—alert, aroused, erect—and her partner has already fallen asleep? She can call upon her own fingers or a vibrator. A more companionable solution, however, is to teach her partner the principle of ladies first. When the man discovers that the woman's orgasm enhances the pleasure of both of them, he may put more effort into manual and oral sex before he comes. A woman might also give her partner a woman-oriented sex manual (like this book!) to read.

If a woman still wants penetration but her partner is no longer erect, she can ask him to use his fingers. Even a man who feels sexually spent can often muster the energy to use his hands. Clittage and G spotting will bring the woman to orgasm and may even give her partner a second wind.

PST!—Place, Style, Time

Athletes know the three ingredients to high-quality physical training indicated in the FIT formula for exercise—frequency, intensity, and time. For good sex, the key is PST—place, style, and time.

- Place indicates *where* to stimulate the body.

- Style is *how* to stimulate the genitals or other body parts.

- Time is *how long* or the duration of stimulation.

A woman and her partner can use the PST acronym as a reminder of how to keep stimulation on a genital track. If a woman's partner veers from the focus of pleasure, all she has to say is "Pst!" This acronym can remind her partner to ask—*Am I going too fast? Is my touch too hard or too soft? Am I on the right spot? Do you want more?*

PLACE, or, Location, Location, Location. Women have orgasms when they are stimulated in the right places. A well-aimed finger or tongue can usually rivet even the most distracted mind right back to the body. A good partner understands that precision and accuracy are crucial to a woman's orgasm: A millimeter to the left can change a woman's whole perspective on the proceedings. That partner can provide adequate stimulus only if the woman lets him know what feels good and offers directions when necessary.

STYLE, or, Steady as She Goes. Once proper location is established, a woman will want a continuous and steady touch. A touch that is too erratic, too rough, or not strong enough will fail to please. A woman needs the same steady stimulation a man gets with fellatio, a hand job, or intercourse. Like men, women enjoy constant, rhythmic clitoral stimulation. In cunnilingus and clittage, women's partners might take a lesson from the tongue vibrator, an electric wand with a flexible vinyl tongue at its tip that wiggles to a steady beat and does not stop until the woman turns it off.

TIME, or, Don't Stop. Most women have had the experience of being on the brink of orgasm only to have their partner suddenly remove his hand or tongue or shift his body so that the stimulation ceases. A woman should not be afraid to say "Keep going," "That feels good," "More," and, finally, "I'm coming! Don't stop!"

Brick-Wall Partners

Most women successfully learn to reach orgasm if they make the effort. Some go to sex therapy, while others follow the exercises in sex manuals for women, or learn to use a vibrator. But when these women try to apply what they have learned in partner sex, they often run into obstacles. The most difficult obstacle is what we call the brick-wall partner. A woman may have a partner she loves but who is unwilling to explore or who is threatened by change. When one woman told a partner that she did not have orgasms from intercourse alone, he told her it must be her fault: "But all the other women I've been with came that way." Although she explained that those women were either part of a very lucky minority or they were faking, this brick-wall partner was not convinced. It is not surprising, since the pop-porn sexual culture would lead anyone to believe in orgasmic intercourse for women, and sometimes women themselves share the view that they must be deficient if intercourse does not do it for them. Other women know that it is the sexual culture and the partner who ignores her pleasure that are mistaken. If a partner completely refuses to try to please a woman, it may indicate a deeper problem in the relationship. When a man is no more resilient than a brick wall, he asserts power over a woman. Part of opening up communication about sex is to help brick-wall men let down their defenses and work with women to break the tie between sex and power.

Getting the (Public and Private) Sex Conversation Started

Brick-wall partners may be impossible to move. But a woman can get a sexual conversation going with more open-minded partners. She may want to change partners to find a man who is willing to talk. She can use any opportunity when sex comes up (in a movie, on TV, in the news) to open the floor for discussion. She can encourage learning more about sex by watching erotic movies or videos together or reading a book. (Most media will present a traditional male-oriented view, but these can serve as icebreakers to critical and creative conversation about how sex could be better.) She can declare a Sadie Hawkins sex holiday. On this day, she initiates sex and it unfolds on her terms. Putting a new spin on sex may introduce lovers to new experiences that change the way they have sex forever.

What'll We Tell the Kids?

Perhaps the most important lesson parents can give is to have healthy sex lives themselves and to talk openly about sex whenever the subject comes up. Parents can also teach their kids to approach pop porn with a critical eye and ear.

Even partners who have a healthy sex life together may find it hard to talk about the specifics of sex with their kids. They can at least provide good written material and let their kids know they are willing to listen. Other parents who hardly talk to each other about sex are even more likely to hesitate about having "the talk" about what is for them a very delicate subject. Besides their own discomfort, many parents believe that the less said about sex, the better, as if by not talking about child or teen sexuality, it will go away.

Sex education in the era of AIDS is no longer an option—it is imperative. To make sure that children (especially girls) are not harmed or waylaid by sex, women need to get serious about providing their own children with good information. And the discussion must go beyond a vague reference to birds, bees, and where babies come from. But most parents just do not know what to say. Nor do they know how to deal with sexual feelings when a child expresses them.

Concerned parents have to go up against the sexual culture and provide the information and support that is not generally available to girls or boys about sex. Children learn from the sexual culture that to touch the genitals is dirty, a message that makes a child doubt and feel shame about her body. It also contradicts what she may know, that self-stimulation can feel good. Girls are discouraged from masturbating, while it is a well-known fact of boys' lives. Boys are generally expected to masturbate and, as long as it occurs in private, they are not deterred. Boys are thought to need to express their sexuality in ways that girls do not. What boys are typically not taught, however, is how to express themselves verbally, that is, they may not learn the skills that will later enable them to get involved in a sex conversation with their partner.

There are age-appropriate books and other materials for children that can help to counteract the influences of misinformed or misguided peers, pop porn, and other negative influences in the sexual culture. Children do best when, instead of sexual blinders, good information about sex is made available to them. An informed child who feels comfortable about her body and who can talk to her parents is given the opportunity to develop a sexual self. Healthy attitudes about sex lead to healthier sexual practices and to an adult sex life that avoids the potential dangers but cultivates the available pleasures of sex.

Parents who do encourage education and open discussion about sex have their work cut out for them though, because the existing names for female genitals especially are inadequate. What is the female counterpart to the penis, for example? What is the male counterpart to the vulva? Vagina? Clitoris? The very practice of comparing the man's penis to women's genital parts reinforces the sexual culture's orientation to the male genitals. The available words are misleading because they make women and men seem more different than they really are, helping to perpetuate the view that men's genitals are for pleasure and women's genitals are for men and making babies.

Parents need better words than "down there," that vague-place-between-the-legs-that-has-a-vagina-and-who-knows-what-else. Our new word, *cligeva,* lets children know that girls and women have a genital *whole* of their own and not just a "hole" or a missing or miniature penis. Further, they learn that their cligeva belongs to them alone and that (in contrast to, say, the ovaries) its only purpose is to provide her with pleasure. The message they get is both novel and important: Sex is fun.

> "Honey, I never had enough fun with sex. You go out and have fun with sex." Who ever heard that from their mother?
> —CAROL QUEEN

Making Noise

Women can replace the pop-porn soundtrack and the sexual culture's silence with women's real voice of orgasmic joy. One woman told us that sex is not right for her unless she is being noisy and expressive: "Sex is a funny thing. . . . I mean, you're farting and laughing and gurgling and huffing and making funny noises and making weird faces." Other women have other styles. Some are quiet, others serious, and still others feel transported to a spiritual dimension. There is no one "right away."

A woman may have concerns about how she looks or sounds during sex, especially when she comes. A woman in the throes of orgasm bears little resemblance to its stereotypical depiction in pop porn or pornography. One woman tells us of a man who believed her fake orgasm when she imitated the soundtrack of a porno movie. But when she let out an authentic moan when she had the real thing, he insisted she was faking. Even after Meg Ryan blew the cover on fake orgasms in that memorable scene from *When Harry Met Sally*, many men still do not seem to know what a woman coming actually sounds like.

A good orgasm can wipe away a woman's concern about how she looks or sounds. She'll feel so good, she won't even care that the neighbors hear. The sound of a woman coming is a far better ambient noise than the traffic, car alarms, and sirens that now fill the air. Part of reinventing sex is women granting themselves the right to make noise—during sex, in conversation, and in the sexual culture. Eventually, if enough women make noise, the sexual culture will have to listen to them. And when women replace silence with frank discussion, with expressions of desire, and with the laughter of sexual joy, everybody will be having more fun.

> A healthy sex life. Best thing in the world for a woman's voice.
> —LEONTYNE PRICE, OPERA SINGER

Don't Stop

A New Sexuality of Pleasure

Today, instead of conforming to the sexual culture, women are changing it. They are reinventing sex by shifting away from a male-oriented view of sex to one that includes both women and men. Such a move involves a tremendous change in the way people think about sex. It requires, first, acknowledging that there is a problem with *sex* (and not with women) and, second, recognizing that because sex is not inherent, but learned, people have the power to change it.

Some women may find it difficult to imagine how sex might be reinvented because, no less than men, they have been socialized in a sexual culture that reduces sex to a beautiful woman and a man's orgasm and frequently dishonors sex by linking it to violence. What would a sexual culture that respected and represented women be like? What would sex feel like in such an environment? For women who are not used to thinking about their own pleasure, it takes a large leap of the imagination to create or build that alternative.

Imagining a new sexuality requires that women move beyond the constraints of their sexual upbringing. It means critically examining the way they have sex, not with an accusatory finger pointed at their male partner, but with an awareness that the answer lies in remaking sex, first from the inside out of their own experience, and, second, by remaking the sexual culture.

Because sex occurs in private, it is often treated as an individual concern. Because it involves the body, sex is often considered to be solely a natural act. It is rarely viewed as a phenomenon affected by a variety of social forces beyond the body and the bedroom. Turning the question back at society is not the usual approach to sex in a culture such as ours, which favors psychological explanations and individual solutions to problems. When a woman wants to address a sexual problem, she is often advised to go, alone or with her partner, to see a sex therapist. Certified sex therapists can be a crucial part of the healing process for a woman who has been sexually abused or who has experienced rape. Professional counseling can also help a woman deal with specific sexual issues or assist a couple in building communication and trust in a relationship. Improving sex and solving problems for individual women and for couples is important; however, private therapy on its own cannot get to the root of a pleasure imbalance that affects sex for everyone. Reinventing sex for more than just a minority of women ultimately requires a broad and fundamental change in the way sex is defined, accompanied by what is nothing less than a revolution in the sexual culture.

The Pleasure Revolution

Initiating cultural change can seem an impossible or daunting task for an individual, yet each woman who improves her own sex life contributes to the revolution in pleasure. Many different kinds of women and men in all sorts of settings and situations are already contributing to the pleasure revolution. The pleasure revolution is being carried out by mothers and fathers who dare to talk honestly and openly to their daughters and sons about sex. It is fostered by people in the fields of reproductive health and in health care who treat women and girls as sexual beings and whole persons rather than as a bundle of reproductive body parts. It is sparked by sex educators such as Betty Dodson, who go beyond the prescribed sex curriculum to teach women self-pleasure and sexual independence. Other people are making women's sexual presence felt by making videos, editing magazines, or writing erotica and sex manuals that deal with sex as women experience it.

Both a sign and source of change is the advent of woman-friendly sex stores and mail-order outlets. People such as Joani Blank, who founded Good Vibrations, helped make vibrators, sex toys, and woman-oriented books and videos more easily available. Whereas only sleazy male-directed "adult" bookstores existed before, these new places have provided an alternative sexual environment that is clean, well-lighted, and that welcomes women, saying, "Come on in. Consider a vibrator. Compare the dildos. If you have any questions, just ask." In a pop-porn culture, the value of having a place that caters to women's sexual needs and desires—which by its very existence sends the message that women deserve a good sex life—cannot be overestimated.

In the less sensual settings of laboratories and universities, researchers and feminist sexologists, struggling against a scientific tradition that has treated women as the deviant case, are beginning to ask new questions about women's bodies, their health, and their sexuality. Neuroscientist and nurse educator Beverly Whipple, for example, has investigated female ejaculation and is now researching the neurology of orgasms. Norma Wilcox, a nurse and sexologist who teaches medical students how to do pelvic exams, tries to make future doctors understand the role of pleasure in sexual health. She teaches them to see women's genitals as not just ovaries, uteruses, and fallopian tubes, but as including the clitoris and G spot as well.

Sex Pioneers

Throughout history, there have always been "wild women" who broke the sexual codes of their day. The loose woman, the prostitute, lesbians and other sex "deviants" were renegades in a society where sexual pleasure was the prerogative of men. Most such women lived on the margins of a society that exploited them. Wild women today no longer lead their lives at the margins and their ideas are beginning to affect how even mainstream media view sex.

Women at the frontier of a new sexuality became pioneers because something in their lives inspired them to reject the model of sex they had been offered. Carol Queen began to explore her own sexuality in response to the absence of sexual joy she observed in her parents' sex life. From a young age she began to follow her sexual curiosity and she continues her sex journey today as a sex educator and writer.

For Louisa Daniels, co-owner of Passion Flower, a sex-toy store in Oakland, California, her sexual journey was motivated by a desire to better understand the connection between sex and violence. With family members who were Holocaust survivors, Louisa first wanted to understand how and why violence comes about in a particular society. When she began to work with women who had been raped and battered, she remembered her own personal experiences with sexual violence. "I began analyzing the interface between sex and violence. . . . [Eventually] I . . . started bringing it home to myself and realizing that I had had experiences that had made me shut down sexually. I had a poor body image which affected my sexuality. I began addressing those [problems] in the context of a relationship."

It is a woman's relationships that usually prompt her to begin thinking seriously (or at all) about sex. The beginning of a really good relationship or the end of a really bad one often inspires a woman to look at what she does (or does not) get out of sex.

When divorce occurs, for example, a woman may look back and realize that she had years or even decades of sex against desire or sex without orgasm, and she gets motivated to explore sexual pleasure. The right partnership can make a woman grow; the wrong one may, at first, turn her off to sex. But a woman eventually realizes that she has a right to enjoy her body's sexuality and to explore how best she can experience its pleasures.

Women who begin a sex journey usually do so because something happens that makes them stop and say, "Hey, wait a minute! This just isn't right!" But there are also women who begin because sex has been really good and they want more, or they want to figure out why their positive experience seems so unconnected to the sexual culture's standard model for sex.

Every woman is, then, a sex pioneer. Her body is her own territory, and she (and not even the most experienced partner) deserves to be its first explorer. Even a grown woman can go back and start again, taking a wholly new approach to her own body and her sexuality with a guidebook she writes for herself. The work of sex pioneers and this book provide some road maps and a cheering section. But it is up to each woman to discover for herself the pleasure that can be hers.

> Each one of us is the first expert and the first explorer of our own sexuality. . . . To skip that step of getting to know yourself erotically, physiologically, and fantasy-wise is a mistake. . . . Take a mirror and find your clitoris right now!
> —CAROL QUEEN

Taking a Sexual Journey

Every woman can gain from embarking on a sexual journey. A sexual journey is a self-exploration and a commitment to sexual growth that can take place no matter what a woman's age and whether or not she has a partner. A sexual journey begins with the woman, but it eventually involves her partner and the support of family, friends, lovers, and the sexual culture.

A few women begin their journey when they first become sexually active as children or as teenagers, but most women do not see the need for cultivating their sexuality until decades later, if at all. It does not matter *when* a woman begins, only *that* she does, and she can enjoy the benefits of this journey for the rest of her life.

Some women embark on a sex journey when they become aware of their attraction to women. Other women, who consider themselves lesbians, begin to rethink sex when they realize that they like sex with both women and men. In fact, the establishment of a bisexual community is a direct result of the pleasure revolution. Women and men who found both sexes attractive stopped trying to conform to existing categories of heterosexual or homosexual that did not describe what they felt or desired.

By takng a sexual journey, heterosexual women realize that the sexual culture did not have them in mind when it defined sex. No wonder they were not having orgasms! A woman has to defy the sexual traditions she has been taught and take sex into her own hands.

[Women] don't learn about their body; they're not giving themselves permission—and they are certainly not given permission—to explore their bodies to find out what is pleasurable to them. I think women first have to be aware of what it is they like, which takes a lot. Then they have to acknowledge it to themselves and say, you know, I really do like that, which is hard for women. Then, the hardest part is to communicate that to a partner, or to show a partner, whether it's verbally or nonverbally. That's real hard for women. They are still getting so many sex-negative messages.

—BEVERLY WHIPPLE

Getting Physical

Although information and advice from sex educators and experts can be useful, a woman ultimately learns most from her own experience. With the mirror and her fingers, a woman can locate her clitoris, U spot, and G spot. By masturbating, a woman can find out how to stimulate each part and see how her cligeva looks and feels when it is erect. One woman told us that she feels more comfortable looking at her genitals after she has had an orgasm. An orgasm helps to clear the mind of negative messages and body images and to focus on the intrinsic power of her own body. Some lube, a plug-in vibrator, and a G spotter or dildo can facilitate the process, providing a delightfully swift path to orgasm.

> I really resent it when people say "Oh, well, the biggest sex organ is between your ears." You can rub my head until I turn 180 years old and I'm not going to have an orgasm. If you don't get down there on my clit, nothin's going to fuckin' happen! . . . I say, get it centered in the body.
>
> —BETTY DODSON

Genital Image and Reality

As women combine self-exploration with a new view of their genitals, they can come up with the images, words, and techniques that work for them. Rather than thinking of their genitals as either a blank mystery spot, as something dirty, or only as "a hole and a bud," women can create a more positive and useful image of their sexual parts and whole. The more a woman learns about herself, the more she can "know and grow," developing her cligeva and her sexuality to their full potential.

Each One, Teach One

Women who expand their own knowledge can enrich others by spreading the word. Rather than allowing false information and damaging stereotypes about women, men, and sex to continue, a woman needs to speak up whenever the opportunity arises (or can be created) and say no to sex as intercourse, yes to manual sex, and no to SAD, yes to the golden age of youthful sexual exploration. She can advocate that a woman's first time be orgasm not intercourse, and that sex never be considered over until *both* partners are satisfied. Each woman needs to tell other women about what she has learned. Exchanging sex tips, like recipes, can spread the pleasure around.

Talking to a Partner

Women often say to us, "Well, this is all fine and dandy, but I cannot even bring up the subject of sex with my partner, much less ask him to give me 'clittage' or tell him I get erections too." For many women, incorporating men into the pleasure revolution is the most challenging step, particularly when they do not yet have a dialog going about sex with their partner.

The surest way to bring men into the pleasure revolution is to make clear to them that there is something in it for them. When men find out that intercourse is a far more exciting experience when *both* partners are erect, or that when women have orgasms, men's orgasms are more intense, they may be more interested in learning, listening, and exploring. A man who is unwilling to develop a sexual self is probably not an appropriate partner for a woman who has begun a sex journey. But a man who is willing to explore sex and who appreciates a sexual woman will soon be waving the new flags of the women's pleasure revolution.

Talking Sex with Friends

Women who have taken a sexual journey can encourage other women to take their own. Several women told us that their sex lives totally changed as a result of participating in discussions with us for this book. One woman told us that our encouragement to get a vibrator and take care of her own sexuality changed her life. She feels sexually independent now. They said they looked at their genitals for the first time or saw them in a completely new way. Some had orgasms or ejaculated for the first time. We were able to see the transformation on their faces and in their bodies. For all, being able to talk openly was a crucial step toward ending the silence that only keeps women from enjoying sexual pleasure.

A New Sexual Culture

In a new sexual culture, sex will have a totally new character. Neither gender will necessarily be more sexually aggressive than the other; the individuals involved and the context will determine who takes the lead. Every young woman will experience a golden age when she can explore clittage and other forms of manual and oral sex. Many sex educators already encourage outercourse—everything but intercourse—but instead of masturbation, oral, and manual sex being presented as a poor substitute for the real thing, these activities would become real sex. The new sexual culture will stop confusing sex with intercourse and instead of focusing solely on the man's experience of sex, will promote mutual erection, mutual orgasm, and mutual pleasure.

Women need not wait for others to announce the pleasure revolution. They can begin changing the sexual culture themselves. Each woman reinvents sex every time she gives herself an orgasm. She changes sex when she reorders the typical sequence by which sex unfolds, rethinks the timing of sex, and expands its contents. She changes sex by no longer accepting orgasmless encounters.

When millions of women are having orgasmic sex on equal terms with their partners, they will transform not only their own lives but men's as well. The beginning of a new millennium seems an especially appropriate time for women to put a stop to pop porn, SAD, sexualized violence, and one-sided sex and create a brand new sexual culture. Women will have truly reinvented sex because they will be saying yes not just to their partners, but to themselves. The sexual revolution will finally have come when women, too, are having fun.

GLOSSARY

caressing the crescent   Simultaneous stimulation of both ends of the orgasmic crescent (the clitoris and the G spot) using manual sex and/or cunnilingus.

cligeva (cli-GEE-va)   Our term for the whole of a woman's genitals derived from the first syllables of its most sensitive sexual parts—the clitoris, the G spot, and the vagina. The final "a" also incorporates the pleasures of the anus. The term provides a name for the whole of women's sexual anatomy where none now exists, and helps remind women and their partners in what order most women want these sexual parts stimulated.

clitoris (CLI-tor-is)   The woman's clitoris is a four-inch Y- or wishbone-shaped sexual organ inside the cligeva that is the key to women's sexual pleasure. The man's clitoris is a five-inch tube-shaped (with the legs together) sexual organ inside the penis that serves the same pleasure function.

clittage (clit-TAZH)   Manual stimulation of the clitoris. This form of manual sex is the most common way women reach orgasm.

clittage intercourse   Intercourse with simultaneous (usually manual) stimulation of the clitoris by either partner.

cul-de-sac   The cul-de-sac is a sexually sensitive area that is created during erection when the woman's cervix lifts and her vagina "tents" up. Firm pressure (rather than thrusting) on the woman's cul-de-sac with the head of the man's penis gives both partners intense pleasure.

cunnilingus   Oral sex on a woman using the tongue and lips to stimulate the tip and shaft of the clitoris, the frenulum, the inner labia, the perineum, and the U spot.

dildo   A silicone or plastic penis-shaped object (varying from short to long, slender to thick, and straight to curved) used for G spotting and vaginal and anal penetration. Dildos for anal penetration are usually smaller and have flared ends to avoid getting lost in the rectum.

do-it-yourself   Self-stimulation to orgasm during partner sex or alone.

ejaculatory orgasm   An orgasm that occurs with ejaculation. In both women and men, orgasm and ejaculation are two separate events. They usually occur simultaneously in men and are therefore typically treated as one event. Currently the sexual culture ignores ejaculatory orgasms in women.

fellatio   Oral sex on a man.

female ejaculation   The ejaculation of fluid from the urethra during sexual excitement. Female ejaculate is similar to male ejaculate without the semen.

forget foreplay   To forget foreplay is to reject the definition of manual and oral sex as optional or marginal warmups for intercourse and to make these activities the focus of sex.

G spot   The female prostate gland, also known as the peri-urethral glands or urethral sponge, is a sexually sensitive area that surrounds the urethra. It can be reached by inserting fingers inside the vagina and feeling along the front vaginal wall. The G spot swells when stimulated and, along with clitoral stimulation, contributes to the pleasure of orgasm. Women who ejaculate expel fluid that is thought to come primarily from the G spot.

G spotting   Stimulation of the G spot. G spotting can be done with the fingers, a curved dildo, a vibrator attachment, or a kegelcisor.

going all the way   Making orgasm, not intercourse, the main event of sex.

kegels   Exercises for the PC muscle. A strong PC muscle enhances erection, orgasm, and ejaculation in both women and men. Women can also strengthen their PC muscle using a kegelcisor, a small vaginal barbell.

know it and grow it   The idea that by knowing and using her cligeva, a woman can actually grow new blood vessels and nerves to increase the sensitivity and the orgasmic capacity of her genitals.

ladies first   The principle that a woman's orgasm should occur before that of her male partner. This assures a woman's satisfaction before the man ejaculates and sex is over. Also, orgasm before intercourse ensures that a woman's cligeva is erect and ready to enjoy proactive penetration.

lubricant   Artificial water-based lubricant, or lube, makes the stimulation of sensitive tissues more pleasurable. It is especially important to use for clittage, anal penetration, vaginal penetration, and for extended sexual sessions. Water-based lube is essential for keeping latex condoms, dental dams, and gloves from breaking and from irritating sensitive tissues.

manual sex   Manual stimulation of the genitals, one's own or a partner's. Manual sex is the most common way people masturbate. It is also a very common activity in partner sex but is neither named nor seen as "sex" on a par with intercourse and oral sex. The most common forms of manual sex for a woman are clittage and G spotting.

multiple orgasms   More than one orgasm in a sexual session. They may occur separated in time or in rapid succession. Both women and men can experience multiple orgasms.

mutual ejaculation   When both partners ejaculate in a sexual encounter. (Compare to simultaneous ejaculation.)

mutual oral sex   When both partners receive oral sex in a sexual encounter. (Compare to simultaneous oral sex.)

mutual orgasms   When both partners have orgasms in a sexual encounter. (Compare to simultaneous orgasm.)

orgasm   The peak experience of sexual pleasure in which contractions of the PC muscle release blood from the genitals. At the moment of orgasm, the climax of excitement is followed by a feeling of release.

an orgasm every time   A motto that asserts a woman's right to orgasm every time she wants one. A takeoff on Mae West's motto, "an orgasm a day."

orgasm gap   The statistical gap between one group's rate of orgasm compared to another's. There is currently a large orgasm gap between women and men and between women who have sex with men and women who have sex with women.

orgasmic crescent   The orgasmic crescent includes the most important sexual parts of the woman's cligeva—the clitoris, U spot, and G spot. Stimulation of the whole orgasmic crescent by clittage or cunnilingus and G spotting, or by clittage and intercourse can give a woman powerful orgasms. Caressing the crescent causes some women to ejaculate.

PC muscle   The PC (short for pubococcygeus, pronounced pew-bo-cox-i-GEE-us) muscle is actually a group of three muscles that are involved in sexual pleasure. A strong PC muscle enhances erection, orgasm, and ejaculation in both women and men and helps make them equal partners in proactive sex.

pop porn   Pop porn is the portrayal of sex and of what is sexy from an exclusively heterosexual male point of view. Pop porn lacks images of sexual women or of sex from a woman's perspective. Pop porn is the much more pervasive, mainstream cousin of pornography.

proactive penetration Vaginal and anal intercourse as well as G spotting, anal-finger penetration, and fellatio in which both partners are full participants. The partner who is penetrated is erect and controls the timing, depth, and speed of penetration. (Contrast to SAD.)

proactive sex Partner sex between two people who have cultivated their sexual selves. In proactive partner sex, either person may choose to play a more passive or a more active role, but does so intentionally rather than by default.

PST An acronym for the principle of place, style, and timing, PST can be used to help partners communicate what they want in sex.

SAD (sex against desire) Sex agreed to out of a sense of obligation or for any reason other than one's own and one's partner's pleasure. Some common forms of SAD are the obligation for a woman to engage in intercourse every time she has sex with a man and sex that does not include the woman's orgasm when she wants one.

sexual culture The sexual beliefs, practices, and conditions of a particular culture or society.

sexual self The quality of sexual self-ownership. A person with a sexual self develops and exerts control over her sexuality and does not allow others or the sexual culture to determine sex for her.

simultaneous ejaculation When both partners control their arousal in order to ejaculate at the same time. (Compare to mutual ejaculation.)

simultaneous oral sex When mutual oral sex is performed at the same time. Also known as "69." (Compare to mutual oral sex.)

simultaneous orgasm   When both partners control their arousal to have an orgasm at the same time. (Compare to mutual orgasm.)

spongiosum   The erectile tissue surrounding the urethra in both women and men.

third shift   Sex as a chore that follows the first (paid work) and second (housework and child care) shifts.

U spot   The sexually sensitive area around the opening of a woman's urethra. The woman's U spot is equivalent to the head of the man's penis, which surrounds his urethral opening.

vibrator   Vibrators are usually used to stimulate the clitoris (usually in women but also in men). Using a vibrator is an easy way for a woman to masturbate to orgasm. Vibrators can also be used in partner sex. Because sex is often equated with intercourse, many people assume that women use vibrators for penetration, but they are primarily for clitoral massage (clittage). The vagina is more sensitive to pressure provided by a penis or dildo, while the tip of the woman's clitoris enjoys vibration.

woman's erection   The primary sign of sexual arousal in both women and men and usually the precondition for orgasm. Erection occurs when the woman's cligeva becomes engorged with blood and the pelvic muscles tense. A woman's erection is necessary to orgasm, intercourse, and ejaculation. A woman's erection is similar to a man's in that the genitals of both become enlarged, full, and taut with excitement.

RESOURCES

Woman-Friendly Stores, Sex Toys, and Books

Good Vibrations. 1210 Valencia Street, San Francisco, CA 94110. (415) 974-8980.

2504 San Pablo Avenue, Berkeley, CA 94110. (510) 841-8987.

Mail order: 938 Howard Street, Ste. 101, San Francisco, CA 94103. (800) 289-8423. (415) 974-8990. Fax (415) 974-8989. E-mail: goodvibe@well.com. Web site: http://www.goodvibes.com.

Passion Flower. 4 Yosemite Avenue, Oakland, CA 94611.

Mail order: (510) 601-7750. Fax (510) 658-9645. E-mail: passion@passionflwr.com.

Eve's Garden. 119 West 57th Street, Ste. 420, New York, NY 10019-2383. (212) 757-8651. Web site: http://www.evesgarden.com.

Educational Videos

Betty Dodson. *Selfloving* and *Celebrating Orgasm.*

Fanne Fatale. *How to Female Ejaculate*
Safe Is Desire.

Annie Sprinkle. *Sluts and Goddesses.*

Recommended Books

Josephine Lowndes Sevely. *Eve's Secrets: A New View of Female Sexuality.*

Shere Hite. *The Hite Report.*

Alice Kahn Ladas, Beverly Whipple, and John D. Perry. *The G Spot.*

Cathy Winks and Anne Semans. *Good Vibrations Guide to Sex.*

Betty Dodson. *Sex for One: The Joy of Selfloving.*

Federation of Feminist Women's Health Centers. *A New View of a Woman's Body.*

Lonnie Barbach. *For Yourself.*

Joani Blank. *Good Vibrations: The Complete Guide to Vibrators.*

Joani Blank, ed. *First Person Sexual: Women and Men Write About Self-Pleasuring.*

Magazines
With Occasional Issues on Sex

BUST. P.O. Box 319, Ansonia Station, New York, NY 10023. E-mail: BUST@AOL.com

off our backs. 2337 B 18th Street, NW, Washington, DC 20009. (202) 234-8072. Fax (202) 234-8092. E-mail: internet:73613.1256 @compuserve.com

Ms. Magazine. 230 Park Avenue, New York, NY 10169. E-mail: ms@echonyc.com

Recommended for Teens

Teen Voices. Published by Women Express, Inc. 316 Huntington Avenue, Boston, MA 02115.

NOTES

Chapter 1   The Orgasm Gap

3   Seventy-five percent of men . . . orgasms only sometimes or not at all.: Laumann et al., p. 116. This study, referred to throughout as the 1994 U.S. sex survey, was carried out in 1992 on a random sample of 3,432 respondents aged eighteen to fifty-nine.

4   The Orgasm Gap: Laumann et al., p. 116.

4   Women who have sex with a female partner come 83 percent of the time.: Lever, p. 26.

5   Women's Orgasms: The orgasm rate in masturbation is an average for women who masturbate regularly. The orgasm rate for all women in partner sex is for those who say they "always have an orgasm," in Laumann et al., pp. 85, 116. The orgasm rate for lesbians in partner sex is for the most recent sexual encounter, in Lever, p. 26. Lever analyzed 2,525 responses to a survey published in *The Advocate,* a magazine for gays and lesbians.

9   "I don't think orgasms are . . . live without them.": Interview with Betty Dodson, May 9, 1996.

9   Other examples of the view that sex is socially constructed include Laqueur, Vines, Fausto-Sterling, Gagnon, and Tuana.

17   "There are very few absolute . . . we cannot know for sure what they are.": Fausto-Sterling, p. 269.

21   "What do women want. . . . Everyone knew that. . . .": Shields, p. 246.

31   (Women can get "prostate" cancer . . . usually not life-threatening.): Zaviacic and Whipple, p. 148.

Chapter 2 *Sex Undressed*

51 "What if you have tried . . . manually stimulate your clitoris during intercourse.": Keesling, p. 199.

51 In her survey of British women . . . what she calls an "orgasm hierarchy.": Quilliam, p. 152.

53 In "Dyke Hands," . . . "sexual organ of lesbian love.": Bogus, p. 198.

53 In one survey, 75 percent of lesbians said . . . having their own stroked . . . : Lever, p. 26.

53 . . . "Use your hands like they're your tenderest parts.": Bright, p. 20.

56 "I think that for many women . . . is the ultimate satisfaction.": Dell Williams quoted in Monagle, p. 54.

58 . . . more men than women . . . enjoyed to the same degree.: Laumann et. al., pp. 152, 157.

58 The sex survey found that 20 percent . . . while 28 percent of men reported receiving fellatio.: Michael et al., p. 140, and Laumann et. al., p. 98.

58 The survey researchers point out . . . less frequently than men do.": Laumann et. al., p. 168.

58 At the same time, they acknowledge . . . "the 'fairness' of the typical sexual event.": Laumann et. al., p. 168.

58 The survey researchers' results . . . cunnilingus is not for men.": Laumann et. al., p. 157.

59 Giving Oral Sex: Laumann et al., p. 152 and Michael et. al., p. 140.

61 Twenty percent of all women . . . the last time they had sex.: Michael et. al., p. 140 and Lever, p. 26. In Lever's survey, 53 percent of lesbians reported giving oral sex to their partner and 48 percent said they received it in their last encounter.

63 . . . "Lubricant [is] one of life's more enjoyable essentials . . . a decent cup of coffee.": Winks and Semans, p. 67.

Chapter 3   *Learning Desires*

77   "[First intercourse] was quick. . . . I broke off our relationship shortly thereafter. . . .": Bouris, pp. 92–93.

77   The 1994 National Opinion Research Center (NORC) sex survey reports that . . . intercourse the first time.": Laumann et. al., p. 328.

79   "I didn't tell anyone. . . . I don't believe I know what sex is. What it's for.": Bouris, p. 117.

80   Writer Jane Kramer recalls attending the wedding . . . "proof" that her son had gotten "his money's worth.": Kramer, p. 139.

80-81   The 1994 NORC sex survey found that . . . sought intercourse out of curiosity.: Laumann et. al., p. 329.

82   College students surveyed . . . 7 percent of the women and 79 percent of the men reported having an orgasm with first intercourse. . . . : Sprecher, Barbee, and Schwartz, p. 9.

83   "He, instead of dealing with it like there was obviously something wrong . . . our time together started getting more and more rushed.": Thompson, p. 35.

84   In Sharon Thompson's study, one girl says that her boyfriend "tried very hard. . . . 'Don't wear yourself out.' ": Thompson, p. 225.

84   Another told her boyfriend . . . " 'It's great for me.' ": Thompson, p. 248.

84   Bouris's first-time stories . . . "I didn't have an orgasm . . . but I felt loved. . . .": Bouris, p. 162.

84   A majority of boys make a point of . . . only 40 percent of girls masturbate.: Laumann et al., p. 84.

85   " 'You need to make sure the girl comes first. . . . Then you won't leave her hung up.' ": Rhodes, pp. 22–23.

87   The study of college students . . . equal sexual experience.: Sprecher, Barbee, and Schwartz, p. 13.

87   Several decades ago, anthropologist Margaret Mead . . . learning about sexual activities.: Mead, 1928.

90   "Orgasms—as rare as hen's teeth . . . saw orgasm as a feat.": Thompson, p. 184.

91 The women's health classic . . . "one more performance pressure." . . . : Boston Women's Health Book Collective, p. 209.

92 Sexologist Naomi B. McCormick . . . Learn *relational* ones. McCormick, p. 19.

92 . . . researcher John M. Gagnon notes ". . . while girls learn about love and the importance of boys.": Gagnon, p. 164.

92 One girl told of feeling like . . . their body "says yes yes yes yes" and feels "ready to burst" with erotic excitement.: Tolman, pp. 255, 257.

93 One girl was the exception . . . when she is turned on.": Tolman, p. 257.

93 Sharon Thompson concludes that girls who focused on romance . . . social, emotional, and financial dependence on a man or men.: Thompson, p. 285.

93 Girls had sex . . . what Thompson calls "progress in love.": Thompson, p. 8.

93 Some girls Thompson interviewed . . . sought out relationships with older men that were purely erotic.: Thompson, p. 243.

97 Writer Ana Castillo notes how a "woman is taught . . . to negate sexual desire.": Castillo, pp. 148–149.

97 Psychotherapist Olivia M. Espín concurs, noting . . . ". . . lack of sexual pleasure or desire.": Espín, pp. 141, 143.

98 Pamela H., an Asian American writer, says that there is an extreme sexual double standard. . . . ". . . encouraged by peers to be sexually active.": Pamela H., p. 284.

98 Poet and playwright Ntozake Shange writes, "If some of us are wont . . . without our knowledge or consent.": Shange, p. 211.

100 Lesbians are coming out with greater ease and at younger ages than in previous generations. . . . : Lever, p. 24.

100 Pamela H. writes that her lesbianism is additionally problematic . . . do not even have a word that means "lesbian.": Pamela H., pp. 284–285, 287.

100 "The most difficult thing a handicapped person . . . I gained greater freedom to be myself.": Chan, p. 272.

102 The 1994 edition of a textbook . . . an optional unit on sexual behavior and pregnancy prevention.: Sizer et al., pp. A1–B30.

103 In sexual intercourse . . . into the uterus and fallopian tubes.: The American College of Obstetricians and Gynecologists, 1992.

106 As sex educator Betty Dodson says, "Lovers come and go . . . ongoing love affair with yourself.": Dodson in her *Bodysex* video (see Resources).

107 The women sat on their partner's lap . . . of their skirt to give them clittage.: Flandrin, p. 275.

108 "Teenage girls (and all of us!) . . . '. . . here's how I want it.' ": Bouris, p. 4.

Chapter 4   Pop Porn

118 A magazine like *Playgirl* survives . . . popularity among gay men.: Dirk Shafer, *Playgirl* magazine's 1992 "Man of the Year" and a gay man, estimates that 25 percent of readers are gay men, and says that the women who work at the magazine know but do not talk about it. See Stack, p. E1.

132 Even though "Some days . . . never that free.: Tannen 1993, p. 20.

143 "A naked babe on a computer screen . . . People do.": Palac, p. 252.

Chapter 5   Sexual Self

149 Writer Sally Kempton . . . "who has outposts in your head." In *Quotable Women.*

151 "Sometimes I allow my unprotected vagina . . . overpowers my fear of AIDS.": Hadleigh-West, p. 95.

154 A wife's lower income . . . the "second shift"—child care and housework.: Hochschild, 1992.

157 One survey found that a common complaint . . . two-thirds said they wanted sex more often.: Lever, pp. 25, 26.

158 Nelson reports that . . . while other men cheered: Nelson, p. 84.

158 The physical and social adrenaline that goes into both playing . . . players or fans "celebrate" a win or avenge their loss.: Nelson, pp. 129–130.

158 A *Ms.* survey of more than seven thousand . . . rape or attempted rape.: Stan, p. 285–286.

158 In a study cited by Catharine MacKinnon, Diana E. H. Russell . . . usually by men who were friends, relatives, or acquaintances.: cited in MacKinnon, pp. 121–122.

159 . . . British researcher . . . "a vast undercurrent of unwilling sex" in society.: Quilliam, p. 185.

163 . . . Helen Brown Norden revealed . . . "Latins Are Lousy Lovers.": See Lawrenson, 1968.

163 "It is *pleasure* . . . that is still denied many wives.": Heyn, p. xv.

165 "The message from both . . . as a woman, you're empowered.": Hutton, p. 21.

166 Shere Hite found that women who regularly had orgasms . . . their own bodies. . . .: Hite, 1981, pp. 311–312, 385–386.

167–8 "When we live outside ourselves . . . responsible to ourselves in the deepest sense.": Lorde, p. 58.

Chapter 6   *The Parts and the Whole*

170 Writer Sandra Cisneros describes how religious . . . ". . . perhaps through the walls of my skin.": Cisneros, p. 44.

170 . . . what sex educator Carol Queen describes as "a hole and a bud.": Interview with Carol Queen, June 8, 1996.

171 "Really that little dealybob . . . should be built right in.: Loretta Lynn quoted in Stephens, p. 85.

172 "Sex is dirty . . . somebody you love?": Interview with Beverly Whipple, May 22, 1996.

173 In 1995, the Women's Tennis Association . . . distasteful fact of menstruation.: "Sensitivity Over Image," pp. B6, B8.

174 "Around the age of ten . . . and love my little brothers.": Dodson, p. 57.

175 "At the age of thirty-five . . . on top of me for 'normal sex.' ": Dodson, p. 58.

175 "What a difference it would have made . . . adult genitals in a sex book.": Dodson, p. 59.

179 Western critics such as Alice Walker say . . . not "culture" but torture.: Alice Walker, in *Warrior Marks,* her documentary on female genital mutilation.

179 In the 1860s, . . . considered indicated today. See Tuana, pp. 104–5 and Laqueur, p. 176.

179 Though becoming less frequent today . . . surgery to correct "urinary incontinence.": Ziviacic and Whipple, p. 50.

180 . . . "physicians often connect the uterus . . . that indeed you might.": Federation of Feminist Women's Health Centers, p. 148.

182 In Nicholson Baker's novel . . . female counterpart offers no endearing nicknames for her own genitals.: Baker, p. 11.

185 Norma Wilcox, a nurse and sexologist who teaches medical students . . . could benefit from human sexuality instruction from a sexologist.: Interview with Norma Wilcox, August 28, 1996.

186 "Think of a penis as . . . a woman's interior bulbs and clitoral network,". . . : Hite, 1981, p. 181.

187 . . . "one of organization, not of substance.": Sevely, p. 21.

187 The word *clitoris* . . . "little hill.": Richter, p. 46.

191 After the sensitive clitoral tip, the next stop . . . is the frenulum. . . . : Sevely and the women at the Federation of Feminist Women's Health Centers describe the woman's frenulum as a sexually sensitive area, but most other books mention only the male frenulum.

192 Barbara Keesling is one of the few . . . treats it as a sexual part.: Keesling, p. 118.

197 There are disputes about whether it exists. . . . : Doubters about the existence of the G spot include Tavris, pp. 232–242, and Irvine, pp. 161–169.

201 . . . on the Pacific atoll of Truk, . . . a "small projection below the clitoris," . . . : According to an anthropological report sponsored by the U.S. government, cited in Sevely, p. 102.

202 Going for the Turn-on: See Ladas et al. for more on kegels.

202 Barbara Keesling is the only writer . . . meaning "bottom or end of the sack.": Keesling, pp. 117–118.

203 Sevely suggests that "the arch is very close . . . stimulation of these nerves." Sevely, pp. 119–120.

Chapter 7   Orgasm or Bust

208 "I believe that this is true. . . . it's nice, really, but one can do without it.": Hite, 1981, pp. 407–408.

209 When women say they do not care about orgasm . . . ". . . *then* saying they are not important.": Hite, 1981, p. 137.

210 "Do you think cake . . . kind of cake?": Hollander, 1992.

210 . . . "unquestionably better than cake" . . . : Roz Warren, the editor of *What Is This Thing Called SEX?: Cartoons by Women,* which features Sylvia's question on the cover, dedicates the book to her husband, Richard, "who is unquestionably better than cake."

210 The large-scale 1994 U.S. sex survey . . . women's much lower rates of orgasm.: Michael et al., p. 124.

211 "It might be a revelation. . . . I won't bother having sex.": Maurer, p. 111.

214 One woman told . . . made her feel "slim.": Quilliam, p. 147.

215 . . . orgasm is usually due to some form of clitoral stimulation,: see for example, Hite, 1981, p. 199.

215 . . . the "bridge maneuver," . . . : See for example, Keesling, pp. 199–200.

215 . . . the coital alignment technique . . . : See Eichel and Nobile.

216 One woman told Susan Quilliam . . . "usually shorter but more intense" . . . "not so intense but softer and longer.": Quilliam, p. 145.

220 The 1994 U.S. sex survey researchers suggest ". . . report experiencing orgasm when masturbating.": Laumann et al., p. 84.

222 Orgasm from Masturbation: Laumann et. al., p. 85.

226 The 1994 sex-survey researchers note . . . the sexual event for heterosexuals.": Laumann et. al., p. 157, 167.

229 ... "Orgasms are a simple pleasure. ... taking less seriously.": Winks and Semans, p. 34.

229–30 "I figured out from a women's magazine. ... how are we going to know?": Interview with Carol Queen, June 8, 1996.

236 "I usually need clitoral contact. ... soaked my husband's feet.": Meshorer and Meshorer, pp. 144–145.

Chapter 8   A Lingo for Love

243 ... survey researchers report is ... less than once a week.: Laumann, et al., p. 399.

246 "In America sex ... is a fact.": Marlene Dietrich quoted in Stephens, p. 89.

248 "The language we use to describe sex ... negative undertone is so pervasive.": Hutton, p. 60.

250–1 "If I was famous and my name ... but a female one which changes it all. ...".: Dworkin, pp. 224, 225–226.

251 "I love CUNT. ... correctly used, at your fingertips?": Air, p. 81.

252 *Cock* (from British English for a "watercock" or faucet) ... spurts fluid ...: Richter, p. 47.

254 Linguist Julia Penelope calls reinventing language ... a "sifting process. ...: Penelope, p. 215.

257 "What is wrong with sex in America. ... people you are having it with.": Interview with Joani Blank, July 10, 1996.

257–8 As Deborah Tannen suggests in her book ... a man may think he is being asked to answer it or to solve a problem, ... when all she wants is simply to talk.: Tannen 1990, pp. 49–73.

260 "What's the worst thing. ... you certainly won't get it.": Interview with Joani Blank, July 10, 1996.

267 "A healthy sex life ... for a woman's voice.": Leontyne Price quoted in Stephens, p. 74.

Chapter 9   Don't Stop

271   "I began analyzing the interface between sex and violence. . . . addressing those [problems] in the context of a relationship.": Interview with Louisa Daniels, November 16, 1995.

272   "Each one of us is the first expert. . . . Take a mirror and find your clitoris right now!": Interview with Carol Queen, June 8, 1996.

273   "[Women] don't learn about their body. . . . They are still getting so many sex-negative messages.": Interview with Beverly Whipple, May 22, 1996.

274   "I really resent it when. . . . get it centered in the body.": Interview with Betty Dodson, May 9, 1996.

SOURCES FOR ANATOMICAL ILLUSTRATIONS

The woman's clitoris   Based on drawings by Regnier deGraaf and Johannes Sobotta, Frank Netter, and Suzann Gage and reconceptualizations by the Federation of Feminist Health Centers and by Josephine Lowndes Sevely.

The man's clitoris   Based on the conceptualization of Josephine Lowndes Sevely and on drawings by Johannes Sobotta, Frank Netter, and Suzann Gage.

The G spot   Based on drawings by J.W. Huffman, Frank Netter, Suzann Gage and descriptions from Regnier deGraaf and Josephine Lowndes Sevely.

The U spot   Based on drawings by J.W. Huffman and Robert Latou Dickinson and on descriptions and conceptualization by Sevely. Drawings of vulva and U spot based on photographs of vulvas by Tee A. Corrinne, Michael Perry, Jill Posner, and Michael Rosen in *Femalia*.

Drawings of the cligeva   is a composite and conceptualized by the authors.

Drawings of the vagina, PC muscle, perineum, bulbs, spongiosum, cul-de-sac, frenulum, anus, and male prostate   based on drawings by Suzann Gage and Frank Netter and descriptions from Josephine Lowndes Sevely.

REFERENCES

Corinne, Tee A., et al. Photographs by Joani Blank (ed.). *Femalia*. San Francisco: Down There Press, 1992.

deGraaf, Regnier. *On the Human Reproductive Organs: Treatise Concerning the Generative Organs of Women,* 1672. In Jocelyn and B.P. Setchell, trans. *Journal of Reproduction and Fertility.* Supplement 17, 1972.

Dickinson, Robert Latou. *Human Sex Anatomy.* Baltimore: Williams & Wilkins Company, 1949.

Gage, Suzann, illustrator of Federation of Feminist Women's Health Centers. *A New View of a Woman's Body.* West Hollywood: Feminist Health Press, 1991.

Huffman, J.W. *American Journal of Obstetrics and Gynecology.* vol. 55 (1): 86–101, 1948.

Netter, Frank, Reproductive Systems. *CIBA Collection of Medical Illustrations.* CIBA Pharmaceutical Company, Division of CIBA-Geigy Corporation, vol. 2, Summit, 1954.

Sevely, Josephine Lowndes. *Eve's Secrets: A New Theory of Female Sexuality.* New York: Random House, 1987.

Sobatta, Johannes. *Atlas of Human Anatomy.* Baltimore-Munich: Urban and Schwarzenberg, vol. 2, 1983.

SOURCES

Air, Jane [pseud.]. "A Vindication of the Rights of Cunt." *Bust,* #6, Summer/Fall 1995, pp. 80–81.

American College of Obstetricians and Gynecologists. "Being a Teenager: You and Your Sexuality." Patient Education Pamphlet. Washington, D.C.: ACOG, 1992.

Baker, Nicholson. *Vox.* New York: Vintage Books, 1992.

Bechtel, Stefan, Laurence Roy Stains, and the editors of Men's Health Books. *Sex: A Man's Guide.* Emmaus, Pa.: Rodale Press, 1996.

Blank, Joani, ed. *First Person Sexual: Women and Men Write About Self-Pleasuring.* San Francisco: Down There Press, 1996.

———, ed. *Femalia.* San Francisco: Down There Press, 1993.

———. *Good Vibrations: The Complete Guide to Vibrators.* San Francisco: Down There Press, 1976.

Bogus, SDiane. "Dyke Hands." In *Erotique Noire/Black Erotica,* edited by Miriam DeCosta-Willis, Reginald Martin, and Roseann P. Bell, pp. 198–9. New York: Anchor, 1992.

Boston Women's Health Book Collective, The. *The New Our Bodies, Ourselves: A Book By and For Women.* New York: Touchstone, 1992.

Bouris, Karen. *The First Time: What Parents and Teenagers Should Know About "Losing Your Virginity."* Emeryville, Calif.: Conari Press, 1995.

Bright, Susie. "How to Make Love to a Woman: Hands-on Advice from a Woman Who Does." In *Susie Bright's Sexwise,* pp. 19–21. San Francisco: Cleis Press, 1994.

Castillo, Ana. "The Distortion of Desire," In *The Sexuality of Latinas,* edited by Norma Alarcón, Ana Castillo, and Cherríe Moraga, pp. 147–150. Berkeley: Third Woman Press, 1993.

Chan, Sucheng. "You're Short, Besides!" In *Making Waves: An Anthology of Writings By and About Asian American Women,* edited by Asian Women United of California, pp. 265–273. Boston: Beacon Press, 1989.

Cisneros, Sandra. "Guadalupe the Sex Goddess: Unearthing the Racy Past of Mexico's Most Famous Virgin." *Ms.,* vol. vii, no. 1 (1996), pp. 43–46.

Dodson, Betty. *Sex for One: The Joy of Selfloving.* New York: Crown, 1996.

Dworkin, Andrea. *Mercy.* New York: Four Walls Eight Windows, 1990.

Eichel, Edward and Phillip Nobile. *The Perfect Fit.* New York: Signet, 1993.

Espín, Olivia M. "Cultural and Historical Influences in Sexuality in Hispanic/Latin Women: Implications for Psychotherapy." In *Race, Class, and Gender: An Anthology,* edited by Margaret L. Anderson and Patricia Hill Collins, pp. 141–146. Belmont, Calif.: Wadsworth, 1992.

Fausto-Sterling, Anne. *Myths of Gender: Biological Theories About Women and Men,* 2d ed. New York: Basic Books, 1992.

Federation of Feminist Women's Health Centers. *A New View of a Woman's Body.* West Hollywood: Feminist Health Press, 1991.

Feinberg, Leslie. *Transgender Warriors: Making History from Joan of Arc to RuPaul.* New York: Beacon Press, 1996.

Fine, Michelle. "Sexuality, Schooling, and Adolescent Females: The Missing Discourse of Desire." *Harvard Educational Review,* vol. 58, no. 1, pp. 29–53.

Flandrin, Jean-Louis. *Sex in the Western World: The Development of Attitudes and Behavior.* Paris: Harwood Academic Publishers, 1991.

Gagnon, John. "On the Sources of Sexual Change." In *Promoting Sexual Responsibility and Preventing Sexual Problems,* edited by George W. Albee, Sol Gordon, and Harold Lietenberg, pp. 157–170. Hanover, N.H.: Press of New England, 1983.

Gray, John. *Men Are From Mars, Women Are From Venus: A Practical Guide for Improving Communication and Getting What You Want in Your Relationships.* New York: HarperCollins, 1992.

————. *Mars and Venus in the Bedroom: A Guide to Lasting Romance and Passion.* New York: HarperCollins, 1995.

H., Pamela. "Asian American Lesbians: An Emerging Voice in the Asian American Community." In *Making Waves: An Anthology of Writings By and About Asian American Women,* edited by Asian Women United of California, pp. 282–290. Boston: Beacon Press, 1989.

Hadleigh-West, Maggie. "Safe Sex." *Ms.* vol. vi, no. 5, March/April 1996, pp. 92–95.

Haskell, Molly. *From Reverence to Rape: The Treatment of Women in the Movies.* Second Edition. Chicago: The University of Chicago Press, 1987.

Heyn, Dalma. *The Erotic Silence of the American Wife.* New York: Signet, 1992.

Hite, Shere. *The Hite Report: A Nationwide Study of Female Sexuality.* New York: Dell Publishing, 1981.

————. *Women as Revolutionary Agents of Change: The Hite Reports and Beyond.* Madison: University of Wisconsin Press, 1993.

Hochchild, Arlie, with Anne Machung. *The Second Shift.* New York: Avon Books, 1992.

Hollander, Nicole. "Sylvia." Sylvia Syndicate, 1992.

Hughes, Holly. *Clit Notes: A Sapphic Sampler.* New York: Grove Press, 1996.

Hutton, Julia. *Good Sex: Real Stories from Real People.* Pittsburgh: Cleis Press, 1992.

Irvine, Janice M. *Disorders of Desire: Sex and Gender in Modern American Sexology.* Philadelphia: Temple University Press, 1990.

Keesling, Barbara. *Sexual Pleasure: Reaching New Heights of Sexual Arousal & Intimacy.* Alameda, Calif.: Hunter House, 1993.

Kinsey, Alfred C., Wardell B. Pomeroy, Clyde E. Martin, and Paul H. Gebhard. *Sexual Behavior in the Human Female.* Philadelphia: W. B. Saunders Co., 1953.

Koedt, Ann "The Myth of the Vaginal Orgasm." In Ellen Levine and Anita Rapone (eds.), *Radical Feminism,* New York: Quadrangle, 1973.

Kramer, Jane. "The Invisible Woman." *The New Yorker,* Feb. 26 and Mar. 4, 1996, pp. 136–147.

Ladas, Alice Kahn, Beverly Whipple, and John D. Perry. *The G Spot and Other Recent Discoveries About Human Sexuality.* New York: Dell, 1982.

Laqueur, Thomas. *Making Sex: Body and Gender from the Greeks to Freud,* Cambridge: Harvard University Press, 1990.

Laumann, Edward O., John H. Gagnon, Robert T. Michael, and Stuart Michaels. *The Social Organization of Sexuality: Sexual Practices in the United States.* Chicago: University of Chicago Press, 1994.

Lawrenson, Helen. *Latins Are Still Lousy Lovers.* New York: Hawthorn Books, 1968.

Lever, Janet. "Lesbian Sex Survey." *The Advocate,* August 22, 1995, pp. 21–30.

Locker, Sari. *Mindblowing Sex in the Real World: Hot Tips for Doing It in the Age of Anxiety.* New York: HarperCollins, 1995.

Lorde, Audre. "Uses of the Erotic: The Erotic as Power." In *Sister Outsider: Essays and Speeches.* Freedom, Calif.: Crossing Press, 1984.

Lutz, Catherine A. and Jane L. Collins. *Reading National Geographic.* Chicago: University of Chicago Press, 1993.

MacKinnon, Catharine A. "Does Sexuality Have a History?" In *Discourses in Sexuality: From Aristotle to AIDS,* edited by Domna C. Stanton, pp. 117–136. Ann Arbor: University of Michigan Press, 1992.

Mead, Margaret. *Coming of Age in Samoa.* New York: Morrow, 1928.

Maurer, Harry. *Sex: An Oral History.* New York: Viking, 1994.

McCormick, Naomi B. *Sexual Salvation: Affirming Women's Sexual Rights and Pleasures.* Westport, Conn.: Praeger, 1994.

Meshorer, Marc, and Judith Meshorer. *Ultimate Pleasure: The Secrets of Easily Orgasmic Women.* New York: St. Martin's Press, 1986.

Michael, Robert T., Edward O. Laumann, John H. Gagnon, and Gina Kolata. *Sex in America: A Definitive Survey.* New York: Little, Brown and Company, 1994.

Monagle, Katie. "All About Eve's Garden." In *Ms.,* vol. VI, no. 3, November/December, 1995, pp. 53–55.

Moore, Lisa Jean and Adele E. Clarke. "Clitoral Conventions and Transgressions: Graphic Representations in Anatomy Texts, c1900–1991." *Feminist Studies* 21, no. 2 (Summer) 1995, pp. 255–301.

Morin, Jack. *Anal Pleasure and Health: A Guide for Men and Women.* San Francisco: Down There Press, 1986.

Nelson, Mariah Burton. *The Stronger Women Get, the More Men Love Football: Sexism and the American Culture of Sports.* New York: Harcourt Brace & Company, 1994.

"Sensitivity Over Image Sinks a Women's Tennis Sponsor." *The New York Times,* February 16, 1995, pp. B6, B8.

Palac, Lisa. "How Dirty Pictures Changed My Life," In *Debating Sexual Correctness,* edited by Adele M. Stan, pp. 236–252. New York: Delta, 1995.

Penelope, Julia. *Speaking Freely: Unlearning the Lies of the Fathers' Tongues.* New York: Pergamon Press, 1990.

Queen, Carol. *Exhibitionism for the Shy: Show Off, Dress Up and Talk Hot.* San Francisco: Down There Press, 1995.

Quilliam, Susan. *Women on Sex.* New York: Barricade Books, 1994.

Quotable Women: A Collection of Shared Thoughts. Philadelphia: Running Press, 1989.

Rhodes, Richard. *Making Love: An Erotic Odyssey.* New York: Touchstone, 1993.

Richter, Alan. *Dictionary of Sexual Slang: Words, Phrases, & Idioms from AC/DC to Zig-zag.* New York: John Wiley & Sons, 1993.

Rothblatt, Martine. *The Apartheid of Sex: A Manifesto on the Freedom of Gender.* New York: Crown Publishers, 1995.

Sevely, Josephine Lowndes. *Eve's Secrets: A New Theory of Female Sexuality.* New York: Random House, 1987.

Sevely, J. Lowndes and J. W. Bennett. "Concerning Female Ejaculation and the Female Prostate." *Journal of Sex Research* 14 (1) Feb. 1978, pp. 1–20.

Shange, Ntozake. "However You Come to Me." In *Wild Women Don't Wear No Blues,* edited by Marita Golden, pp. 207–211, New York: Anchor, 1993.

Sherfey, Mary Jane. *The Nature and Evolution of Female Sexuality.* New York: Vintage Books, 1973.

Shields, Carol. *The Stone Diaries.* New York: Penguin, 1992.

Sizer, Frances Sienkiewicz, Eleanor Noss Whitney, and Linda Kelly deBruyne. *Making Life Choices: Health Skills and Concepts.* Minneapolis: West Publishing Co., 1994.

Sprecher, Susan, Anita Barbee, and Pepper Schwartz. " 'Was It Good for You, Too?': Gender Differences in First Sexual Intercourse Experiences." *Journal of Sex Research* 32 (1) (1995), pp. 3–15.

Stack, Peter. "Centerfold in the Closet." *San Francisco Chronicle,* March 2, 1996, p. E1.

Stan, Adele, ed. *Debating Sexual Correctness: Pornography, Sexual Harassment, Date Rape, and the Politics of Sexual Equality.* New York: Delta, 1995.

Stephens, Autumn, comp. *Wild Words from Wild Women: An Unbridled Collection of Candid Observations & Extremely Opinionated Bon Mots.* Berkeley: Conari Press, 1996.

Tannen, Deborah. *You Just Don't Understand: Women and Men in Conversation.* New York: Ballantine Books, 1990.

———. "Wears Jump Suit, Sensible Shoes. Uses Husband's Last Name." *New York Times Sunday Magazine,* June 20, 1993, pp. 18–20.

Tavris, Carol. *The Mismeasure of Woman: Why Women Are Not the Better Sex, the Inferior Sex, or the Opposite Sex.* New York: Simon & Schuster, 1992.

Thompson, Sharon. *Going All the Way: Teenage Girls' Tales of Sex, Romance & Pregnancy.* New York: Hill and Wang, 1995.

Tiefer, Leonore. *Sex Is Not a Natural Act & Other Essays.* Boulder: Westview Press, 1995.

Tolman, Deborah L. "Daring to Desire: Culture and the Bodies of Adolescent Girls." In *Sexual Cultures and the Construction of Adolescent Identities,* edited by Janice M. Irvine, pp. 250–279. Philadelphia: Temple University Press, 1994.

Tuana, Nancy. *The Less Noble Sex: Scientific, Religious, and Philosophical Conceptions of Women's Nature.* Bloomington, Ind.: Indiana University Press, 1993.

Vines, Gail. *Raging Hormones: Do They Rule Our Lives?* Berkeley: University of California Press, 1993.

Warren, Roz, ed. *What Is This Thing Called SEX? Cartoons by Women.* Freedom, Calif.: Crossing Press, 1993.

Winks, Cathy and Anne Semans. *The Good Vibrations Guide to Sex: How to Have Safe, Fun Sex in the 90s.* San Francisco: Cleis Press, 1995.

Zaviacic, M. and Beverly Whipple. "Update on the Female Prostate and the Phenomenon of Female Ejaculation." *Journal of Sex Research,* 30 (2), (1993), pp. 148–151.

The authors gratefully acknowledge the following individuals and publishers who permitted us to quote from their work:

Page 17. Quote from *Myths of Gender* by Anne Fausto-Sterling. Copyright © 1986 by Basic Books, Inc. Reprinted by permission of BasicBooks, a division of HarperCollins Publishers, Inc.

Page 21. Excerpts from *The Stone Diaries* by Carol Shields. Copyright © 1996 Penguin Books Inc. USA. Reprinted by permission.

Pages 77, 79. Excerpts from *The First Time: What Parents and Teenage Girls Should Know About "Losing Their Virginity"* by Karen Bouris. Copyright © 1993, 1994. Reprinted by permission of Conari Press: Berkeley, CA.

Pages 83, 84, 89. Excerpts from *Going All The Way: Teenage girls' tales of sex, romance & pregnancy* by Sharon Thompson. Copyright © 1995 by Sharon Thompson. Reprinted by permission of Hill & Wang, a division of Farrar, Strauss & Giroux: New York.

Page 85. Excerpt from *Making Love: An Erotic Odyssey* by Richard Rhodes. Reprinted with the permission of Simon & Schuster. Copyright © 1992 by Richard Rhodes.

Pages 92, 93. Excerpts from Deborah Tolman's "Daring to Desire: Culture and the Bodies of Adolescent Girls" from *Sexual Cultures and the Construction of Adolescent Identities* edited by Janice M. Irvine. Copyright © 1994 by Deborah Tolman. Reprinted by permission from Temple University Press.

Page 100–101. Excerpts from "You're Short, Besides!" by Sucheng Chan. Copyright © 1989 by Sucheng Chan. Reprinted by permission of author.

Page 151. Excerpt from Maggie Hadleigh-West's "Safe Sex" reprinted by permission of *Ms.* Magazine, © 1996.

Page 165, 248. Excerpts from *Good Sex: Real Stories From Real People* by Julia Hutton, Copyright © 1992 by Cleis Press: Pittsburgh, PA. Reprinted by permission.

Page 167–168. Excerpts from "Uses of the Erotic: The Erotic as Power," *Sister Outsider: Essays and Speeches*, p. 58, by Audre Lorde, © 1984. Published by The Crossing Press: Freedom, CA.

Pages 174, 175. Excerpts from *Sex For One: The Joy of Selfloving* by Betty Dodson. Copyright © 1996 reprinted by permission from Crown Publishers, Inc.

Page 210. Excerpts from a "Sylvia" cartoon by Nicole Hollander. Used by permission of author. Copyright © 1992.

Page 208. Excerpts from *The Hite Report: A Nationwide Study of Female Sexuality* by Shere Hite reprinted with the permission of Simon & Schuster. Copyright © 1976 by Shere Hite.

Page 211. Excerpts from *Sex: An Oral History* by Harry Maurer. Copyright © 1994 by Harry Maurer. Used by permission of Viking Penguin, a division of Penguin Books USA Inc.

Page 236. Excerpts from *Ultimate Pleasure: The Secrets of Easily Orgasmic Women* by Marc and Judith Meshorer reprinted by permission of St. Martin's Press Incorporated. Copyright © 1986 by Marc and Judith Meshorer.

Pages 250–1. Excerpt from *Mercy* by Andrea Dworkin was reprinted with permission from Four Walls Eight Windows: New York.

Page 251. Excerpts from "A Vindication of the Rights of Cunt" by Jane Air © 1995. Reprinted by permission of author.

INDEX